Introduction to
monetary economics

Introduction to monetary economics

Stanley M. Besen

Rice University

HARPER & ROW, Publishers

New York, Evanston, San Francisco, London

Sponsoring Editor: John Greenman
Project Editor: Eleanor Castellano
Designer: Frances Torbert Tilley
Production Supervisor: Will C. Jomarrón

Library of Congress Cataloging in Publication Data
Besen, Stanley M
  Introduction to monetary economics.
  1. Money.   2. Economics.   3. Financial institutions.   I. Title.
HG221.B537   332.4   74-14096
ISBN 0-06-040656-9

To Roberta Ann
and
Elizabeth Rebecca

Contents

INDEX   225

Preface

Almost ten years ago, I was asked to teach a course in money and banking. My students, I was told, would come from varied backgrounds, some having had substantial work in economics while others had completed only the principles. Having decided that an understanding of the role of money in affecting prices, output, and employment would be my central theme and being convinced that an understanding of microeconomic foundations was essential, I set about the task of designing the course. This book is an outgrowth of my experience over the past decade.

The organization of this book

The book is constructed somewhat like a sandwich. The core (to mix a metaphor) consists of Chapters 7 and 8, in which a complete model of the economic system is developed and is used to analyze the factors which determine output, employment, and prices, and Chapters 9, 11, and 12 in which the model is extended to allow for the presence of government, banks, and other financial institutions respectively. (Chapter 10 treats some special cases of the basic model.)

These chapters are preceded by a set of five, Chapters 2 through 6, in which the behavior of individual economic units is explored in some detail. Thus, we are concerned in Chapter 3 with the way in which wealth-holders choose to allocate their holdings among competing assets. In Chapter 4 we examine the determinants of investment by business firms, and in Chapter 5 we consider the spending of households. In Chapter 6, we develop an explanation of the behavior of labor markets and of the production and employment decisions of business firms.

The justification for looking at these individual decisions in some detail prior to incorporating them into a model of the complete economic system is first, to motivate an understanding of why the particular assumptions made in constructing the model were employed, and second, to see what factors are omitted from the complete model. The assumptions about individual decision-making contained in our models of the economy are necessarily less complicated than those examined when the individual decisions themselves are analyzed. Since the various pieces of the model are to be manipulated simultaneously, it makes things a good deal simpler if the components are themselves not excessively complicated. The reader interested in extending the model to permit such complications will find much grist for his mill in the extended discussions of the individual decisions in the early chapters of the book.

Chapters 14 through 16 and—to some extent—Chapters 11 and 12, consist of putting the model through its paces to illustrate its usefulness in analyzing some real world problems. (Chapter 13 contains a discussion of American financial institutions although institutional material appears in other chapters as well.) Thus, in Chapter 14 we examine the making of monetary policy in the real world where information available to policy-makes is incomplete. Here the model is employed to illustrate some of the basic difficulties which the Federal Reserve faces and to describe some of the ways in which it attempts to deal with them. Chapter 15 examines the process of inflation and the ways of dealing with it, and Chapter 16 explores problems in the balance of payments. The proof of the pudding is in the eating, and by the time you get this far you should—if this book is successful in its aim—be convinced of the usefulness of economic models in understanding the behavior of money, output, and prices.

How to use this book

There are a variety of ways in which this book can be used. The instructor who does not share the author's belief that considerable attention must be paid to microeconomic considerations may begin with Chapters 7 and 8. Some instructors may find that they do not wish to examine all of the subjects covered in Chapters 9 through 15. The book is designed so that once the basic model has been developed in Chapters 7 and 8, any of the subsequent chapters can be considered separately. Finally, all instructors should consider the use of a supplementary book of policy-oriented readings. There are many excellent books of readings and these, combined with references to the daily newspaper or the *Wall Street Journal* will provide sufficient institutional material against which the usefulness of the analytical models provided in this book can be tested.

Acknowledgements

My indebtedness to others in the writing of this book is all too apparent. As a graduate student, I was privileged to study under Arthur M. Okun and James Tobin. And, like other monetary economists of my generation I have benefitted greatly from exposure to the seminal works of Milton Friedman, John Gurley and Edward Shaw, and Don Patinkin. Due to my hopeless eclecticism, some influences of the work of each of these writers will be found in these pages. Vera Wallis cheerfully typed several early drafts. Finally, I wish to express my appreciation for the patience and understanding of my wife, Marlene.

STANLEY M. BESEN

Introduction to
monetary economics

1
Introduction

The American economy entered the 1970s plagued by the twin problems of unemployment and inflation. The rate of unemployment for 1971 stood at 5.9 percent of the labor force, higher than it has been for any year since 1961. And despite a control program begun in 1971, prices continued to rise at a very rapid rate. Between September 1972 and September 1973 the rate of inflation, as measured by the consumer price index, exceeded 7 percent per year.

What were the sources of the rapid inflation that built up during the 1970s? How did policy attempt to deal with it, and how successful were the measures applied? What explains the coexistence of unemployment and rapidly rising prices? Can full employment and price stability be restored? If so, how?

By now, most economists attempting to answer these questions would assign a role to money. But despite a vast amount of research during the past two decades, substantial disagreement still exists about the importance of monetary factors. Although it is unlikely that any economist believes that "money doesn't matter," and few if any believe that "money is all that matters," there remains a wide range of views about the significance of money. One of the principal aims of this book is to assess the role of money in determining output, employment, and prices. We deal with such questions as: Why do people hold money? What causes changes in the quantity of money? What effects do changes in the stock of money have on unemployment and inflation? What are the channels through which changes in the stock of money operate? What factors determine the effect of a change in the stock of money?

Unfortunately, a good deal of public debate about the causes of unemployment and inflation proceeds without benefit of a framework to explain how the economy functions. It is a basic contention of the author that such an approach is wrongheaded. Without an appreciation of the structure of the economic system, one is limited in what he can intelligently say about the causes and possible cures for the economic maladies that may befall our country.

1

In place of the usually informal ways in which problems of inflation and unemployment are examined, this book employs a series of simplified representations—models, if you like—of the economic system. Those unused to working with models to examine real-world phenomena often complain that the schemes are too simple, that they do not describe reality very well. But the critics fail to realize that such simplifications are the inevitable—and indispensable—results of trying to represent a complicated world in a way that can be comprehended by man. The question is not whether to simplify, for simplify we must, but which simplifications are most useful to employ. The use of models forces us to be explicit about the methods we choose and to scrutinize both their logical consistency and their ability to explain events. And this explicitness is the principal advantage of the approach taken here.

None of the foregoing is meant to suggest that all models are good ones. Some elegant and consistent models bear little or no correspondence to reality. Model building is something of an art and one must know how much to include to be accurate and how much to exclude to be simple. The models employed in this book are representative of a widely used class, and most economists would accept their broad outlines. Where economists differ, we try to make precise the sources of their disagreement, and the use of formal structures makes this task easier.

As result of its emphasis on models, this book contains somewhat less than the conventional amount of descriptions of the financial system and institutions. Institutional information is far from unimportant, nor is it neglected entirely. The justification for our approach is that understanding what effect a particular institution has is more important than simply knowing that it exists. The limited number of institutions that are discussed are analyzed. Thus, for example, when we examine the Federal Funds market, in which banks make loans of reserves to one another, we do so in the context of an explanation of the factors that determine the supply of money. And when we treat the behavior of savings and loan associations, it is in connection with an analysis of the effect of their existence on commercial banks and on the rate of interest. Many more institutions can be understood with the tools developed in this book than are in fact examined. But you should be able to understand them if you have mastered the tools.

Still another reason for not providing detailed descriptions of the American financial system is that the system itself is in a flux. The Federal Funds market did not exist 20 years ago, but the tools to analyze its possible effects did. The author believes that you should be prepared to understand the evolution of the financial system and that such comprehension is more important, in the long run, than having a complete catalog of institutions from the 1970s.

Some students, and perhaps their instructors, may regard this book as "too theoretical." And, indeed, much of the book focuses on rather abstract descriptions of reality. But any explanation is necessarily simpler than the phenomenon it describes, if only because of man's limited capacity to fashion comprehensible descriptions. The principal aim of teaching should be to provide to students, not answers but a way of looking at the world. To limit discussions to descriptions of today's institutions or policies, without bringing about understanding of how they operate and interact, is to leave students with no knowledge, if those institutions or policies change. A look at the important policy questions with which this course was concerned 10 years ago shows how quickly such knowledge becomes outdated. I ask you to judge this book by whether the theoretical models presented prove useful in understanding the real-world phenomena that you think are important.

A MONETARY ECONOMY

Money has often been referred to as a "social contrivance." My dictionary defines *contrivance* as "something which is fabricated as a work of art or ingenuity" and *social* as "involving cooperative and interdependent relationships with one's fellows." Apparently, then, "social contrivance" is something cleverly or artfully created to facilitate cooperative interactions with other members of society. The particular form of cooperative interaction that is facilitated is, of course, exchange. Without the social contrivance of money, exchange would necessarily involve the transfer of goods for goods—that is, barter. What money does, and precisely how it does it, is still a matter of serious scientific investigation. To begin, however, we can say that money improves the opportunities available to the members of society by permitting indirect exchange—that is, the transfer of money for goods and goods for money. It is a good thing that money exists; otherwise we would have to invent it.

But the movement from a barter economy to a money economy is not an unmixed blessing: Money must somehow be brought into being and, as we shall see, its quantity must be regulated. The excessive creation of money has led to serious inflations, and the destruction of money has created situations of massive unemployment. At other times so much money was created that it ceased to have any value and to serve its intended function, to facilitate exchange.

In early times money consisted of commodities, frequently precious metals. Because of its divisibility, durability, and stable value, money was a commodity that was generally agreed on a medium of exchange. By agreeing on one such commodity, members of a society enabled indirect exchange to replace barter. But it became apparent that the production of money in this manner was expensive, since the resources required could be employed to produce other things. Why not, people might have asked, replace the commodity that served as a medium of exchange but is expensive to produce, with something that can be produced more cheaply? Thus paper money came into being. Once money was cheap to produce, however, what was to prevent the production of so much currency that it became worthless? In response to this difficulty, government came to control the amount of money in the system, sometimes sharing the role with the banking system. But now a new problem arose. What was to prevent the government from producing too much money? At times, nothing, as experiences in the Confederate States during the Civil War and in Germany during the early 1920s attest. And although not all government policies are as bad as those just alluded to, there is still considerable debate over whether governments are creating, or are permitting to be created, too much or too little money.

This book picks up the story long after the switch from barter to the use of money and long after paper money had replaced commodities as a means of exchange. It seeks simply to understand how such an economy functions and to discover the role played in the process by changes in the amount of money.

THE MONETARIST CONTROVERSY

For some time now a group of economists who call themselves monetarists have taken a prominent role in the debate about the determinants of employment and prices. The monetarist position contains many components, and monetarism is not a monolithic system of thought, but the members of the group share the belief that movements in the stock of money are the principal driving force in the determination of output and prices in the short run. Clearly, over long periods of time the growth of output in an economy depends on the productive resources it has available and on the level of technology it can employ. But there can be substantial shortfalls from an economy's potential output, as evidenced, for example, by the massive unemployment and lost output in the Great Depression in the 1930s. And at times the demand for output substantially exceeds the capacity of the economy to produce, leading to rising prices. Monetarists attribute these failures of the demand for output to conform closely to the capacity of the economy to produce largely to movements in the money supply. If money grows too rapidly, they argue, demand will exceed capacity, and inflation will occur. If money grows too slowly, demand will fall short of capacity, and unemployment of resources will occur. The evidence marshaled for this viewpoint, particularly for situations of massive unemployment and rapid inflation is indeed impressive. During the Great Depression there was a very substantial reduction in the stock of money, and periods of very rapid inflation have always been accompanied by very rapid increases in the stock of money.

The author shares the view that changes in the money stock are important and that in some instances they can be overwhelmingly important, but he is not a monetarist. That is, he believes that at certain times factors other than money can have an important role in the determination of output and prices. The model employed throughout this book, therefore, allows us to assign roles to both monetary and nonmonetary factors. The model can be modified to permit monetaristic results or to exclude the importance of money altogether. Since the author believes that the truth lies somewhere between these extremes, and that it is yet to be found, the framework is explicitly agnostic on the monetarist question.

Although no monetarist would deny the potential importance of nonmonetary factors in influencing spending, the group seems to be saying that whereas other factors *could* be important in determining output and prices, in fact they are not. Monetarists point to data that can be explained by movements in the money supply; others call attention to evidence that cannot be accounted for by monetary factors. This debate is a lively one and promises to keep many economists employed for a considerable period of time.

⣎ 2 ⣾
Characteristics of assets

The first of the building blocks in our model of income determination is the theory of *asset choice*. At each point in time, every wealth holder must decide how to allocate his wealth among the types of assets that compete for a place in his portfolio. In an economy like that of the contemporary United States, in which the financial structure is highly developed, this choice must be made from a very large number of alternatives.

Wealth can be held in the form of currency and coin, which are readily acceptable as means of payment and are indispensable for carrying out small transactions. They are not an important form in which wealth is held, however, because deposits against which checks can be drawn (*demand deposits*) possess the same ready acceptability as currency and are far less vulnerable to loss or theft. In the United States, deposits against which checks can be drawn may be placed only at commercial banks. They are called demand deposits because the banks are obligated to redeem the instruments on demand in currency either to the deposit holder or to the holder of his check. In terms of the volume of transactions, the check is a far more important means of payment than currency.

Wealth also can be held in the form of deposits for which notice may be required before redemption. All such deposits, which include time deposits at commercial banks, deposits at mutual savings banks, and deposits at savings and loan associations, earn interest for their holders, unlike demand deposits, and all must be converted to either currency or demand deposits before they can be employed to make a purchase. A portion of a person's savings deposit cannot be transferred directly to someone else, as is the case with checking deposits. This category of assets is sometimes called *thrift deposits* because it represents a convenient form of saving for households. Recently banks have begun to issue certificates of deposits (CDs) in large denominations. These are usually held by business firms and are exchanged among holders prior to maturity.

6

Wealth can be held in the form of the liabilities of governments or firms. (Still another way is, of course, the liabilities of individuals. This is an important form of holdings for financial institutions but not for households or nonfinancial firms.) One familiar form of institutional liability is the nonmarketable government bond. Series E bonds, which are most common, are purchased at a discount from the face value—you pay $18.75 for a $25 bond—and, after a fixed period of time, they can be redeemed for face value. These bonds can only be purchased directly from the government or from a financial institution acting as its agent. Similarly, they can be redeemed only by the government. Series H bonds are also nonmarketable, but they come in larger denominations and instead of selling at a discount from face value, the holder receives periodic interest payments.

Marketable government bonds provide another alternative to wealth holders. Typically, short-term obligations of the government such as Treasury bills sell at a discount from the face value, whereas long-term bonds yield explicit interest. But these bonds differ from Series E and H bonds in that holders can convert them to other assets prior to maturity only by finding willing purchasers. A highly developed market in government bonds exists, and the potential seller of a bond has a fairly large number of potential buyers. A number of firms serve as government securities dealers, and they supply regular price quotations. In addition, current quotations appear in the financial pages of most newspapers. On the date of maturity of a marketable bond, the government is obligated to pay the face value to the person then holding the bond.

Corporate bonds are similar in many respects to government bonds. They promise the holder fixed and regular interest payments. They have a specific maturity date. And, if they are the obligations of major business firms, they can be bought and sold in highly organized markets. The bonds of most major firms trade on either the New York Stock Exchange or the American Stock Exchange. As a result, buyers can obtain "old" bonds simply by offering to pay the going price. Moreover, newly issued bonds can be purchased directly from the issuing corporation or from the collection of firms acting as underwriters. Maturing bonds are redeemed by the corporation.

Still another alternative to wealth holders is ownership shares of businesses. This means direct holding of common stock or indirect holdings through mutual funds of the shares of corporations or, for smaller firms, direct ownership. Both common stock and direct business ownership represent claims on the earnings of businesses. Holders of these assets are residual claimants on the receipts of firms being paid after the suppliers of factors of production and the holders of bonds.

Wealth is also held in the form of the cash surrender value of life insurance policies. The purchase of an ordinary (as opposed to a term) life insurance policy involves the simultaneous acquisition of a life insurance policy and a savings program. A portion of each premium is set aside in the policy-holder's name, providing a pool of funds he can borrow against or, if he wishes to cancel the insurance contract, convert to cash. By electing to purchase an ordinary life insurance policy a person is, in effect, rejecting the alternative of purchasing term insurance and employing the difference in premiums to buy other assets. Thus he has decided to hold a portion of his wealth in the form of the cash surrender value of life insurance policies.

Pension funds are another form of wealth holding. A worker and his employer may set aside funds to be invested in stocks or bonds to provide income in retirement. This represents an increasingly important form of wealth holding for households.

Finally, wealth is held in the form of physical assets. For households these include owner-occupied houses, land, and consumer durables such as refrigerators, washing machines, and automobiles. Business firms acquire machine tools, trucks, and assembly lines, and similar assets.

Table 2-1 presents, for a not very recent year, the distribution of asset

─────── **Table 2-1   Asset holdings of nonfarm households (1958)** ───────

	$ billion	% of Total assets
Tangible assets		
Residential structures	347	22
Land	92	6
Consumer durables	165	10
Other	28	2
Total tangible assets	632	40
Intangible assets		
Currency and demand deposits	61	4
Other banks deposits and shares	141	9
Life insurance reserves	100	6
Pension funds	93	6
U.S. government securities	59	4
Common stock	333	21
Business equity	98	6
Other securities	46	3
Other	29	2
Total intangible assets	960	60
Total assets	1592	

Source: R. W. Goldsmith and R. E. Lipsey, *Studies in the National Balance Sheet of the United States*, National Bureau of Economic Research, Princeton University Press, Princeton, N.J., 1963, vol. II, table III-1, pp. 118–119. Percentages do not add to total because of rounding.

holdings of nonfarm households in the United States. Approximately 40 percent of total assets were held in the form of tangible (real, physical) assets, and 60 percent were in the form of intangible (financial, monetary) assets. By far the largest portion of tangible assets was in the form of houses, about 20 percent of total assets, whereas consumer durables and land represented the bulk of the remainder. Common stock, coming to about one-fifth of all assets, was the single largest intangible asset held. Other important assets were thrift deposits (almost 10 percent of total assets), life insurance reserves and pension fund assets (which together account for about an eighth of total assets), and business equity (about 6 percent of total assets).

CHARACTERISTICS OF ASSETS

In the remainder of this chapter we consider the numerous characteristics of the various assets that a wealth holder might choose for his portfolio, taking into account the way in which these differences influence the choice among assets.[1] In Chapter 3 we examine the decision regarding which assets to hold.

Liquidity

Suppose you wish to dispose of an asset that you hold, taking this action because you need the proceeds of the sale to make a purchase. For most assets, there will be a large number of potential purchasers. The asset may have widely differing values for each of the potential purchasers, some valuing your asset highly and others placing a lower value on the asset. Naturally, you will want to find the person willing to pay the highest price. The question is, How easily can he be found?

Let us contrast two alternatives: Suppose that the asset you wish to sell is a share of a company listed on the New York Stock Exchange. Finding the highest bidder is then a simple matter. You instruct your broker to make the sale, the sell order reaches the floor of the New York Stock Exchange, and of all the people who might possibly buy the share, the person willing to pay the highest price *at that time* is the one who makes the purchase. All the people who are potential or actual purchasers of the share know where all transactions in the share occur. Some people may leave instructions to purchase shares in the company whose share you wish to sell at particular prices. When your share reaches the market, it is sold to that person whose instructions contain the highest offering price.[2] If you went to sell the share tomorrow, however, it might fetch a higher price: This is precisely what would happen if someone decided overnight that he would like to hold a share in the company and is willing to pay more than the previous high bidder had offered. But given the conditions at the time you decided to make the sale, you were able to find the high bidder almost immediately.

Contrast this with a decision to raise the same amount of money by the sale of your automobile. Just as in the case of your share of stock, there are a number of potential purchasers and each is willing to bid a particular price. As in the case of the share of stock, you would like to find the highest of these bidders. Unfortunately, there is not a well-developed used automobile market. Thus you may advertise in a newspaper, indicating that you have an automobile for sale, or you may call a dealer in used automobiles and ask him what he would be willing to pay for your car. You may quickly get several offers, but it is likely that there exists someone who would be willing to pay a higher price than any yet announced. The problem is, of course, to find him. The longer you wait, the greater the likelihood becomes of finding this high bidder. But suppose that you need your funds now. To sell your automobile quickly, you may not set the price in the advertisement at the level this potential high bidder would offer. Instead, you may ask a lower price, to achieve a quicker sale. If you needed the money by a given date and you were willing to sell only to the highest bidder, you would have to begin to plan the transaction well in advance of the date of the sale.

Clearly, in terms of the characteristic we have been considering, shares of companies listed on the New York Stock Exchange and used automobiles are significantly different. The difference is attributable to the nature of the markets in which the two assets trade. The New York Stock Exchange is highly organized, all potential buyers and sellers can find out about all transactions that occur, and at any time the highest bidder for an asset can be found. The automobile market is poorly organized, and the amount of time one would have to employ to find the highest bidder may be extremely great. We can array assets along a spectrum ranging from those in which it takes little time to find the high bidder and those in which it takes a great deal of time. The characteristic we are measuring along this array can be called *liquidity*.

It is clear that most financial assets are more liquid than are real assets such as automobiles. The markets for United States government securities or municipal securities are better developed than are the markets for houses or used automobiles. Finding the high bidder is a less time-consuming process. There are many financial assets in which there is only one potential bidder. The United States government is the only entity to which you can sell your Series E bond. You can only redeem your savings and loan shares at the savings and loan association that issued them. But, in general, you can redeem them immediately. If your savings and loan association insisted on 60 days notice in writing before redeeming your shares, as it has legal right to do, you might say that the shares are completely illiquid for 60 days and completely liquid thereafter. If you could arrange a loan equal to 50 percent of the value of the shares against the collateral of the shares for the first 60 days, you could say that the shares were partially liquid for the first 60 days and liquid thereafter.

One important thing to notice here is that we are not classifying assets as either liquid or illiquid. All, or almost all, assets possess the characteristic that some portion of the price that the highest bidder would be willing to pay can be achieved immediately. If you are willing to make a substantial sacrifice, almost any asset can be quickly turned into cash. Liquidity or illiquidity has been defined in terms of this sacrifice relative to the time allocated to make the sale. The sacrifice can take two forms. First, the sale may be made to a bidder other than the highest because that person cannot be found immediately. In addition, the seller may bear the cost of engaging the services of an agent to aid in the search for the highest bidder. Presumably because of his expertise, the agent will be able to locate the highest bidder sooner than the seller would have found him. The seller must decide whether the advantages (in terms of the more rapid sale at a given price, or a higher price for a given sale period) justify the cost of the agent's services. In some transactions—those involving shares listed on the New York Stock Exchange, for example—virtually everyone has decided that the use of the agent's services is the correct policy. In the case of the sale of houses, however, some people use real estate brokers to promote the sale but others prefer to sell the house themselves. Apparently the latter believe that the agent's commission is not justified in terms of the higher selling price obtained and/or the more rapid sale made possible. A perfectly liquid asset would be one for which the highest bidder could be found immediately and at no cost.

That most financial assets are at the highly liquid end of the spectrum and most real assets are not is part of the reason for believing that there is greater substitutability within the category of financial assets than between financial and real assets. But even within the financial asset grouping, not all assets are equally liquid. A United States government security is more liquid than the debt instrument that your friend gives you when you lend him money. This is true, not necessarily because the United States government is less likely to default on its obligation than is your friend; if you must sell your friend's note in a hurry, however, you are unlikely to realize its full market value, whereas you can always do so in the case of the United States government security. The difference has to do with the extent of development of the market in which the asset is traded. The more highly developed the market, the more liquid the asset.

Clearly, liquidity is a desirable characteristic for an asset. If you had to choose between two assets that were alike in every other way, you would undoubtedly choose to hold the one that was more liquid.

Reversibility

Suppose that I am considering switching a portion of my holdings from one kind of financial asset to another. Costs are always associated with making such a switch. Even if one ignores the value of the time involved in deciding to rearrange one's portfolio, one must consider the cost of using the facilities of a market to make the exchange. In addition, there is the time needed for consummating the transaction. For example, if one wishes to sell a share of a company listed on the New York Stock Exchange, he must spend time contacting his broker, who must be paid a brokerage commission. Because people are aware of these transaction costs, some transactions or asset rearrangements do not take place. Thus even though you would not choose the portfolio you are currently holding if you were starting anew, you might refrain from rearranging your portfolio if the costs of transactions were sufficiently high. Even when these transactions costs do not eliminate asset switches, they may serve to limit them.

A measure of the transactions costs involved in dealing in an asset is the difference between the current price at which one could buy the asset and the price at which one could sell the asset. If the asset were a share of stock, one would have to pay the current market price plus a brokerage commission to acquire the stock, whereas he would receive the current market price minus the brokerage commission if he sold the stock. The difference between these two amounts is a measure of the irreversibility of the asset.[3] (This calculation ignores the value of time taken to consummate the transaction.) If the commission on the New York Stock Exchange were $6 per transaction, the sale of a share worth $100 would bring $94, whereas it would take $106 to acquire it, a difference of $12. Other assets, such as United States government securities, are far more reversible; that is, the brokerage costs of buying them or selling them are considerably smaller per dollar of asset traded. Similarly, if one traded in lots of 100 shares of common stock, the brokerage costs per dollar of transaction would be significantly reduced. An example of an asset that is quite irreversible is a mutual fund with a so-called front-end load. If one sent $100 to the mutual fund to acquire shares and the load was, as is typical, 8.5 percent, one would receive $91.50 worth of shares. A person selling the same number of shares at the same time would receive $91.50.

Thus switching from one fund to another would cost $8.50 per $100 switched, which is a measure of the extent of irreversibility. Other assets are highly reversible. The only cost of exchanging a share in one savings and loan association for a share in another is the value of the time lost in making the transaction. There are no brokerage charges. On the other hand, a person who holds a Series E bond with one year to run, can sell it at a price previously prescribed; but it is impossible—the price is literally infinity—to acquire such an asset. One can think of such an asset as being completely irreversible.

Thus one can array all assets along a spectrum displaying the degree of irreversibility. If we assume that the time involved in making such transactions is the same for all assets, we can ignore it in arraying assets. If we use as a measure of irreversibility, the difference between the price one would receive if one sold the asset and simultaneously tried to acquire it (i.e., the size of the loss one would incur if he engaged in such a transaction), we would make the following ratings: savings and loan shares—perfectly reversible (no loss in making the transaction); sale of United States government securities on the open market—slightly less reversible; sale of large amounts of stock on the New York Stock exchange—still less reversible; mutual funds—still less reversible; and United States Government Series E Saving Bonds—completely irreversible. Actually, reversibility might be applied to transactions of particular kinds rather than to particular assets. If one is considering switching from a mutual fund to a savings and loan association, he can ignore the commission charged to buy shares in the mutual fund. On the other hand, if one wishes to sell shares in a savings and loan association and purchase shares in a mutual fund, the commission cannot be ignored.

We can close this discussion by contrasting reversibility and liquidity. A share of a company listed on the New York Stock Exchange is perfectly liquid. One can find the highest bidder almost immediately. But since brokerage costs are incurred in selling the security, as well as a bid–ask differential, such a sale is not completely reversible. Thus the characteristics are distinct. For another example, consider shares in a mutual fund in which sales commissions are charged. The shares are perfectly liquid because the fund, which is the only bidder for the shares, will in general redeem them immediately for cash. But the shares are not reversible, since a sales commission is attached to the purchase of the shares. In addition, there may be a redemption fee, which adds to the irreversibility. On the other hand, almost all, if not all, the assets that will be classed as highly reversible will be highly liquid. Markets that are imperfect insofar as one cannot quickly find the highest bidder, typically involve significant disparities being buying and selling prices, as well. In these markets, intermediaries (brokers) earn large commissions for bringing buyers and sellers together. Where markets are highly developed, on the other hand, the highest bidder can be quickly found, and brokerage charges are typically small. Undoubtedly, all markets are highly imperfect to start. If large profits can be earned by those performing a brokerage function, however, additional resources will be attracted to the brokerage industry. The entry of new firms serves simultaneously to improve the functioning of the market, to make the assets traded more liquid, and to drive down brokerage commissions; thus the assets become more reversible.

Divisibility

A third characteristic of assets that must concern us is divisibility. It is not always possible to hold exactly the desired amount of a given asset, since many assets exist only in units of large value. For example, it is impossible to hold $100 of shares in International Business Machines Corporation, since at present IBM shares sell for more than $200 apiece. Similarly, United States Treasury bonds sell in denominations of $10,000. The more indivisible are assets, the less likely it is that each individual will hold in his portfolio the exact quantities of various assets that he wishes. The lumpiness of the assets that he is considering will force him to allocate his portfolio in a way that differs from the most preferred combination. Some assets are completely divisible. That is, one can hold the amount desired, to the penny. Examples are currency, bank deposits, and savings and loan shares. At the other end of the spectrum, as indicated, are Treasury obligations and high-priced shares of stock.

Issuers of assets use a variety of devices to make them divisible, thus to increase their attractiveness to potential holders. For example, a company can split its stock so that there are more shares outstanding, each worth less than one of the original shares. The shares of IBM have been split several times. A company called Superior Oil Corporation whose shares sold for up to $2000 apiece during the 1950s split 10 for 1, thus making its shares accessible to a larger number of wealth owners. Similarly, many banks are currently attempting to increase persons holding CDs by selling them in much smaller denominations than the $10,000 units in which they were originally issued to corporations. Similarly, the sale of Series E bonds by the government in amounts of $18.75 was a device to increase the participation of small investors in the holding of federal debt. The smaller investors were previously excluded because government debt was available only in large denominations.

The indivisibility of common stock is one of the factors responsible for the growth of the mutual fund industry. Previously, if an individual wished to hold a widely diversified portfolio but had small total wealth, he would have been disappointed, since he could acquire, for example, no less than $200 of IBM if he wished to hold it at all. On the other hand, by acquiring shares in a mutual fund he can now hold the same proportion of IBM that the mutual fund holds, thus allocating less than $200 of his portfolio to that company's stock.

In a world in which assets are not completely divisible, individuals may not be able to allocate their wealth among competing assets in the way they would have chosen if they could hold as much or as little of each asset as they wished. This is the significance of the indivisibility of assets for the asset holding decision.

Predictability

A fourth important characteristic of assets is the predictability of the value of the asset over time. An asset that has a perfectly predictable value (so long as the general level of prices does not change) is a Series E bond. By consulting the schedule on the back of instrument, the holder of the bond can tell what the price of the bond will be at any given date in the future. If, on the other hand, one buys a marketable United States Treasury obligation, one knows the value of the bond at one point in the future, the maturity date. For dates between the date of purchase and the maturity date, the value of the bond cannot be known with certainty. The closer the bond is to maturity, the more predictable the price of the bond will become, since it probably will not sell for a price very different from the maturity price. At the opposite extreme from a Series E bond is a common share in a corporation. The price of the share at every point in the future is uncertain, and investing in the stock market involves the attempt to predict the course of future prices.

The increase in the price of the Series E bond over time represents the assured interest income earned by the holder. For marketable government bonds, there is also an assured interest payment, which unlike the case of a Series E bond, is paid to the holder of the bond on a regular basis. (In this respect, these bonds are identical to the nonmarketable Series H bond, which pays a fixed interest payment on a regular basis. They differ from a Series H bond in that the price of the latter is perfectly predictable. A Series H bond can be sold back to the government at par.) Thus the element of unpredictability that accompanies the holding of marketable government bonds concerns not the payment of interest, which is fixed and assured, but the fluctuations in the price of the bond. In the case of a common share, however, there is uncertainty both about the price of the share and about the dividend payment that will reward the holding of the share. In the case of private bonds, even though the interest payment is fixed in the loan contract, there is some uncertainty about receiving the payment, given the risk that the borrower will default. This condition also affects the predictability of the price of the bond. If the borrower defaults, the bond will not pay its par value at maturity. We can summarize these sources and types of unpredictability of assets in tabular form as follows:

Type of Asset	Interest or Dividend Payment	Price
Series E or H bond	Predictable	Predictable
Marketable government bond	Predictable	Unpredictable; predictable at maturity
Marketable private bond	Predictable (in the absence of default)	Unpredictable; predictable at maturity (in the absence of default)
Common share	Unpredictable	Unpredictable

SUMMARY

Several characteristics can be used to distinguish among the assets that compete for places in wealth holders' portfolios. Liquidity is the characteristic measuring the speed with which the seller of an asset can locate the potential buyer willing to pay the highest price. Reversibility is a measure of the cost of buying and selling an asset. Divisibility denotes the size of the units in which an asset can be obtained. Predictability is a measure of the ease with which we can determine variations in the price of an asset or its yield. Each of these characteristics plays a role in the selection of the assets in a wealth holder's portfolio.

NOTES

[1] The source of these distinctions is the work of James Tobin. See, e.g., "The Theory of Portfolio Selection," in F. H. Hahn and F. P. R. Brechling, ed., *The Theory of Interest Rates,* Macmillan, London, 1965.

[2] Actually the share may be purchased by the specialist, the trader of the shares of the company at the stock exchange, whose principal function is to smooth out price fluctuations by purchasing from sellers and selling to buyers as their orders reach the market. However, what the specialist is willing to pay depends on the highest price at which he thinks he can subsequently resell the shares.

[3] Since the seller would receive the highest price anyone is willing to pay (the bid price) and the buyer would pay lowest price anyone would accept (the ask price), the difference between the bid and ask prices would add to the irreversibility of an asset.

Asset choice

In the previous chapter we examined the significance of certain characteristics of the various assets that wealth holders may select. Since choice among
assets can have important effects on the behavior of the economy as a whole,
we must include an explanation of asset choice in the model of the determination of national income and the price level toward which we are working.
This chapter treats in some detail a few simple models of asset choice to
serve as an input to the model constructed in Chapter 7.

AN ELEMENTARY ANALYSIS OF ASSET CHOICE

Let us imagine a world in which there are only two kinds of asset, money
and bonds. A bond represents a promise to pay its holder fixed amounts at
various times in the future. The most common kind of bond is one that pays
annual interest and also repays the face value, the principal, at a specified
date, the maturity date. There are, in addition, bonds that offer only fixed
annual payments but no repayment of principal and others that promise only
a single payment at maturity.

Suppose that a bond being offered promises a payment of $5 at the end
of one year, another $5 payment at the end of the second year, and payment
of the face value of the bond, $100, also at the end of the second year. What
will the price of the bond be? How much would you be willing to pay for
it?

Let us consider each of the components of the payment stream that the
bond promises: the $5 payment at the end of the first year and the $105
payment, principal and interest, at the end of the second year. What would
you be willing to pay for the promise that you will be paid $5 at the end
of a year? You clearly should be willing to pay less than $5, since instead
of purchasing the promise you have other places in which to put your funds
and these other places may offer a positive return. If you have the option

of investing funds for a year at a 4 percent rate of return, your $5 will have grown to $5.20 by the end of the first year. Therefore you will be unwilling to pay $5 for the promise to repay you only $5. But what amount should you be willing to pay? You should be willing to offer the amount you would have to invest at 4 percent to have your investment grow to $5 by the end of the year. The amount, call it X, invested at 4 percent will be worth $X(1.04)$ at the end of the year. That amount is, therefore, $5/(1.04)$ or $4.81.

What about the promise to pay $105 at the end of the second year? The procedure is the same as for the first payment, but now we must allow for the alternative uses of the funds during the second year. How much would you have to invest today to be repaid $105 at the end of two years if the rate of interest is 4 percent. The amount, call it Y, will have grown to $Y(1.04)$ at the end of the first year. If that amount is reinvested at the end of the first year, it will have grown to $Y(1.04)(1.04)$ at the end of the second year. But this amount $Y(1.04)^2$ must be equal to $105. The value of the promise to pay $105 at the end of the second year is $97.08. The total value of the bond is, therefore, $101.89, the value of the $5 payment due at the end of the first year and the value of the $105 payment due at the end of the second year.

Clearly the value of the promise depends on the return on available alternatives. The value we would place on the same bond, given a 6 percent rate of interest on alternative assets during its two-year life, is

$$\frac{\$5}{(1.06)} + \frac{\$105}{(1.06)^2} \quad \text{or} \quad \$4.72 + \$93.45 = \$98.17$$

The value of the various promises clearly declines as the return on alternatives increases.

The foregoing procedure is applicable to the calculation of the value of any bond. Some bonds (e.g., United States Treasury bills) provide no annual payment. The holder is promised only the face value at maturity. What would you be willing to pay for the promise to pay you $100 in one year if your best alternative was a bond with a rate of interest of 6 percent? You clearly should be willing to pay no more than $100/(1.06)$, or $94.34.

A third kind of bond takes the form of a promise to pay a fixed amount of money, per year, in perpetuity. This form of debt obligation, which does not exist in the United States but does exist in the United Kingdom, is called a *consol* or *perpetuity*. Even though the bond has no maturity date and no repayment of principal, it is possible to place a value on the stream of payments it promises. Suppose that a bond promises to pay $1 per year forever and that the rate of interest on the best alternative asset is 7 percent per year. The value of the first $1 payment is $1/(1.07)$, or 94 cents; the value of the second payment is $1/(1.07)^2$, or 87 cents; the value of the third payment is $1/(1.07)^3$, or 82 cents, and so on. Although the payments go on forever, the sum of these values is finite. The value of a bond promising to pay $1 per year forever if the best alternative yields 7 percent is simply $1/(.07)$ or $14.29.

Suppose that bonds and money are perfectly liquid, completely reversible, and infinitely divisible. In other words, they can be quickly converted, at full value, into each other, in any amount desired, and at no cost. By definition, the price of money is perfectly predictable. The price of one dollar is always equal to one dollar. But even if the interest payment to be received from holding a bond is perfectly predictable, so long as there is no risk of default, such promises are in no way constrained to sell for the same price forever: When they are popular to hold, their prices will be high; during periods of disfavor, their prices will fall. Increases in the supply of bonds will reduce their prices and decreases in supply will raise their prices. If someone holds a perpetuity when a large additional amount is sold on the market, he will suffer a loss. Thus there are risks involved in holding consols due to unpredictability in price.

Suppose that on January 1 you buy a consol with a $1 annual coupon for $20. If you sell the bond at the end of the year and its price is still $20, you will have earned the $1 interest payment for holding the bond. (We assume that the interest payment is made on December 31.) The rate of return earned for holding the bond is 5 percent, $1/$20. Suppose, instead, that its price changes during the period of time that the instrument is held. Clearly, if the price of the bond rises during the period in which it is held, the rate of return earned by the bond holders is greater than 5 percent. Of course, a rise in the price of the bond is equivalent to a fall in the rate of return that will be earned by those holding bonds in the future. If, for example, the price of the bond was $25 on December 31, those holding the bond during the year would earn a 30 percent return during the year of their holding: $($1 + $5)/$20$. However, assuming that there were no further changes in bond prices, bondholders during the next year would earn 4 percent, $1/$25.

Of course, the price of the bond may fall during the period in which it is held, thus reducing the return below 5 percent. If the price falls to $19, the rate of return earned is zero, since the loss of $1 in the price of the asset exactly matches the $1 interest coupon. For larger declines in the price of bonds (i.e., larger increases in the rate of interest), the return from holding the bond for a year is actually negative.

Suppose that a person is assured that there will be no change in bond prices (i.e., in interest rates) during the forthcoming period. Thus if bonds are selling for $20 he will earn 5 percent per period on the proportion of his portfolio held in the form of bonds. On the proportion of his portfolio held in the form of money, he earns a zero return. Under our assumption that the price of bonds will not change, assuming also that the individual will hold an unchanged quantity of wealth at every point throughout the period, he should therefore hold his entire portfolio in the form of bonds. To hold money would involve needlessly foregoing the interest income from holding bonds. (Actually, the assumptions employed here are too restrictive. Even if the individual is assured that the price of bonds will fall but the decline will be smaller than the interest earned, he should hold bonds. The same argument holds, a fortiori, for rises in bond prices.) In other words, if an investor is certain that he will hold a portfolio of unchanged size during a given period and if he knows the return he will earn from holding various kinds of asset (in our example, bonds and money), he will choose to put his entire portfolio into that asset which provides the largest return.

TRANSACTIONS DEMAND FOR MONEY

People do not hold portfolios of unchanged size during each period. Their total holdings fluctuate as they engage in purchases and sales of goods and services. Let us suppose that an individual who holds a given stock of wealth at the beginning of a period knows that for the forthcoming period he will receive income payments on various dates and that he will be called on to make payments at other dates. Assume that the payment and receipt dates and the amounts of the transactions are known. Since as a rule, bonds are not media of exchange—that is, they are not generally acceptable means of payment—the individual will receive money at various dates during the period and will have to make payments in the form of money at others. To make the example more specific, suppose that an individual receives wage payments in the form of money on the last day of each month, that he is called on to make rental payments on the same day, and that his purchases of food take place at a constant rate throughout the month.[1] Assuming that payment and receipt dates and amounts are fixed and certain, how will an individual manage his portfolio? At any given time, how will he decide on how much money and how many bonds will be held?

Let us examine the stream of receipts and expenditures just described. On the last day of a given month, the individual has a given quantity of wealth (money and bonds) in his portfolio, a legacy from the past. He receives his wages from the previous month's work and makes a rental payment for the coming month's occupancy of his home. He also anticipates making the same payment for food on each day of the coming month. Let us call the amount of wealth left over from the past W, the amount of the wage payment Y, the rental payment R, and the food expenditure per day F. Thus in terms of the total amount of funds to be allocated between money and bonds, the individual, on the first day of the month has $(W + Y - R)$ and on the mth day of the month he has $(W + Y - R - mF)$. What alternative strategies might the individual follow in determining his portfolio position—the distribution of his portfolio between money and bonds—on any given day during the month?

Let us consider two extreme cases. In the first, the individual never holds any bonds in his portfolio. At the beginning of the period he holds $(W + Y - R)$ in the form of money, and at the end of the month he holds $(W + Y - R - tF)$ if there are t days in the month. Of course, the interest earned following this strategy is zero. At the other extreme, the individual always keeps his entire portfolio in the form of bonds. If he receives income, he immediately converts the money received into bonds. If he must make a payment, he holds bonds up until the moment that the payment is due, then converts the bonds into money and makes the payment. If the interest payment is at the rate of $1 for each $20 invested for the entire period the individual receives $(\$1/\$20) [(\$W + Y - R) + (\$W + Y - R - tF)]/2$. In other words, he earns 5 percent on the average amount of wealth held during the period because the whole portfolio is always held in the form of bonds.

Is either of the strategies outlined optimal? To answer this question, we return to our analysis of asset reversibility. Suppose there were a very large fixed charge for buying and selling bonds, that is, bonds were reversible only at a very large cost. Under these conditions, although the strategy of holding only bonds in the portfolio and converting from bonds to money only at the instant of transaction would maximize interest income, it might produce a negative return on the portfolio as a whole, after transaction costs had been deducted. On the other hand, suppose that bonds were completely reversible; that is, they could be converted to money and money could be converted to bonds at no cost. Then the strategy of maximizing interest income—holding only bonds in the portfolio—is equivalent to maximizing the total returns from the portfolio. Clearly, the world lies somewhere between the extremes of prohibitively high transaction costs and no transaction costs at all; thus we must consider the role of these costs in the determination of the optimal portfolio.[2]

Since an individual's policy of allocating his portfolio between bonds and money depends on the cost of converting money to bonds, and vice versa (i.e., on the degree of reversibility), as well as on the interest to be earned from holding bonds, we must ask how these two factors enter into the decision.[3] Before proceeding to consider this question, we examine two facets of one element of the portfolio management process, the time of sales and purchases. First, whatever the number of bonds held during the period and whatever the number of conversions of bonds into money, all conversions of money to bonds will be made at the beginning of the period. In other words, the maximum holdings of bonds are at the beginning of the period. To do otherwise would involve holding money during a part of the period, a subsequent conversion of the money to bonds, and a conversion from bonds to money. This sequence would mean income needlessly foregone during the period when the money being held was not needed for transactions but was not earning interest income. Second, no conversions of bonds to money will be made before the moment of need. So long as some money is held, bonds will not be converted to money. The assumed liquidity of bonds means that no preparation is required for the conversion. To convert before the money is needed will also involve foregoing interest income.

Let us first fix the number of transactions and determine, for a given number of transactions, the optimal amount of bonds to be held and the optimal time of transactions (i.e., the amount and time of transactions that will maximize *interest* income).

The downward sloping line ZT in Figure 3-1 represents the holdings of bonds and money at various points during the period. The amount of money and bonds held at the start of the period, time O, is Z and this sum declines at a constant rate to zero at the end of the period time T. (Recall that any funds which will be held beyond the period will be held in bonds and are not considered here.) The height of the horizontal line represents bond holdings at that point; therefore, the difference between the horizontal line and ZT is money holdings. Thus if there are no bond holdings, money holdings are the difference between the horizontal axis and the ZT. When money holdings reach zero, a conversion from bonds to money must be undertaken so that subsequent payments can be met.

The strategies represented in Figure 3-2 for two transactions cannot be optimal. In Figure 3-2(a) the asset holder holds his entire portfolio in money until time t_1, whereupon he converts OA to bonds. These bonds are held until time t_2, when money balances are exhausted and a conversion from bonds to money must be made. Clearly, for the same number of transactions, thus the same transaction costs, interest income could have been increased

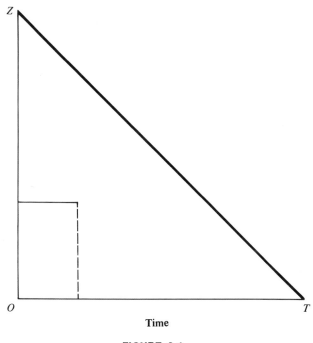

Time

FIGURE 3-1

by converting OA from money to bonds at time O. Thus the strategy in Figure 3-2(a) is suboptimal.

In Figure 3-2(b), another kind of suboptimal behavior is illustrated. The conversion from money to bonds of OB occurs at time zero. But at time t_3, before money holdings are exhausted (they are still BC), the bonds are converted to money. Interest income, thus total income, could have been raised simply by delaying the conversion until time t_4.

If transaction costs are dependent only on the number of transactions and not on their size, and if for a given number of transactions we determine which pattern of transactions maximizes interest income, that pattern will also maximize net income after transactions costs. If we do this for every possible number of transactions, we can determine the number of transactions that maximizes total income.

Let us consider two transactions. Remembering that all conversions from money to bonds will occur at the beginning of the period and that there will be a single conversion from bonds to money (the second transaction), we must determine how large the initial conversion should be. If the individual places a large fraction of his portfolio in the form of bonds at the beginning

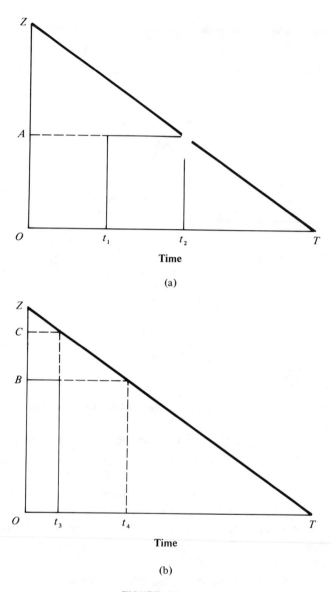

FIGURE 3-2

of the period, he will earn interest income on a large fraction of his portfolio. However, he will be called on to convert from bonds to money early in the period, since the small portion of the portfolio initially held in the form of money will quickly be dissipated. If, on the other hand, a small proportion of the portfolio is held in the form of bonds at the beginning of the period, the conversion from bonds to money will take place late in the period but interest will be earned on a relatively small number of bonds. Finding the optimal policy clearly depends on balancing the starting with a large proportion of the portfolio in bonds against the early conversion date, which such a policy requires. Since interest earned depends on the amount of funds held in the form of bonds *and* on the amount of time for which the bonds are held, we must find that transaction pattern that maximizes the amount held, multiplied by the time for which it is held. The quantity Z is the amount the individual will spend during the forthcoming period. Thus one-quarter of the way through the period the total resources (money and bonds) held by the individual will be $(3Z/4)$, halfway through the period it will be $Z/2$, and so on. If the individual chose to put three-quarters of his portfolio into bonds at the beginning of the period, he would be forced to convert them to money one-quarter of the way into the period. If he put one-half of his wealth into bonds, the conversion would take place at the midpoint of the period. Possible patterns of bond holdings for two transactions are illustrated in Figure 3-3.

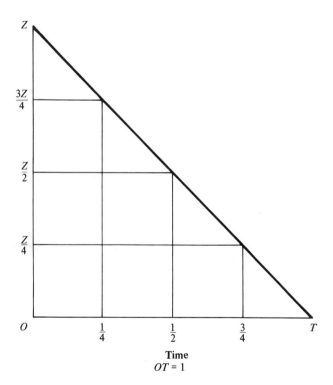

FIGURE 3-3 Some possible patterns of two transactions.

If p is the fraction of Z initially held in the form of bonds, $(1 - p)$ is the conversion date, and interest income earned is thus pZ (the amount held in the form of bonds) times $(1 - p)$ (the period for which the bonds are held) times the interest rate. Thus if the initial conversion of money to bonds is three-fourths of Z, the subsequent conversion of bonds to money must occur one-fourth of the way through the period. If the initial conversion is $Z/2$, money holdings will be exhausted at time $1/2$. And if only $Z/4$ is initially converted to bonds, money balances will last for three-fourths of the period. For two transactions, interest income is maximized if half the portfolio is held in bonds at the beginning of the period and the bonds are converted to money halfway through the period.

The case of three transactions may help us to develop a general rule. Again, there will be a conversion from money to bonds at the beginning of the period, but now there will be two conversions of bonds to money. When the initial cash holdings run out, only a fraction of the remaining bond holdings are converted to money, and only when the latter money holdings are spent are the remainder of the bonds finally converted to money. This policy clearly permits the earning of higher interest income than in the two-transaction case, but there are larger transaction costs. Whether the extra costs are larger than the extra interest income earned is a subject we consider shortly. Now we are concerned with the optimal pattern for someone who wishes to engage in three transactions. The individual will place pZ in bonds at the beginning of the period. At time $(1 - p)$ he will be forced to convert some of the bonds to money. At that point his total wealth will be pZ, of which he will continue to hold pqZ in the form of bonds. At time $(1 - p) + p(1 - q)$ the individual will once again be forced to convert the remaining bonds to money. Interest income from this policy is equal to the interest rate times $pZ(1 - p) + pZ(q)(p - pq)$. Using this expression to determine the values of p and q that maximize interest income, we find $p = \frac{2}{3}$ and $q = \frac{1}{2}$. This means that a person will place two-thirds of his wealth in bonds at the beginning of the period, convert one-third to money at time $1/3$, continue to hold one-third of his wealth in bonds $(pq = (2/3)(1/2) = 1/3)$ until time $2/3$, at which point the remainder of the bonds are converted to money. This policy maximizes interest income for three transactions.[4]

The general rule for n transactions is as follows: At time zero, buy $[(n - 1)/n]Z$ bonds and sell them in equal installments of Z/n at times $1/n, 2/n, \ldots , [(n - 1)/n]$. Using this policy, the average holdings of bonds are equal to half the initial bonds held. Clearly, interest income is larger, the larger number of transactions, the larger the initial bond holdings, and the larger the average bond holdings. However, increasing the number of transactions also increases transaction costs. We turn next to the determination of the optimal number of transactions.

The foregoing analysis indicates for any given number of transactions the optimal size and time of the transactions needed to maximize interest income. To determine which level of transactions is optimal, we must construct a formula that permits us to take into account transaction costs. As we know, if these costs were zero the optimal number of transactions would be infinite and the entire portfolio would be held in bonds, with liquidation of bonds for money occurring only when the need for an expenditure arose. The simplest assumption to make is that there is a fixed cost per transaction, independent of transaction size. From our previous analysis we know that the relation between the number of transactions and the interest income earned is

$$\frac{n-1}{2n} Zi \tag{3-1}$$

where n is the number of transactions, $[(n-1)/n]Z$ is the value of bond holdings at the beginning of the period, $[(n-1)/2n]Z$ is the average bond holdings for the period, and i is the interest rate per period. Net earnings for n transactions after allowing for transactions costs are (3-1) minus nb, where b is the fixed cost per transaction. The problem is to find, for a given Z, i, and b, the number of transactions for which the net income earned from the portfolio is a maximum. The solution or the value of n that maximizes net income is[5]

$$n = \sqrt{\frac{Zi}{2b}} \tag{3-2}$$

Since average money holdings, $\bar{M}$, are determined once the optimal number of transactions has been learned, we can also solve for $\bar{M}$ in terms of Z, i, and b. Since average holdings of money and bonds are $Z/2$ and average holdings of bonds are $[(n-1)/2n]Z$ average money holdings, the difference between these is $Z/2n$. Substituting (3-2) for n we get

$$\bar{M} = \sqrt{\frac{bZ}{2i}} \tag{3-3}$$

As (3-3) indicates, average money holdings are an increasing function of transaction costs and expenditures and a decreasing function of the rate of interest.

To illustrate the workings of these formulas, let us see how the number of transactions, average bond holdings, and net income vary as we change the rate of interest, transaction costs, and total expenditures.

Let us first examine the relationship between money holdings and the rate of interest. The formula indicates that other things equal, the higher the rate of interest, the higher will be average holdings of bonds and the smaller will be average holdings of money. In other words, the transactions demand for money is interest elastic. For expenditures of $100,000 per month and a cost of transactions of $6, average bond holdings rise from $40,000 to $44,444 when the interest rate rises from 3 to 12 percent per year. Since average wealth holdings are $50,000, this implies that average money holdings decline from $10,000 to $5,556. Table 3-1 shows the optimal number of transactions and the average bond holdings for a number of interest rates. It also shows the net income earned by pursuing the optimal policy.

The second important result is that other things equal, the higher the cost imposed for a transaction, the smaller will be the number of transactions engaged in, the smaller will be the average holdings of bonds, and the larger will be the average holdings of money. A rise in transaction costs will cause individuals to increase their average holdings of money because doing so reduces the transaction cost incurred. This result is illustrated in Table 3-2.

Table 3-1   Optimal transactions and bond holdings: total expenditures, (Z) = $100,000, transaction costs, (b) = $6

Interest rate i	Number of transactions n	$\bar{M}$	Average bond holdings $\dfrac{n-1}{2n}Z$	Net income $\dfrac{n-1}{2n}Zi - nb$
.0025 (3% per year)	5	$10,000	$40,000	$ 70.00
.0050 (6% per year)	6	$ 8,333	$41,667	$172.33
.0075 (9% per year)	8	$ 6,850	$43,750	$280.12
.0100 (12% per year)	9	$ 5,556	$44,444	$390.44

Table 3-2   Optimal transactions and bond holdings: total expenditures, Z = $100,000, interest rate, i = .005 (6% per year)

Transaction cost b	Number of transactions n	$\bar{M}$	Average bond holdings $\dfrac{n-1}{2n}Z$	Net income $\dfrac{n-1}{2n}Zi - nb$
$ 5	7	$ 7,143	$42,857	$179.29
$ 6	6	$ 8,333	$41,667	$172.33
$10	5	$10,000	$40,000	$150.00
$25	3	$16,667	$33,333	$ 91.67

For example, if expenditures are $100,000 per month and the interest rate is 6 percent per year, the number of transactions engaged in declines from 7 to 3 as transaction costs rise from $5 to $25.

The third important facet of the result, which is related to the assumption that transaction costs are independent of the size of the transactions, is that for given interest rates and transaction costs, not only do average bond holdings increase as total expenditures increase, but the rate of increase of bond holdings is faster than that of expenditures. In other words, wealthy people will hold a smaller *percentage* of their portfolio in money than will poor people. Table 3-3 illustrates this relationship. For an annual interest rate of 6 percent and the cost of a transaction of $6, average bond holdings for a person with expenditures of $25,000 are $8,333, which is 67 percent of average wealth holdings of $12,500. For a person with expenditures of $100,000, average wealth holdings are $50,000 and average bond holdings are $41,667, or 83 percent. For a person with $200,000 of expenditures, the ratio of bond holdings to total holdings rises to 89 percent.

Our analysis of the decision to hold money and securities is not set forth as a definitive answer to the question of portfolio management. It is intended to give the student insight into the components of the decision that an individual must make. In the world we have analyzed, in which the decision maker is assumed to know the return that will be earned by holding a portion of his portfolio in bonds and the amounts and timing of his receipts and payments are also known, the decision must take into account: (1) the rate of interest, (2) the nature of transaction costs, and (3) the pattern of receipts and payments. If we assume that the individual wishes to maximize the return from his portfolio net of transaction costs, we are able to determine what his portfolio decision will be. In much of the analysis to follow, it is assumed that transaction costs are not subject to substantial change in the short run;

Table 3-3 Optimal transactions and bond holdings: interest rate, $i = .005$ (6% per year), transaction cost, $b = \$6$

Total expenditures Z	Number of transactions n	$\bar{M}$	Average bond holdings $\dfrac{n-1}{2n} Z$	Net income $\dfrac{n-1}{2n} Z - nb$
$ 5,000	0	$ 2,500	0	0
$ 25,000	3	$ 4,167	$ 8,333	$ 23.67
$100,000	6	$ 8,333	$41,667	$172.23
$200,000	9	$11,111	$88,889	$390.44

thus we are particularly concerned with the impact of changes in interest rate and the rate of expenditures on the portfolio selection decision.

PRECAUTIONARY DEMAND FOR MONEY

The foregoing analysis must be modified if we assume that instead of transactions being known with respect to both timing and amount, there is uncertainty about these factors. In the analysis of the transactions demand for money, if we had retained all our assumptions except the assumption that bonds are perfectly liquid, only one element would have changed: namely, households would have had to begin preparation for the sale of bonds prior to the date on which the money would be needed. The proceeds of the conversion would arrive exactly when money holdings ran out, a result assured by our assumption that the amount and timing of payments is known.

When there is uncertainty about the nature of the payments stream, however, the assumption of perfect liquidity becomes crucial. If bonds are perfectly liquid, the correct policy for a household trying to maximize the net income from its portfolio involves converting bonds to cash whenever cash balances reach zero, the amount of the conversion being the same as if the "expected" value of transactions over the coming period was actually known. Such a policy will maximize "expected" income from managing the portfolio. The determination of the optimum policy will involve balancing expected transaction costs and expected interest income.

When bonds are not perfectly liquid, however, a new element enters the analysis. The imperfect liquidity of bonds requires that preparation for sales be made if the full value of bonds is to be realized and the proceeds are to arrive when money balances reach zero. But since the payments stream is uncertain, one cannot know precisely when to time the beginning of the conversion to ensure that its proceeds arrive when money balances are zero. If the conversion begins too late, the household will run out of money balances, leaving it with one of three choices: (1) to sell the bond and accept less than its full value, (2) to borrow from another source to tide the household over until the full value of the bond can be realized, or (3) to default on making the payment until the full value of the bond can be realized. Each alternative involves a cost the household would like to avoid. However, the only way to prevent such a situation from arising is to begin conversions well in advance of reaching zero money balances. But such a policy would entail holding large amounts of non-interest-bearing money, which also involves a cost—namely, the earnings foregone from holding bonds. The existence of uncertainty with respect to the timing and amount of transactions together with the less-than-perfect liquidity of bonds forces the household or firm to hold larger money balances than it would hold if the payment stream were certain. These additional balances will be greater, the less liquid the bonds, the higher the interest cost involved in borrowing to meet payments, and the larger the cost of being unable to meet payments.

SPECULATIVE DEMAND FOR MONEY

To this point we have assumed that the investor believes with complete certainty that the rate of interest will not change during the period under consideration. We wish now to consider the impact of changing this assumption.

As our previous discussion indicated, the return an investor obtains from holding a bond depends both on the promised interest or coupon payment and on any change in the value of the bond during the period in which it is held. Thus if during the period the interest rate rises, i.e., bond prices fall, the return to an investor from holding a bond is less than the coupon. In fact, a sufficiently large fall in bond prices can completely wipe out any return from holding the bond, and one may even earn a negative return from holding bonds.

Suppose that an individual holds with certainty an expectation about the interest rate that will prevail at the end of the period. In other words, he believes, or behaves as if he believes, that there exists only one possible future rate of interest. Then, given the current rate and the expected future rate, the individual determines whether holding bonds or holding money will be more rewarding, and he places his entire portfolio into that asset with the highest return. Money has a return of zero. Bonds have a return that can be negative if there is a capital loss larger than the coupon amount earned from holding the bond. If the return expected from holding bonds is positive, the individual will hold all bonds. Otherwise, his entire portfolio will consist of money.

The calculation of the decline in bond prices that produces a zero rate of return on bonds is a straightforward matter. As before, we are considering perpetual bonds, consols, which are promises to pay $1 per year in perpetuity. Let us consider a number of hypothetical interest rates and ask what rise in the rate of interest would be sufficient to just overcome the interest earnings from holding bonds. Alternatively, what is the level to which the rate of interest must rise, we might call this the *critical rate,* for the rate of return from holding bonds to equal zero?

Let us consider a consol when the rate of interest is 1 percent. The price of a bond promising to pay $1 per year in perpetuity is $100. Clearly, if the price of the bond falls to $99 during the period, the capital loss incurred, $1, is just equal to the coupon, and a zero rate of return is earned. Thus if the rate of interest rises to 1.01 percent, 1/99, the rate of return earned from holding the bond is zero. Thus at the low interest rate of 1 percent, a relatively small rise in the interest rate is sufficient to produce a zero rate of return. Alternatively, let us suppose that initially the interest rate is 10 percent. The price of the perpetuity described above is thus $10. Clearly, if the bond price falls to $9 the rate of return will be zero. To produce a capital loss of $1 on the bond, the rate of interest must rise from 10 to 11.1 percent. Thus when interest rates are high it takes a relatively large rise in the interest rate to produce a zero rate of return. In other words, the critical rate is a much larger percentage of the current rate when rates are high than when they are low. Table 3-4 indicates critical interest rates for various levels of the current rate.

The derivation of the critical interest rate can be viewed in the following manner. The return R from holding a bond for one period is equal to the coupon C plus any capital gain which is equal to the end-of-period bond price P_1, minus the initial bond price, P_0.

$$R = C + (P_1 - P_0) \tag{3-4}$$

The problem is to find the P_1, thus the end-of-period interest rate i_1, for which R is zero. Setting R equal to zero and dividing through (3-4) by P_0, we have

$$i_c = \frac{i_0}{1 - i_0} \tag{3-5}$$

Table 3-4   Critical interest rates for various levels of the current rate
—————————————————bond coupon = $1—————————————

Current interest rate i	Current bond price	Critical bond price (current price: $1)	Critical interest rate i_c (1/critical bond price)	$\dfrac{i}{i_c}$
.01	$100	$99	.0101	1.010
.02	$ 50	$49	.0204	1.020
.03	$ 33.33	$32.33	.0309	1.030
.04	$ 25	$24	.0417	1.042
.05	$ 20	$19	.0526	1.052
.06	$ 16.67	$15.67	.0638	1.063
.07	$ 14.29	$13.29	.0752	1.074
.08	$ 12.50	$11.50	.0870	1.087
.09	$ 11.11	$10.11	.0989	1.099
.10	$ 10	$ 9	.1111	1.111

If for a given current rate, the expected interest rate exceeds i_c, the individual will hold his entire portfolio in money, since holding bonds involves a loss. If the expected rate is less than i_c, the individual can expect a positive return from holding bonds; therefore he will hold his entire portfolio in bonds.

There is an equivalent way of looking at the same problem. Given the expected rate, we can find the current rate for which the investor will just break even (i.e., earn a zero return) from holding bonds. Again using (3-4), replacing P_1 with P_e, and dividing through by P_0', the current price for which an individual just breaks even by holding bonds, we can solve for i_0', C/P_0'.

$$i_0' = \frac{i_e}{1 + i_e} \qquad (3\text{-}6)$$

If the current interest rate is less than i_0', the individual will hold his entire portfolio in the form of money. If the current rate is greater than i_0', the individual will hold his entire portfolio in the form of bonds.

AN ALTERNATIVE VIEW OF THE SPECULATIVE DEMAND FOR MONEY*

The model of the speculative demand for money employed thus far has one glaring defect. It implies that depending on the relationship between current and expected future interest rates, an individual decides to hold his entire portfolio in either bonds or money. This follows from our assumption that the individual wishes to maximize the expected return for his portfolio. He does so by holding his entire portfolio in the asset with the highest expected return. Differences in expectations about the future course of interest rates determine how any given amount of money and bonds will be distributed among individuals. However, the model does not allow an individual to hold a *diversified* portfolio, consisting of both bonds and money, and to change the *proportions* of his portfolio held in bonds and money in response to changes in the current rate of interest. Let us turn now to a description of such a model.[6]

We shall assume that an individual can buy bonds with a current yield of 5 percent. The price of a bond that promises to yield $1 per year in perpetuity is thus $20. Let us suppose that the individual believes it to be equally likely that the price of the bond will fall to $18 or rise to $22 i.e., that the rate of interest will rise to 5.56 percent or fall to 4.54 percent. The expected return from holding a bond is clearly 5 percent, since the possible capital gains and losses are of equal size and are equally likely. The expected return

* This section can be omitted with no loss in continuity.

is obtained by taking a weighted average of each possible occurrence, the weights being the probabilities of occurrence. In this case the calculation is:

$$1/2(3/20) + 1/2(-1/20) = .05$$

where the probability of each outcome is 1/2, since the events are deemed equally likely, and the rate of return is 3/20 if the price of the bond rises by $2 and $-$ 1/20 if the price falls by $2.

At the same time, there is clearly a dispersion about the expected outcome. One measure of the dispersion is the *standard deviation,* which is obtained by computing the squared deviation of each possible outcome from the mean, weighting the result by the probability of its occurrence, summing over all possible outcomes, and taking the square root. In this case the standard deviation is obtained as follows:

Outcome	Rate of return	Squared deviation from mean	Probability of occurrence	Squared deviation weighted by probability
$i = .0556$	$-.05$	.01	1/2	.005
$i = .0454$	.15	.01	1/2	.005
				.010

$$\text{Standard deviation} = \sqrt{.01} = .1$$

The individual can clearly hold a portfolio for which the standard deviation of the outcome is zero. He can hold all cash. But to have the possibility of earning a positive return, he must accept the risk of obtaining outcomes that differ from the expected one. A portfolio in which only bonds are held will, of course, have the largest expected return, but it will also be the portfolio with the largest standard deviation. If S_M is the share of the portfolio in money, S_B is the share of the portfolio in bonds, μ is the expected return from holding bonds and σ is the standard deviation of the return from bonds then the expected return of the portfolio is $S_B\mu$ and the standard deviation of the portfolio is $S_B\sigma$. The opportunities available to the individual are illustrated in Figure 3-4(a). The origin represents a portfolio consisting entirely of money, $S_B = O$. The point T represents a portfolio consisting entirely of bonds, $S_B = 1$. At T, the expected return and the standard deviation of the portfolio is at a maximum. At point M, the midpoint of OT, the portfolio is equally divided between holdings of money and bonds. At M, the expected return from the portfolio is $\mu/2$ and the standard deviation of the portfolio is $\sigma/2$. Any point on T is available to the individual.

Given the alternatives available to the individual, what determines his choice? To answer this question, we must consider his attitudes toward risk. We assume first that he regards large standard deviations as bad—that is, to induce him to increase the risk associated with the portfolio he holds, he must be compensated by a larger expected value. Second, we assume that the increment to expected return he demands as inducement to accept additional risk increases as the amount of risk he undertakes increases.

Such an individual will have indifference curves that slope upward, as in Figure 3-4(a), where I_3 represents a higher level of satisfaction than I_2. In addition, since he requires larger and larger increments of return as he is asked to undertake additional risk, his indifference curves will be convex from below. Given these indifference curves, the possibility exists that an individual will choose a diversified portfolio in reaching the highest attainable indifference curve, such as portfolio G in Figure 3-4(a). On the other hand, even with such indifference curves all bond or all money portfolios are possible. Such cases are illustrated in Figures 3-4(b) and 3-4(c).

If the individual is initially at point G in Figure 3-4(a) and the interest rate changes but the standard deviation from holding bonds does not change, how does the array of choices available to the individual change? A rise in the rate of interest pivots the line OT through the origin to OT'. Now the individual can obtain the same return as before with smaller risk, or larger return for bearing the same risk. If the new equilibrium is to the right of G, the rise in the rate of interest induces the individual to hold less money. If it is to the left of G it induces him to hold more money. Either outcome is possible. The substitution effect of a rise in the rate of interest induces the individual to hold less money. If the individual wishes, however, he can increase the expected return from his portfolio and reduce the risk involved by increasing his holdings of money. The effect of a change in the rate of interest on the demand for money cannot be stated unambiguously.

One factor may tend to increase the likelihood that a rise in the rate interest will lead to a decrease in the quantity of money demanded. A rise in the rae of interest reduces the value of each bond held. Thus even if an individual wishes to hold a reduced proportion of his portfolio in bonds after a rise in the rate of interest, he may have to hold a larger *number* of bonds than previously. If this is the case, he will have to reduce his money holdings.

EMPIRICAL EVIDENCE RELATED TO THE DEMAND FOR MONEY

The demand function for money has been one of the most closely studied of all economic relationships. Attempts to estimate it empirically have been

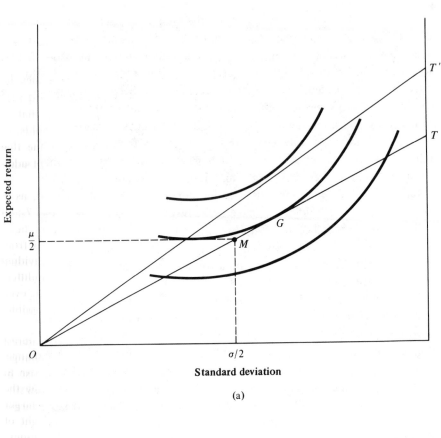

(a)

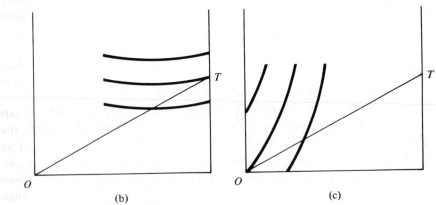

(b)   (c)

FIGURE 3-4

carried on by many investigators. These researchers have employed a variety of definitions of money, the rate of interest, and the level of transactions; but in spite of failure to agree on a common set of variables, there has been reasonable consensus that the quantity of money demanded is affected by income and the rate of interest. Given the tremendous amount of research that has been performed, it would be impractical to review more than a small fraction of it here. It is useful, however, to consider a typical set of results.[7]

David Laidler has estimated a demand function for money in which aggregate holdings of money, defined as currency and demand deposits at commerical banks, are related to the long-term rate of interest and against "permanent" income. The use of the latter instead of actual income stems from the belief that transitory variations in income do not affect the demand for money. Permanent income is a measure that we use in attempting to abstract from the effect of such transitory changes in income. One of the equations estimated by Laidler was:

$$\log_e M = 3.145 + 0.523 \log_e Y_p - 0.516 \log_e i$$

where M is currency plus demand deposits, Y_p is permanent income, and i is the long-term rate of interest. This equation, estimated using annual data for the period 1946 through 1960, explains about 80 percent of the variation in the demand for money.[8] The equation implies that a 10 percent increase in permanent income increases the quantity of money demanded by 5 percent, whereas a 10 percent increase in the rate of interest reduces the quantity of money demanded by 5 percent. The equation reported here is not the best of Laidler's results, but it illustrates the types of demand functions for money that have been estimated by a great many people, with a fair degree of success, over the past decade.

SUMMARY

Money is held for the services it provides. Holding money permits one to avoid the costs of continually converting earning assets to money. Holding money permits the avoidance of the uncertainty with respect to the unpredictability of the prices of earning assets.[9] Finally, one who holds money can avoid the costs associated with being unable to make unexpected payments.[10] The value of the services provided by money can, of course, change. When the value of the services declines, so will the amount of money that people will desire to hold. This chapter is concerned with the factors that determine the value of the services that can be secured by holding money, therefore, with the factors that determine the quantity of money that will be demanded.

NOTES

[1] The payment and receipt dates of various kinds of transaction are conditioned by customs, which themselves may have origins in economic factors. In our society, workers receive wage payments after their services have been rendered. Thus a worker can be thought of as extending credit to his employer during the period of work until the date of payment. However, by custom, the implicit debt from the employer to the employee bears no explicit interest and is not negotiable. Of course, borrowing until payday is customary in some circles. On the other hand, rental payments are made before the premises are used. Thus the renter is extending credit to the landlord during each rental period. Presumably if wage payments were made more frequently, wage payments would fall, since they would include a smaller implicit interest payment for the credit extended by the employee to the employer. Similarly, rentals would rise if rental payments were more frequent, since there would be a smaller amount of credit extended from renter to landlord. The custom in our society is for payments for groceries to be made at the time the goods change hands, although an increasing number of grocers extend credit either explicitly or in the form of check-cashing privileges. The result of these developments is presumably to raise the cost of groceries over what they would be if transactions were on a cash-and-carry basis. It is important to note that although at any given point the date of payment in relation to the date of the transactions is usually fairly closely fixed, over time these transaction "customs" may change as economic conditions change.

[2] The composition of the entire portfolio is not under consideration here. If the income received by the individual plus the wealth with which he enters the period exceeds his payments for rent and food, he will end the period with wealth to be carried over into the next period. Under our assumptions, this increment to wealth will be held in the form of bonds. We are concerned with the proportion of the portfolio that will exist during the period but will be gone at the end of the period.

[3] This analysis has been developed by W. J. Baumol, "The Transactions Demand for Cash: An Inventory Theoretic Approach," *Quarterly Journal of Economics* (1952), and J. Tobin, "The Interest-Elasticity of Transactions Demand for Cash," *Review of Economics and Statistics* (1957).

[4] We could have stated bond holdings after the initial conversion of bonds to money in terms of initial asset holdings, say, rZ. The time at which money holdings would be depleted for the second time then becomes $(1 - r)$. If we solve for p and r that maximize interest income, we get $\frac{2}{3}$ and $\frac{1}{3}$.

[5] This is obtained by setting the partial derivative of (3-1) minus nb with respect to $n = 0$ and solving for n. An economic interpretation of the result is that the number of transactions is increased until the extra cost of a transaction b is just equal to the extra interest income made possible by the additional transaction.

[6] This analysis has been developed in James Tobin, "Liquidity Preference as Behavior Toward Risk," *Review of Economic Studies* (1958).

[7] More evidence is reported in David E. W. Laidler, *The Demand for Money,* International Textbook, Scranton, Pa., 1969.

[8] David Laidler, "The Rate of Interest and the Demand for Money—Some Empirical Evidence," *Journal of Political Economy* (1966).

[9] In a financial system in which there are other alternatives than bonds, this motive for holding money may be particularly weak. If a person believes that bond prices will fall, rather than holding money he can hold assets that provide a return but fluctuate little, if at all, in price. Examples of such assets in the United States are nonmarketable government bonds, savings deposits at commercial or mutual savings banks, shares in savings and loan associations, and short-term marketable government bonds such as Treasury bills. All these provide a return to the holder with little or no possibility of capital loss as interest rates fluctuate.

[10] Again, in a financial system featuring a wide variety of highly liquid assets other than money which provide returns to the holder, precautionary balances may well be held in these forms rather than in money.

4

The investment decision

In this chapter we consider the determinants of investment spending by business firms. Investment spending represents the acquisition by business firms of commodities that enable companies to expand their production in the future. For example, purchases of buildings, machine tools, and vehicles, all represent expenditures that permit a firm to produce more in the future than it can at present. In the same sense, spending by firms in research and development activities can be viewed as a form of investment, as can the acquisition of inventories of raw materials. Each of these permits the firm to produce more in subsequent periods than it would have been possible without their acquisition.[1]

The investment decision for a firm stems from the decision relating to the amount of capital goods it wishes to hold. If there is a disparity between the amount of capital that a firm wishes to hold and the amount that it actually holds, there is an incentive for the firm to invest to close the gap. Since the entire gap may not be closed in a single period, a theory of investment behavior should include explanations of the determinants of the desired stock of capital and of the speed with which the gap is closed.

Let us consider a firm holding a given stock of capital goods and now considering a number of possible additions to that stock.[2] It is considering an array of possible investment projects. We make the following assumptions:

1. For each potential investment project the firm knows the additions to receipts and the additions to costs that will be produced by having and using the investment good. In other words, the firm can tell with certainty the amount by which production can be increased in each period as a result of possessing the capital good and the additional costs of labor and raw materials that must be incurred to make use of the investment good. Knowing this, it can calculate for each future period the net increment to receipts of the firm which result from having and using the capital good.

2. Project outcomes are independent. The return obtained from any one project is unaffected by whether any other project is undertaken. The existence of other projects neither raises nor lowers the return from any given project. This assumption rules out the existence of mutually exclusive projects.
3. The rate of interest at which the firm can borrow or lend in each of the periods during the useful life of the project is known. The firm may borrow to obtain the capital good, or it may use funds that otherwise could have been invested in bonds. We must allow for either the explicit cost of borrowing or the opportunity cost of not holding bonds in the firm's decision of whether to acquire the capital good.
4. The firm is not limited in the current period to any fixed quantity of investment, but if it has desirable projects, it can borrow to finance them at the going rate of interest. In other words, there is no rationing of credit.
5. There are no taxes.

The undertaking of an investment project produces a stream of additional receipts and expenditures for the firm. Because it owns a new piece of capital equipment, it can produce and sell more in subsequent periods than if it had not acquired the equipment. In addition, the use of the equipment involves the firm in additional expenditures for complementary inputs such as labor and raw materials, which must be used in conjunction with the capital equipment if the latter is to produce output. Since the incremental receipts and expenditures resulting from the acquisition of the capital good occur at various times, the problem for the firm is to somehow make them comparable.

As the discussion of the valuation of bonds in Chapter 3 makes clear, a $1 receipt at one point is not equivalent to a $1 receipt at another. And a $1 receipt at one point need not be exactly offset by a $1 expenditure at another. Ask yourself whether you are indifferent to the prospects of a $1 payment today and a $1 payment one year from today. Would you be willing to pay $1 today for the promise to repay you $1 one year from today? Since the answer to both questions is clearly no, this implies that you value the early payment of $1 more highly than the $1 payment a year from now and that a $1 expenditure today carries a larger weight in your calculations than a $1 receipt a year from now. This is true because the earlier $1 receipt can be placed in some income-earning asset, say bonds, as soon as it is received, and by the time the later receipt has arrived, the first receipt has grown to more than $1 through the payment of interest. Similarly, a $1 expenditure today involves funds that must be taken out of bond holdings. The original $1 would have grown to more than $1 after one year, thus the repayment of $1 at the beginning of the next year does not completely offset the original expenditure.

For the firm, earlier receipts are "more valuable" than later receipts because the firm can place the earlier receipts in bonds, earning interest over the period between the earlier and later receipts. Alternatively, the earlier receipts can be used to pay off loans earlier, thus permitting the firm to avoid interest payments. Similarly, later payments are "better" than earlier payments because the funds that must be made available to meet the later payment can be invested in bonds during the period between the earlier and the later payment dates, or loans made for the purpose of meeting the payment can be postponed.

How then does the firm make commensurate earlier and later receipts and expenditures? The procedure employed, called *discounting,* is exactly the same as that involved in the valuation of bonds. Future receipts and expenditures are discounted—given smaller weights per dollar—to make them comparable to current receipts and expenditures. The discount to be applied to a future receipt is determined by asking, How much would I be willing to accept in the present for a receipt of a given amount at a particular point in the future? The amount obtained, called the *present value* of the future receipt, depends, of course, on the interest rates prevailing during the intervening period. The higher the interest rates, the more valuable will be early receipts as compared to late ones, and the larger must be the discount applied to future receipts. This is because the return that can be had by obtaining the receipts early and placing the proceeds in bonds will be high when the rate of interest is high. When the rate of interest on bonds is low, the amount by which future receipts must be discounted to make them commensurate with present receipts is low. A similar logic holds for the discounting of future payments. Since the funds used to make a payment can be placed in bonds before the payment is required, the higher the rate of interest, the smaller the weight that should be applied to a future payment as compared to a present one.

The same logic again requires that given future rates of interest, the further into the future any receipt (or payment) is, the smaller its assigned weight should be in comparison with any earlier receipt (or payment). This, of course, is because during the period between the earlier and later receipt, the proceeds of the earlier receipt can be placed in bonds to earn interest.

The preceding discussion permits us to obtain a precise formula for making comparable the items in a stream of future receipts and expenditures occurring at various points of time. It permits the aggregation of all the receipts and payments into a single measure, the present value of the investment project, which tells us the maximum amount anyone would be willing to pay in the present to obtain that particular stream of receipts and expenditures. By definition, all receipts and expenditures incurred in the present receive a weight of one; that is, they are not discounted. Suppose the rate of interest prevailing in the first period is designated i_1. What is the current equivalent, the present value, of a $1 payment received at the end of the first period? Equivalently, how much would you be willing to accept in the present in place of a $1 payment at the end of the first year? Since the amount you would be willing to accept, call it X, can be placed in bonds at the beginning of the period, it will have grown to $X(1 + i_1)$ by the end of the period, which is, we are assuming, equivalent to a $1 receipt at the end of the period. Since $X(1 + i_1) = 1$, $X = 1/(i + i_1)$. Thus $1/(1 + i_1)$ is the weight that should be attached to a $1 receipt at the end of the first period if the rate of interest prevailing during that period is i_1, and this value is clearly lower, the higher the rate of interest. If the rate of interest is .05 you would be willing to pay $.95 for a promise to be paid $1, one period from now. If the rate of interest is .10, the value of such a promise, its present value, declines to $.91.

A similar rationale pertains to the treatment of receipts and expenditures still further into the future. We illustrate the procedure for a receipt two periods into the future. If the interest rate prevailing in the first period is i_1 and the interest rate prevailing in the second period is i_2, then Y invested in bonds for two periods will be worth $Y(1 + i_1)(1 + i_2)$, on the assumption that all the proceeds from the holdings of the bonds during the first period are placed in bonds during the second period. Thus the rate of discount to apply to a receipt two periods from the present is $1/(1 + i_1)(1 + i_2)$. In a similar manner, rates of discount can be applied to receipts (and expenditures) further and further into the future, the weight being attached being smaller, the further into the future is the receipt (or expenditure). And, of course, the rate of discount depends on the rates of interest prevailing into the future, as well.

After calculating the present value of each of the future receipts and expenditures resulting from undertaking the investment project, including the initial outlay, it is possible to determine the present value of the entire stream simply by aggregating, or adding up, all the elements of the stream. The following equation shows the calculation of a projects value:

$$V_0 = -C_0 + \frac{S_1}{(1 + i_1)} + \frac{S_2}{(1 + i_1)(1 + i_2)} + \cdots$$

$$+ \frac{S_n}{(1 + i_1) \cdots (1 + i_n)} \qquad (4\text{-}1)$$

where C_0 is the initial outlay required to start the investment project, $S_1, S_2, \ldots, S_n$ are net receipts in each period, including any potential scrap value of the investment good in period n, and i_1, i_2, . . . , i_n are the interest rates prevailing in each of the periods during the investment good's life.

When each element in the stream is appropriately discounted, the sum of these elements determines whether the investment project will be undertaken. If the present value is positive, the firm will undertake the project, since doing so adds to the value of the firm.[3] And this is what happens, whether the firm borrows the funds or employs funds it would otherwise have placed in bonds.

It should be stressed here that the calculation of a project's present value involves the discounting of the stream of actual receipts and payments that characterizes the project. Each receipt (or payment) is recorded as of the date it is received (or incurred) and is discounted to the present. No special allowance is made for the amortization of the project cost or the depreciation of the investment good. All that is relevant is the amount and timing of actual receipts and payment. Since the undertaking of a project involves the acceptance of the stream of receipts and payments that it produces, the stream fully describes the outcome of the project.[4]

INVESTMENT AND THE RATE OF INTEREST

If the rate of interest is constant over the life of a project (i.e., if $i_1 = i_2 = \cdots = i_n$), it may be possbile to describe the relationship between the quantity of investment undertaken and the rate of interest. If the only negative term in the present calculation is the first or undiscounted term (i.e., if incremental receipts exceed incremental expenditures in all future periods), a decline in the rate of interest i will raise a project's present value. A decline in the rate of interest will lower the discount applied to any future receipt or payment, thus raising the absolute value of all future receipts and payments in the determination of the present value. But since receipts exceed payments in all future periods, the result must be to raise the present value of a project. Thus a project that has a negative present value at a high interest rate and will not be undertaken at that interest rate, may be undertaken if the rate of interest falls sufficiently to raise the present value of the project above zero.[5]

Following is an illustrative calculation of the present value of an investment project. The initial cost of the capital good is $10,000. The good can be used by the firm for two years, at which point it can be sold for $1,000. In the first year of its use it will produce additional receipts of $20,000 and involve additional costs of $10,000. In the second year it produces additional

─────Table 4-1─────

Rate of interest i	Present value of first year's net receipts $\dfrac{S_1}{(1+i)}$	Present value of second year's net receipts $\dfrac{S_2}{(1+i)^2}$	Present value of project $V_0 = -C_0 + \dfrac{S_1}{(1+i)} + \dfrac{S_2}{(1+i)^2}$
.05	$9524	$1814	$1338
.10	$9091	$1653	$ 744
.15	$8696	$1512	$ 208
.20	$8333	$1389	−$ 278
.25	$8000	$1280	−$ 720
		$S_1 = \$10,000$	
		$S_2 = \$\ 2,000$	
		$C_0 = \$10,000$	

receipts of $15,000 and involves additional costs of $14,000. Thus net receipts in the first period are $10,000 higher than they would have been without acquisition of the capital good. In the second period incremental receipts are $2,000, since we have assumed that at the end of the second period the good has a scrap value of $1,000. The initial expenditure of $10,000 produces a stream of receipts of $10,000 in the first period and $2,000 in the second, and these amounts are S_1 and S_2, respectively. We can calculate the present value of the investment project for a number of possible interest rates. To facilitate the comparison, we assume that the interest rate is constant during the two periods. Table 4-1 gives some sample values.

At interest rates of .05, .10, and .15, the project has a positive present value. Following the rule already described, for those rates of interest the firm will undertake the project. For an interest rate of .20 the present value is negative and the project will not be undertaken. The *break-even interest rate,* for which the present value of the project is zero, is approximately .17.

INTERDEPENDENT INVESTMENT PROJECTS

The foregoing analysis applies only when investment projects are independent. In such cases, all projects having a positive present value will be undertaken by a firm wishing to maximize its present value. However, some investment projects a firm undertakes may affect the return that can be obtained from others. This section examines some of these cases.

The simplest example of project interdependence concerns projects that are mutually exclusive. If one such project is undertaken, the other project adds nothing to the receipts of the firm. Mutual exclusivity of projects can arise for a variety of reasons. One project may add nothing to total revenue if another is undertaken because both are designed to do the same task. Two projects may require the use of a particular scarce resource, and if that resource is devoted to one it cannot go to the other. In such cases, how does the firm decide which project to choose? Given our assumptions, the correct policy for a firm wishing to maximize its present value is to choose, from among a number of mutually exclusive projects, the project having the largest present value.

Mutual exclusivity is the simplest type of interdependence. In other cases, the undertaking of one project may improve the performance of some projects and worsen the performance of others. How can we allow for such interdependence in making the investment decision? In principle, we would list all possible combinations of projects, calculate the present value of each such *combination,* and choose the combination having the largest present value. If X, Y, and Z are the projects being considered one can list the possible combinations as:

$$X$$
$$Y$$
$$Z$$
$$XY$$
$$YZ$$
$$XZ$$
$$XYZ$$

If the projects are mutually exclusive, the combination with the largest present value must be one of the first three combinations listed. If the projects are independent and each has a positive present value, XYZ will be the combination with the largest present value, assuming that each alone has a positive present value. If more complicated forms of interdependence are permitted, any of the combinations may have the highest present value. For example, the combination XZ may have a larger present value than the sum of the present values of X and Z if the projects are complementary. On the other hand, the present value of XYZ may be smaller than the present value of XY if project Z is to some extent a substitute for X or Y. Table 4-2 illustrates these possibilities.

Clearly, mutual exclusivity of projects is a special case of projects that are substitutes. When projects are mutually exclusive, the incremental returns from undertaking one if another is being undertaken are zero, and since the second project involves investment costs, the present value of the combination of the two projects is smaller than the present value of the project with the

--------------------------------Table 4-2--------------------------------

	Project(s)	V_0
Projects Independent	X	$10,000
	Y	$20,000
	Z	$15,000
	XY	$30,000
	XZ	$25,000
	YZ	$35,000
	XYZ	$45,000
Projects Mutually Exclusive	X	$10,000
	Y	$20,000
	XY	$18,000
Projects Complements	X	$10,000
	Y	$20,000
	XY	$35,000
Projects Substitutes (*a*)	X	$10,000
	Y	$20,000
	XY	$19,000
Projects Substitutes (*b*)	X	$10,000
	Y	$20,000
	XY	$25,000

larger present value. When two projects are partial substitutes, the present value of the combination of the two projects may be larger than, as in the case (*b*), or smaller than, as in case (*a*), the present value of the project with the larger present value, depending on the closeness of the substitution. In the special case of mutual exclusivity, the present value of the combination must be smaller.

CREDIT RATIONING

Let us now examine the effect of dropping the assumption that the firm can borrow any desired amount. To avoid complicating the analysis; we retain the assumption of project independence, but the topics of project interdependence, credit rationing, and methods for dealing with their joint occurrence are the province of capital budgeting in the firm, a subject that is not considered in this book.

Suppose that a firm feels that it has a great many projects that will increase the present value of the firm and that it would be willing to borrow for these projects at the going rate of interest. Furthermore, suppose that instead of raising the interest rate to the firm, to discourage it from borrowing, lending institutions simply maintain the rate of interest at which they will lend but limit the amount they will lend to a sum smaller than that which the firm wishes to borrow. How will the firm decide which among the projects, which all have positive present values, to undertake? Following our previous notation, V_0 is the present value of an investment project and C_0 is the initial outlay associated with undertaking the project (i.e., the cost of the capital good). Suppose that the amount of the firm's own resources together with the amount that the firm can borrow under its credit limit is F. The problem is to allocate F among projects to maximize the present value of the firm. The procedure is as follows: For each project, calculate V_0/C_0, which is the ratio of the increase in the present value of the firm divided by the amount of resources it will take to initiate the project. Array projects by V_0/C_0 from highest to lowest. The projects are now arrayed in terms of the contribution to the present value per dollar invested. Start at the top of the list and undertake projects until F is exhausted. In so doing, the maximum net worth of the firm, subject to the limitation of F to be invested, will be found.[6]

What will be the effect of changes in the rate of interest if there is credit rationing to the firm? Suppose that the rate of interest rises, but there is no change in the firm's credit limit. In a situation of no credit rationing, some projects that previously had positive present values and would have been undertaken now acquire negative present values and are not undertaken, thus reducing investment. With credit rationing, the rise in the rate of interest will reduce the present values of some projects; but while there remain projects with positive present values for which the sum of current outlays exceeds or is equal to F, the amount of investment undertaken by the firm will not change. In other words, over some range, variations in the rate of interest will have no effect on the quantity of investment undertaken by firms facing a credit limit. As we will see later, this has important implications for the effectiveness of monetary policy.

AN "AVAILABLE FUNDS" THEORY OF INVESTMENT BEHAVIOR

We have assumed to this point that the interest rate at which the firm can lend any funds it does not wish to invest in capital goods is the same as the interest rate at which the firm can borrow. Often, however, the borrowing rate of a firm i_B is greater than the rate it can earn by lending i_L. What does this disparity imply for the investment decision?[7]

Let us revert to our previous assumption of project independence, assuming, however, that the firm has F available funds that if not invested in capital goods, can be loaned out at i_L. The firm should first evaluate all projects using interest rate i_L, dropping from further consideration any project having a negative present value at that interest rate. Holding bonds is clearly a superior alternative to undertaking these projects. The remaining projects should be evaluated at i_B. We are assuming that the firm can borrow as much as it wants at i_B. Those projects with negative present values when i_B is used will never be in the collection of projects chosen if undertaking them requires financing through borrowing. They may be in the chosen collection if undertaking them is an alternative to holding bonds. Those projects with positive present values when evaluated at i_B will always be in the collection chosen but may be financed either by borrowing or through the use of "available funds." We have thus divided projects into three groups:

1. Negative present values when evaluated at i_L (therefore, at i_B).
2. Positive present values when evaluated at i_L, negative present values when evaluated at i_B.
3. Positive present values when evaluated at i_B (therefore, at i_L).

Suppose that there are three projects under consideration, X, Y, and Z, and their present values when evaluated at i_L are V_L^X, V_L^Y, V_L^Z. Assume that all these present values are positive, thus none are in group 1. Assume further that of the present values when evaluated at i_B, V_B^X, V_B^Y, and V_B^Z, the first two are negative and the last is positive. Finally, assume that all projects have the same C_0 and that $F = 2C_0$, or in other words, that only two projects can be undertaken if only available funds are employed.

The data just given permit us to exclude from further consideration the following combinations of projects and financing:

1. Projects Y and Z financed by available funds, project X financed by borrowing.
2. Projects X and Z financed by available funds and project Y financed by borrowing.
3. Projects X and Y financed by available funds and project Z not undertaken.
4. All collections of projects involving only one project.
   This leaves for further consideration:
5. Projects X and Z financed by available funds and project Y not undertaken.
6. Projects Y and Z financed by available funds and project X not undertaken.
7. Projects X and Y financed by available funds and project Z financed by borrowing.

Of the collections of projects and methods of finance, items 5 through 7 represent possible outcomes depending on the streams of receipts and payments of each project and on the rate of interest. That collection of projects should be chosen for which the sum of the present values is a maximum. Collection 7 will be chosen if the reduction in the present value of project Z when evaluated at i_B rather than at i_L is smaller than either the present value of X and the present value of Y when each is evaluated at i_L. If this condition does not hold, no borrowing will occur, and available funds will finance project Z and either project X or Y, whichever has the greater present value.

Some examples may help to clarify this analysis. Table 4-3 presents three sets of present values, each one containing the present values of projects X, Y, and Z evaluated using i_L and the present value of project Z evaluated using i_B. These present values are restricted only in that the present value of project Z is smaller when evaluated at the borrowing rate than when evaluated at the lending rate.

In case 1 the optimal strategy is to undertake all three projects, financing project Z by borrowing. The sum of the present values of the projects undertaken is \$18,000. If only projects X and Y are undertaken, their combined present value is \$15,000. And other combinations employing only available funds also yield less than \$18,000. Combinations of X and Z and Y and Z are worth \$17,000 and \$12,000, respectively. In case 2 the optimal strategy is to undertake projects Y and Z, financing both through available funds, which yields a present value of \$12,000. If project X is added and project Z is financed externally, the present value declines to \$10,000. In case 3 projects X and Z are chosen, and both are financed using internal funds, yielding a present value of \$17,000. If project Y is added, the present value falls to \$16,000.

Suppose that we undertake only two projects, say Y and Z, and that both borrowing and lending interest rates decline, but there is no increase in F. What will happen to the quantity of investment undertaken? Clearly, if at the new i_B, $V_B{}^X$ and $V_B{}^Y$ are positive, all three projects will be undertaken. But what if this is not the case? Again we must compare $(V_L{}^Z - V_B{}^Z)$ with both $V_L{}^X$ and $V_L{}^Y$. Since both the latter have risen, it is more likely that both ex-

	Table 4-3		
	Case 1	Case 2	Case 3
$V_L{}^X$	\$10,000	\$2,000	\$10,000
$V_L{}^Y$	5,000	5,000	3,000
$V_L{}^Z$	7,000	7,000	7,000
$V_B{}^Z$	3,000	3,000	3,000

ceed $(V_L{}^z - V_B{}^z)$. But this is by no means guaranteed. If this condition is still not met, the volume of investment will remain limited to F in spite of the decline in interest rates. This result is qualitatively similar to the result obtained under credit rationing (which is a special case of the present analysis), where variations in the rate of interest could but need not alter the volume of investment. This point can be seen by examining case 2. If a decline in the rate of interest raises all present values by $1000, the optimal strategy will still be to undertake only projects Y and Z. Of course, if interest rates fall sufficiently, all the projects will be undertaken.

THE EFFECT OF PRICES AND COSTS

Other variables taken into account in the determination of a firm's investment policy are the price at which the firm's product can be sold and the costs of inputs complementary to and substitutes for the capital good. Other things equal, an increase in the price at which a firm can sell its product increases the net receipts that a firm can expect to obtain from selling the incremental product made possible by the acquisition of the capital good. The result of the price rise is an increase in the number of investment projects having a positive present value. A rise in the price of the product leads to more investment and more output planned in subsequent periods.

An increase in the price of factors used with the capital good in the production process may serve to either decrease or increase investment, depending on whether the other inputs are complementary to or substitutes for the capital good. When the prices of substitute inputs fall, the firm will wish to undertake some projects involving relatively large quantities of the substitute inputs, since these will have positive present values after the decline in the factor price. In the most plausible case in which some projects are mutually exclusive, projects calling for relatively large quantities of capital will be replaced by those having relatively small capital requirements, thus reducing the quantity of investment.

When the price of an input complementary to capital falls, the present values of all projects will rise, and some projects that previously had negative present values may now have positive ones. In the case of mutually exclusive projects, projects involving large quantities of capital will be substituted for those involving small quantities.

TAXES

To take taxes into account in the investment decision, it is necessary to specify several aspects of the tax law. Four are considered here: (1) the rules concerning depreciation, (2) the tax deductibility of interest payments and the tax on interest earnings, (3) the nature of loss offsets, and (4) tax credits for investment.

Depreciation

Assume that a tax is imposed in each period on "profits." For simplicity, we will assume that taxes are a fixed percentage of profits. (By this assumption we avoid having to deal with graduated or progressive tax rates, which may affect the desirability of investment projects by favoring those with relatively smooth flows of profits over those with relatively erratic flows.) It remains to define profits. The tax laws typically permit a firm to make a tax-free recovery of the costs of investment projects before calculating profits, thus profits taxes. The rationale for this is as follows: Like the costs of other inputs (e.g., labor and raw materials), outlays for capital goods represent costs incurred by the firm in the productive process. However, a firm must still determine how much of the cost of using the capital good is borne during each year of its useful life. In principle, one would find the market prices of the capital good at the beginning and the end of the year and treat the difference as the cost of using the capital good during the year. An approximation to this would be the cost of renting the good during the year, on the assumption that a rental market exists. In fact, rental markets frequently do not exist, and it is often impossible to determine the market value of second-hand investment goods on a regular basis, since there are no highly developed markets for such goods. The result is that taxing authorities turn to somewhat arbitrary depreciation rules to enable firms to take account of the costs of capital equipment in computing pretax profits. Since government policy toward depreciation frequently is intended to stimulate or discourage investment, it is not fair to say that the government is attempting to approximate the correct (from an economic point of view) depreciation through these rules.

A number of alternative depreciation methods have been employed by the taxing authority. The simplest is the so-called *straight-line depreciation method*. First, the taxing authority must specify the "useful life" of the capital good. We put "useful life" in quotation marks because the life specified by the taxing authority need bear no exact relationship to the period of time over which the capital good is capable of providing services. The depreciation the firm can take each year is the cost of the capital good divided by its useful life. The firm is permitted to deduct depreciation from sales less other costs incurred, the numerators in (4-1), in computing its taxable profits.

An alternative method sometimes allowed in the United States is the "sum-of-the-years'-digits" method. With this approach, the useful life, in periods, is first determined. Then the digits, starting with 1 and continuing to the useful life, are summed. In the first year of the useful life, the firm is permitted to compute its taxable income by deducting from its revenues the useful life divided by the sum of the digits, times the cost of the capital good. In the second year, it can deduct useful life minus 1, divided by the sum of the digits, times the cost of the investment good. In the final year of useful life, the firm can deduct 1 divided by the sum of the digits, times the cost of the capital good. Thus for a good with a three-year useful life, first year depreciation is $\frac{1}{2}$, second year depreciation is $\frac{1}{3}$, and third year depreciation is $\frac{1}{6}$ of the cost of the good. As compared to the straight-line method, the firm is here deferring tax payments. Taxes are lower in the early part of the useful life and higher at the end. The present value of an investment project is increased by the use of this method as compared with the straight-line method.

A third method is the *"declining balance"* method. Like the sum-of-the-years'-digits method, it permits a faster writeoff of the costs of an investment good, thus permits tax payments to be deferred. Whereas under straight-line depreciation method a capital good with a useful life of 10 years allows the firm to deduct 10 percent of the initial cost of the asset from revenues in each year, use of the *double* declining balance method permits the firm to deduct 20 percent of the value of the asset during the first year of its life, double the straight-line rate, 20 percent of the residual value (80 percent of the initial value) during the second year of its useful life, 20 percent of the residual value (64 percent of the initial value) in the third year, and so on. Since this method will not allow the remaining balance to be reduced to zero, at some point a change to the straight-line method for the remaining balance is permitted. This method, like the sum of the years' digits, permits an increase in the present value of an investment project over that obtained using the straight line.

Tax treatment of interest

The tax treatment of interest payments and receipts is also an important factor affecting the investment decision. Here we assume that all interest earnings on bonds held by the firm are fully taxable and any interest payments made on loans incurred by the firm are deductible from receipts in computing profits taxes. The existence of profits tax on interest income and the deductibility of interest payments from taxable income changes the discount that must be applied to future receipts and payments to make them comparable to current receipts and payments. If the interest rate in period one is i_1, without taxes $1 held in the form of bonds will have grown to $1(1 + i_1)$ by the end of the period. If interest payments are taxed at a rate t, \$1 will have grown to only $\$1[1 + i_1(1 - t)]$ by the end of the year. Thus a smaller rate of discount applies to future receipts and payments when bond interest is taxable. A similar argument holds if the firm borrows at a rate i_1. Since the government permits the deduction of interest payments from income in computing profits taxes, the interest cost incurred by the firm is at a rate less than i_1. In such cases, the rate of discount applied to future receipts and payments is smaller than it would be if the interest payments were not deductible from income.

Loss offsets

Third, we assume that if a firm's taxable profits are negative during any given period, the government pays the firm an amount equal to the tax rate times the loss. This assumption may seem unrealistic, but it requires only that for the years in which the taxable profits on the cited project are negative, the firm have other projects yielding profits sufficient to permit the negative item to be deducted from them, thus producing a tax saving equal to the loss times the tax rate.

Investment tax credit

Finally, we must deal with the *investment tax credit*. This feature of the tax law permits a firm to deduct from its tax a fraction of any new investment made during the year, this deduction being over and above any permissible deduction for depreciation. In other words, in computing the tax payable during a given period, thus in computing the second term in an investment project's payment stream, the firm first calculates its tax disregarding the credit and then deducts from the tax a portion of C_0. The impact of the credit is thus to raise the present value of investment projects, thereby making positive the return from some projects for which the present value would otherwise have been negative. The result is to raise the quantity of investment a firm will wish to undertake.

A PRESENT VALUE CALCULATION WITH TAXES

The calculation of the present value of investment project is shown in (4-2). We assume that the straight-line depreciation method is used, that there is no investment credit, that the "useful life" for tax purposes is two periods, and, to make the point that this need not be equal to the period over which the capital good is capable of yielding services, we make the latter three periods long. For simplicity of exposition, we assume a constant interest rate during the life of the project.

$$V_0 = -C_0 + \frac{(R_1 - P_1) - t(R_1 - P_1 - C_0/2)}{[1 + i(1 - t)]}$$
$$+ \frac{(R_2 - P_2) - t(R_2 - P_2 - C_0/2)}{[1 + i(1 - t)]^2} + \frac{(R_3 - P_3) - t(R_3 - P_3)}{[1 + i(1 - t)]^3} \quad \text{(4-2)}$$

C Cost of investment good
R Receipts
P Payments other than for taxes, interest, and capital goods
t Tax rate
i Interest rate
$C_0/2$ Annual depreciation

The first term in the formula, C_0, represents the initial cost of the piece of capital equipment. This is the payment received by the firm that produced the capital good, whether the purchasing firm pays cash or obtains a loan to make the payment.[8] The second term represents the present value of the payments received in the first year. For simplicity it is assumed that all payments are received on the last day of the year. The cash receipts are represented by R_1, and P_1 designates the cash outlays for expenses other than taxes and interest. However, the firm actually receives less than this amount, since it must make tax payment equal to the tax rate t, times taxable profits. Ignoring interest payments for the moment, taxable income is $R_1 - P_1 -$ depreciation, which in the case of an asset with a two-year useful life and a cost of C_0 is $C_0/2$. Of course, $R_1 - P_1 -$ taxes $= S_1$. The numerator of the second term must be reduced to its present value. To do so, one must discount by the current interest rate i. However, since any interest payments are deductible in computing taxable income, the interest rate as seen by the firm is $i(1 - t)$. Similarly, if the firm is employing its own funds that might otherwise have been invested in bonds at interest rate i, the opportunity cost is also $i(1 - t)$, since the interest income it would have earned would also be subject to income tax. The calculation of the present value of the second year's receipts and payments is carried out in a similar fashion. But in the third year, although the asset still yields services, it can no longer be depreciated, since the useful life as determined by the taxing authorities was two years. Therefore, the fourth term in the calculation contains no term for depreciation. If the capital good has a scrap value, it is included in R_3.

TAX POLICY FOR INVESTMENT

As we can now see, there are a number of ways in which investment may be stimulated through the use of tax policy. Accelerated depreciation formulas, shortened useful lives, investment tax credits, and lower business tax rates all can contribute to increased investment, both by raising the present values of investment projects and by making available additional internal funds. And all these approaches have been used at one time or another in the United States.

An example of the kinds of tax policy the government has pursued in an effort to stimulate investment can be found in the period 1962–1964. Two major changes took place in 1962. First, for many assets, shortened useful lives were permitted in calculating depreciation. Second, an investment tax credit of 7 percent was permitted for many kinds of new investment. In 1964 an additional stimulus to investment was provided by reducing the maximum tax rate on corporate income from 52 to 47 percent. At the time, it was recognized that the stimulus to investment could come from two sources: "First, it (the policy) will strengthen investment incentives by increasing the after-tax profits that businessmen can expect to earn on new productive facilities. Second, it will add to supply of internal funds, a large part of which is normally reinvested in the business. . . ."[9]

In 1970 the government again permitted a reduction in the useful lives of assets that could be used in calculating depreciation and also argued for the restoration of the investment tax credit, which had been suspended in 1969. The government pointed out that the various tax increases enacted in 1969, including the suspension of the tax credit, had "raised the tax burden on investment, through higher levies on corporate profits, and thereby reduced both the supply of internal funds available for business investment and the incentive to invest."[10] Thus it appears to be generally accepted that tax policy can affect investment and that such policy works through two channels, stimulating the demand for investment on the part of business firms and increasing the supply of funds they have available to invest.

As indicated in the Introduction to this book, it is impossible to anticipate all the kinds of change in the economy, including policy changes, that may occur. This chapter provides a general framework within which the effects of these changes can be analyzed and furnishes a number of examples of some actual policies to reveal how the framework can be employed. If a policy that is not considered here is proposed after this book goes to press, the student should be in a position to analyze its effects.

THE INTEREST ELASTICITY OF INVESTMENT DEMAND

The model of investment demand developed in this chapter takes the rate of interest as one of the principal determinants of the volume of investment that firms will undertake. There is, however, considerable controversy over the sensitivity of investment spending to variations in the rate of interest. This controversy is fueled by two kinds of evidence. First, in surveys in which businessmen were questioned about the factors affecting their willingness to invest, the interest rate frequently was not mentioned or was given a small weight. Second, many early empirical studies of investment demand failed to find any important role for the rate of interest. This evidence raises the question of the usefulness of the model developed in this chapter.[11]

We have suggested that variations in the rate of interest might leave investment unchanged for a number of reasons. If credit rationing is an important phenomenon, and that many firms are frequently unable to undertake all the investment projects they have in mind, changes in the rate of interest are frequently outweighed by changes in the availability of funds. By the same token, investment may remain unchanged by a change in the rate of interest that is not accompanied by a change in the availability of funds.

The failure of the rate of interest to appear in studies of investment demand can also be explained by noting that fluctuations in the expected cash flow from a project may well be large enough to offset any changes in the rate of interest. When economic activity is strong, a firm may experience both rising interest rates and rising expected cash flows, and the latter may be large enough to offset the former.

As an example of how the phenomenon just outlined might work, consider a project involving an initial outlay of $2000 and having net receipts of $1000 a year for 10 years; this project will have a present value of $4710 if the interest rate is 8 percent. If, instead, the rate of interest is 10 percent, the present value declines to $4144. But it takes a relatively small increase in the annual net receipts, to $1092, to completely offset the effect of the interest rate rise on the project's present value.

Thus we have a rationalization of why the effect of the interest rate on investment might not be easy to isolate. The reason given is that the effects of variations in the rate of interest are frequently masked by movements in other areas. But for us to be realistically concerned about the effect of the rate of interest on investment, some businessmen, or other spenders, must occasionally be influenced by variations in the rate of interest in their spending decisions. Although other factors may help to determine investment, and at times may be the overriding considerations, unless some investment responds to variations in the rate of interest, we will be better off concentrating directly on such factors as expected profits and available funds as determinants of investment spending. It is the thrust of this chapter that neither these factors nor the rate of interest can safely be ignored in any analysis of investment behavior.

SUMMARY

Business firms acquire capital goods to increase the present value of the firm. The quantity of investment that a firm will undertake during a year depends on the costs and returns entailed by the various projects, on the interdependence among projects, on the supply of funds for undertaking the projects, and on the tax laws. In a world of certainty, a firm will undertake that collection of investment projects which has a larger present value than any other collection.

NOTES

[1] Many actions of the household sector can also be viewed as investment. Examples are the acquisition of an automobile or the obtaining of a college education. These decisions can be analyzed with the same tools employed in this chapter. However, we assume that nonpecuniary factors play little or no part in the decisions of firms, whereas they may be important to the analysis of household behavior.

[2] For an excellent discussion of the logic behind the investment decision, covering some of the same ground as this chapter, see Jack Hirshleifer, James C. DeHaven, and Jerome W. Milliman, *Water Supply,* University of Chicago Press, Chicago, 1960, chap. VII.

[3] Sometimes the decision rule is stated somewhat differently, although the logic involved is identical. If the initial outlay for the investment project is excluded from the calculation of the present value of the investment project, the rule can be stated as follows: Adopt an investment project if its present value exceeds its initial cost. Since the initial cost carried a weight of 1 in our calculation, the rule is clearly identical to including the initial cost in the determination of the present value and requiring that the present value exceed zero.

[4] In more complicated situations (e.g., those involving taxes), more complicated present value calculations will be presented. But that should not obscure the fundamental rationale involved in the decision of whether to undertake an investment project that calls for an evaluation of the stream of actual receipts and outlays with respect to both timing and amount.

[5] If we had assumed, instead, that there are some negative terms in the calculation (i.e., that in some future periods additional expenditures resulting from the project exceed additional receipts), we could not establish definite relationship between the rate of interest and the present value of a project, thus between the rate of interest and the amount of investment undertaken.

[6] The analysis implicitly assumes that there will be no effective credit rationing in subsequent periods, either because firms will be able to obtain all the funds that they need or because they will have no fund requirements.

[7] For a discussion of the significance of the disparity between borrowing and lending rates, see James Duesenberry, *Business Cycles and Economic Growth,* McGraw-Hill, New York, 1958, chap. 5.

[8] When the capital-good-producing firm sells on credit, it can be regarded as simultaneously engaging in the businesses of producing goods and financing their purchase. The two functions need not be combined in the same business.

[9] *The Annual Report of the Council of Economic Advisers,* January 1963, p. 47.

[10] *Economic Report of the President,* February 1971, p. 90.

[11] For a critical view of the evidence from businessmen's surveys, see William H. White, "Interest Inelasticity of Investment Demand—The Case from Business Attitude Surveys Re-examined," *American Economic Review* (1956). Empirical evidence on the determinants of investment is surveyed in Robert Eisner and Robert Strotz, "The Determinants of Business Investment," in Daniel B. Suits et al., editors *Impacts of Monetary-Policy,* Prentice-Hall, Englewood Cliffs, N.J., 1963. Recent empirical evidence has cast doubt on the earlier findings of a small or nonexistent interest elasticity of investment.

5

Consumer behavior

The third building block of our model of income determination examines how households decide what portion of their current income they will consume and what proportion they will save.[1] To illustrate the problem, we make a number of simplifying assumptions:

1. We assume that the household knows its current income Y_1 and also that it expects its income in the next period to be Y_2; it holds with certainty the expectation that Y_2 will prevail.

2. We assume that the household makes its consumption plan for both periods simultaneously. Clearly, this kind of analysis is illustrative of the decisions a household might make about a long-term consumption pattern, if all future incomes were certain. Since we consider only two periods, the problem can be approached using geometric techniques.

There is no need for a household to consume at the same rate that its income accrues if it has some freedom to borrow or lend. A household always has the option of consuming exactly its income in each period, but it may obtain a higher level of satisfaction from consumption from a given income stream if it engages in borrowing or lending at various times. Suppose, for example, that a household has an income that is expected to grow over time: It need not wait for the higher income levels to be reached before consuming at high levels if it has the opportunity and the desire to borrow against future income. Similarly, a household with widely fluctuating incomes need not have widely fluctuating consumption levels if it borrows during periods of abnormally low incomes and repays its borrowings when incomes are abnormally high. Finally, a household need not severely reduce its consumption level when its breadwinner retires if it has consumed less than its income while he was employed. The point here is not that the household needs to spend at a rate different from that at which it receives income, but that it has the option to do so and may find it advantageous to exploit this option.[2]

3. We assume that the household enters the first period with no assets

other than the human capital embodied in its members. The value of this human capital, if there are only two periods over which it will produce income, is the present value of the income stream it can produce. We also assume that the household ends the second period with no assets and that the household begins the first period and ends the second period with no liabilities.[3]

4. We assume (*a*) that the household can borrow as much as it wishes during the first period so long as it can repay the principal and interest out of the income of the second period and (*b*) that the rate of interest at which it can borrow or lend is known with certainty.

5. We assume that the household has a consistent set of preferences and can choose its preferred combination of first and second period consumption from among the available alternatives.

Given the first four assumptions, what are the attainable consumption patterns for a household? How much consumption can a household undertake in the first period if second period consumption is zero? How much second period consumption can it have if consumption in the first period is zero? What other alternatives are available?

How can a household maximize first period consumption? Clearly, the answer is as follows: Borrow the maximum that can be repaid with interest with the income of the second period and use the proceeds of the loan to finance first period consumption. Since borrowing will entail an interest payment of the rate of interest i, times the amount borrowed, the maximum amount that can be repaid when second period income is received is $Y_2/(1 + i)$. If that amount is borrowed, first period consumption will be $Y_1 + [Y_2/(1 + i)]$, which is the present value of the household's income stream, its *net worth*.

In a similar manner, second period consumption can be maximized by lending the entire first period income Y_1 at a rate of interest of i, such that second period consumption is $Y_1(1 + i) + Y_2$ and first period consumption is zero. Clearly, combinations between these two extremes are also possible. For example, one possible combination is Y_1 of consumption in the first period and Y_2 of consumption in the second period, a point at which the household neither borrows nor lends during the first period. The line AB in Figure 5-1 illustrates the attainable combinations of consumption for first and second period incomes of Y_1^* and Y_2^* and for a rate of interest of i^*. Point A represents maximum first period consumption, point B represents maximum second period consumption; at point E the household neither lends nor borrows in the first period. The slope of AB is $1/(1 + i^*)$. Any combination of first period and second period consumption along AB is possible.

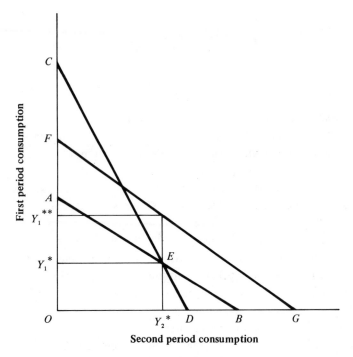

FIGURE 5-1

$$OA \quad \frac{Y_1{}^* + Y_2{}^*}{1 + i^*} \qquad\qquad OD \quad Y_1{}^*(1 + i^{**}) + Y_2{}^*$$

$$OF \quad Y_1{}^{**} + \frac{Y_2{}^*}{1 + i^*} \qquad\qquad OB \quad Y_1{}^*(1 + i^*) + Y_2{}^*$$

$$OC \quad Y_1{}^* + \frac{Y_2{}^*}{1 + i^{**}} \qquad\qquad OG \quad Y_1{}^{**}(1 + i^*) + Y_2{}^*$$

A change in the rate of interest, given fixed values of Y_1 and Y_2 is represented by a pivoting of the opportunity locus through point E. Point E .remains a possible consumption point even after a change in the rate of interest, since consumption of exactly the income earned in each period is still feasible. However, a change in the interest rate changes the consumption possibilities for households that are borrowers or lenders. A decline in the rate of interest increases possible first period consumption levels for any given level of second period consumption for households that are borrowers. The borrowers now can undertake a larger loan to increase first period consumption, since a smaller portion of second period income need be devoted to meeting interest payments on the loan. On the other hand, for any given level of first period consumption, the level of second period consumption is reduced for house-holds that are lenders: These households now receive smaller interest returns from any funds loaned out during the first period. A decline in the interest rate is represented by a change in the opportunity locus from AB to CD. Since the slope of the opportunity locus is $1/(1 + i)$, the slope of CD, which is drawn for interest rate i^{**} which is less than i^*, is larger than the slope of AB.[4]

It is also instructive to consider the change in the opportunity locus that occurs in response to a change in current income. A change in Y_1 produces a parallel displacement of the opportunity locus. Suppose that Y_1 rises to Y_1^{**} while the interest rate remains at i^*. Maximum first period consumption rises by the difference between Y_1^* and Y_1^{**}, since the maximum amount that can be borrowed and repaid out of second period income is unchanged. Maximum second period consumption rises by the difference between Y_1^* and Y_1^{**} times $1 + i^*$. Such a shift is represented by the shift from AB to FG in Figure 5-1, where we have assumed that Y_2 is unchanged.[5]

Some numerical examples may help to clarify the foregoing points. Suppose that a household's income is $10,000 in period 1 and $15,000 in period 2 and the rate of interest is 10 percent. One alternative is to consume at the maximum rate in the first period and nothing in the second period. Maximum first period consumption is equal to first period income, $10,000, plus the discounted value of second period income $15,000/(1.10), or $13,636, a total of $23,636. Maximum second period consumption is second period income $15,000, plus the amount that would be available if the household loaned out first period income at the going rate of interest $10,000(1.10), a total of $26,000. Of course in this situation, first period consumption would be zero. As a third choice, the household might consume exactly its income in each period, $10,000 in the first period and $15,000 in the second.

The three alternatives are illustrated in Figure 5-2. For every dollar below $10,000 that the household consumes in the first period, it is able to expand second period consumption by $1.10. Similarly, for every dollar above $10,000 that the household consumes in the first period, it must reduce second period consumption by $1/(1.10), or $.91. The rate of interest thus tells us the rate of exchange between first period and second period consumption.

If the rate of interest falls to 5 percent, the reward for deferring consumption is decreased and the loss from accelerating consumption is also decreased. Instead of adding $1.10 to second period consumption as a result of deferring $1 of consumption in the first period, the household can expand consumption in the second period only by $1.05. Similarly, an attempt to increase first period consumption by $1 now costs $.95, $1/(1.05), instead of $.91. Maxi-

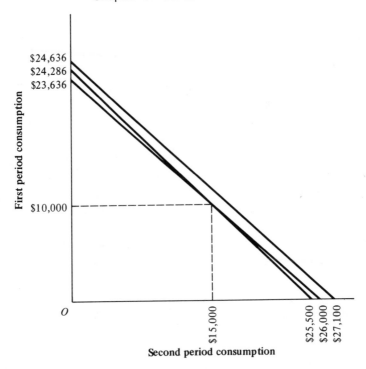

FIGURE 5-2

mum first period consumption is $24,286 and maximum second period consumption is $25,500.

We can also illustrate the effect of a change in income. Suppose that the rate of interest remains at 10 percent while income in the second period stays at $15,000 but first period income rises to $11,000. Maximum first period consumption goes up to $24,636, and maximum second period consumption rises by $1,100 to $27,100. The slope of the set of consumption alternatives remains the same as in the initial case, since the rate of interest is still 10 percent. The shift in the opportunity locus is parallel to the original locus, since the rate at which first period consumption can be exchanged for second period consumption has not changed.

Before we proceed further, one additional assumption is required:

6. We assume that whenever the opportunity locus shifts everywhere outward, a phenomenon that might be called an unambiguous increase in wealth, consumption in *both* the first and second periods will rise. That is, a household is assumed to respond to an increase in wealth by increasing expenditures in all periods for which plans are being made, not merely for the period in which the income increase will·occur. In addition, even when the shift in

opportunity locus is not outward everywhere, when it can be inferred that wealth has increased, we assume that the effect of the rise in wealth is to increase consumption in every period. In some cases, it will be impossible to make any unambiguous statement about the change in the wealth position of the household, therefore it will be impossible to make an unambiguous prediction about the change in its consumption pattern.

Changes in wealth can result either from a change in current or expected future income or from a change in the rate of interest. Changes produced by a change in income, current or expected, lead to parallel shifts in the opportunity locus, since they do not involve a change in the rate at which current consumption can be exchanged for future consumption. They thus produce unambiguous changes in wealth, and the expected responses to these "wealth effects" are contained in assumption 6. An increase in wealth from such a source raises consumption in all periods, whereas a decrease in wealth reduces consumption in all periods.

A change in the rate of interest produces two effects. First, it changes the wealth of the household, even though the direction of change is not always unambiguous. Second, the change in the rate of interest produces a "substitution effect," since it changes the terms on which consumption in the first period can be exchanged for consumption in the second period. For example, a rise in the rate of interest increases the return from deferring consumption into the second period. The amount of first period consumption that must be given up to increase second period consumption by a given amount is reduced. The substitution effect of a rise in the rate of interest is thus to reduce first period consumption at the expense of second period consumption. The substitution effect of a decline in the rate of interest is to raise first period consumption at the expense of second period consumption, since the reward for deferring consumption is reduced. The overall effects on consumption patterns of changes in the rate of interest thus include the response of the households both to changes in wealth and to changes in the terms under which consumption can be exchanged from one period to another.

THE SIGN OF THE SUBSTITUTION EFFECT

It is easy to illustrate that the substitution effect of a rise in the rate of interest increases consumption in the second period and reduces consumption in the first period. Suppose that the household faces the set of consumption alternatives depicted as *AB* in Figure 5-3. If the household consumes more than its income in the first period, it is at a point such as *X*. Now, suppose the rate of interest rises, causing the opportunity locus to pivot to become

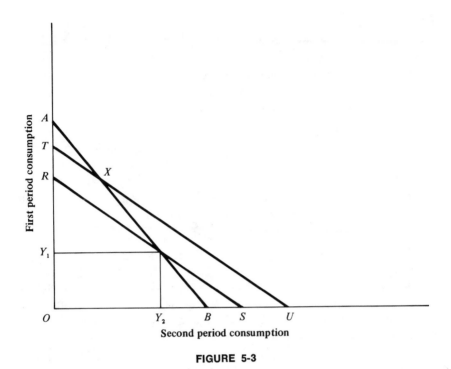

FIGURE 5-3

RS. The household cannot continue to consume at *X,* since it is no longer on its opportunity locus. The rise in the rate of interest has made the borrowing household "poorer."

Now let us restore the loss in wealth by giving the household additional income sufficient to permit continued consumption at *X,* but retaining the higher rate of interest. In other words, we replace the wealth that the higher rate of interest took away but keep the new rate of interest to isolate the substitution effect. This situation is represented as the opportunity locus *TU,* parallel to *RS.* Now we can show that the household will consume more in period 2 and less in period 1 as a result of the change in the rate of interest. That is, it will consume along *TU* to the southeast of *X.*

The opportunity locus available to the household is *TU.* For every point along *TX* there is a point along *AX* that is preferred by the household because it involves more first period consumption and the same quantity of second period consumption. But we can see that point *X* is preferred by the household to every point along *AX,* because the household chose *X* when it could have chosen any point along *AB.* Therefore, *X* must be preferred by the household to any point along *TX.* But what about points along *XU*? We cannot be sure that the household would have preferred X to these points because we have not had an opportunity to observe the household when it had to choose among them. Thus the effect of a rise in the rate of interest, when we correct for any effect of the rise on wealth, must be to increase second period consumption and to reduce first period consumption, or at worst, to leave both unchanged. The substitution effect unambiguously works to induce the household to expand consumption in later periods and to reduce it in earlier ones. This result can easily be extended to cases in which the rate of interest declines and to cases in which the household initially consumes less than its income in the first period, the wealth effect of a rise in the rate of interest being then to make the household "richer."

CONSUMPTION AND THE RATE OF INTEREST

We can now analyze the response of consumption to a rise in the rate of interest.[6] There are two possible initial situations. In the first, a household is a net borrower before the rate of interest goes up. In other words, it plans to consume more than its current income in the first period and less than its income in the second period. In the second situation, the household is a net lender. It plans to consume less than Y_1 in the first period. The first situation and changes in it are depicted in cases A.1 to A.4. The second situation is explored in cases B.1 to B.3. In all the diagrams in this section, XY represents the initial set of consumption alternatives and WZ represents the set of alternatives after the rise in the interest rate.

Household initially a net borrower

Case A.1

In case A.1, illustrated in Figure 5-4, the chosen consumption patterns move in a northwesterly direction. The original consumption choice was A on opportunity locus XY. We know that the substitution effect of a rise in the rate of interest should produce a fall in the first period consumption C_1 and a rise in second period consumption C_2. In addition, the rise in the rate of interest reduces the wealth of a household, which is a net borrower both before and after the change in the rate of interest. Other things equal, this reduction in wealth should produce a decline in consumption spending in both periods. Thus both the wealth effect and the substitution effect should operate to reduce first period consumption. But as the diagram indicates, this case involves an increase in C_1. Thus we have the implication that the wealth effect

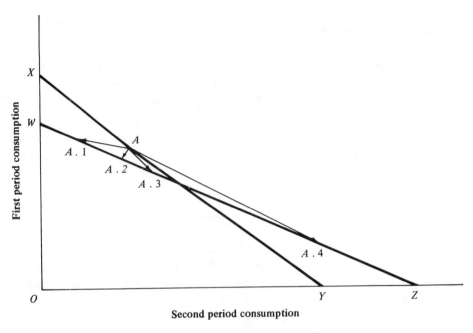

FIGURE 5-4

is operating perversely, a case that has been excluded by assumption 6. For this reason, movements such as those to point A.1 are excluded from further consideration.

Case A.2

In case A.2 the consumption choice moves to the southwest. Again, the substitution effect operates to raise C_2 and to reduce C_1. As in case A.1 the wealth effect should produce a decline in consumption in both periods. The net effect on C_1 must be a decline, which in fact occurs. Consumption in the second period may rise or fall, depending on the relative size of the wealth and substitution effects. In this case, the wealth effect dominates and C_2 declines. Thus the possibility remains that we will encounter cases such as A.2 in which, for a borrower, consumption in both periods declines as a result of a rise in the rate of interest.

Case A.3

In case A.3 the consumption choice moves to the southeast but not by enough to change the household from a net borrower to a net lender. As in the previous cases, the substitution effect operates to reduce C_1 at the expense of C_2. In addition, since the household remains a net borrower, its wealth is reduced as a result of a rise in the rate of interest. Unlike case A.2, however, the substitution effect dominates the wealth effect for C_2, causing second period consumption to rise. Of course since both the substitution and wealth effects of a rise in the rate of interest operate to reduce first period consumption, C_1 declines. This case also remains a possibility.

Case A.4

Case A.4 is similar to A.3 except that the southeasterly movement induced by a rise in the rate of interest is so great that the household, which was initially a net borrower, is induced to become a net lender. The substitution effect operates to raise C_2 at the expense of C_1. However, it is not possible to say anything about the nature of the wealth effect because of the shift of the household from the status of a borrower to that of a lender.[7] The rise in second period consumption is due either to a positive wealth effect combined with a substitution effect that induces an increase in C_2 at the expense of C_1, or to a negative wealth effect with a stronger substitution effect, overcoming the wealth effect to produce a rise in C_2. The decline in C_1 results from the operation of the substitution effect and either a wealth effect operating in the same direction or a positive wealth effect of a lesser magnitude than the substitution effect. Cases such as A.4 are thus also possible.

Household initially a net lender

Case B.1

Case B.1, as well as cases B.2 through B.3, are illustrated in Figure 5-5. The effect of a rise in the interest rate is to move the equilibrium to the northwest. However, this case can be excluded from further consideration on grounds similar to those employed in excluding case A.1. The effect of a rise in the rate of interest is to increase the wealth of a household that is a net lender both before and after the rise. The wealth effect thus serves to raise consumption in both periods. The substitution effect of a rise in the rate of interest serves to reduce consumption in the first period and to increase consumption in the second period. Since both effects operate to raise C_2, westward movement is not possible. Thus this case can be excluded from further consideration.

Case B.2

In case B.2 the effect of a rise in the rate of interest is to move the equilibrium position of the household to the northeast. The wealth effect operates

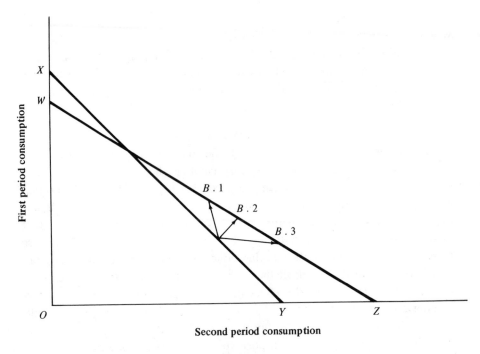

First period consumption

X

W

$B.1$

$B.2$

$B.3$

O

Y

Z

Second period consumption

FIGURE 5-5

to raise consumption in both periods, while the substitution effect serves to raise consumption in the second period and reduce it in the first period. A movement to the northeast involves an increase in first period consumption, which occurs because the substitution effect is overcome by the wealth effect, and an increase in second period consumption due to the combined forces of the wealth and substitution effects. This case is thus a possible outcome of a rise in the rate of interest for a lending household.

Case B.3

In case B.3 the equilibrium position of the household is moved southeast by the rise in the rate of interest. As in case B.2, both the wealth and substitution effects operate to raise C_2. And as in case B.2, the wealth and substitution effects operate in different directions on C_1. Unlike case B.2, however, the substitution effect dominates the wealth effect, and C_1 declines.

The use of the assumption that consumption in both periods change directly with changes in wealth has permitted us to exclude cases A.1 and B.1 from further consideration. However, we are left with the following possible responses to a rise in the rate of interest.

Case	C_1	C_2
A.2	−	−
A.3	−	+
A.4	−	+
B.2	+	+
B.3	−	+

Thus the only possible response that has been eliminated by this analysis is a rise in C_1 and a fall in C_2. If the rate of interest rises, current consumption may rise or fall. Even knowing whether the household is a net borrower or lender is not sufficient to allow us to determine whether consumption in the first period will rise or fall in response to a rise in the rate of interest.

CONSUMPTION AND INCOME

We can employ the analysis developed here to examine the impact on current consumption of a change in the first period income. As indicated by the previous discussion and illustrated in Figure 5-1, a change in first period income that leaves expected second period income unchanged produces a parallel shift in the array of possible consumption choices. The opportunity locus shifts upward by the increase in first period income and the rightward by the increase times $1 + i$. With a constant interest rate, the rate of exchange of first period consumption for second period consumption is unchanged. Therefore, we need consider only the wealth effect. The rise in income produces positive wealth effects. From assumption 6 we predict that both current and future consumption will increase. It would thus be incorrect to treat a change in current income as if it affected only current consumption, even if the change produced no modification in expected future income. If expected future income is increased if current income increases, the shift in the opportunity locus is larger than in the previous case. If a rise in current income produces a rise in expected future income, the household behaves as if it has received a larger increase in wealth. These cases are depicted in Figure 5-6.

Suppose that a household with first period income of Y_1^* and second period income of Y_2^* can borrow or lend at interest rate i^*. The array of possible consumption choices is represented by AB. Suppose that it now learns that its first period income will not be Y_1^* but the larger income Y_1^{**}. As a result, the line representing the array of possible consumption choices shifts to FG. Such a shift permits the household to increase consumption in either or both periods without having to reduce consumption in either. If in the

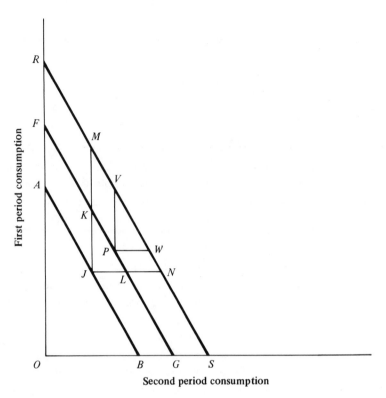

FIGURE 5-6

$OA \quad Y_1{}^* + \dfrac{Y_2{}^*}{1 + i^*}$ $\qquad OB \quad Y_1{}^*(1 + i^*) + Y_2{}^*$

$OF \quad Y_1{}^{**} + \dfrac{Y_2{}^*}{1 + i^*}$ $\qquad OG \quad Y_1{}^{**}(1 + i^*) + Y_2{}^*$

$OR \quad Y_1{}^{**} + \dfrac{Y_2{}^{**}}{1 + i^*}$ $\qquad OS \quad Y_1{}^{**}(1 + i^*) + Y_2{}^{**}$

initial situation it chose the consumption pattern represented by point J, by assumption 6 we are able to predict that its new consumption choice will be along the line KL, which means that the household will increase consumption in both periods.[8] If the rise in first period income from $Y_1{}^*$ to $Y_1{}^{**}$ causes the household to revise upward its estimate of second period income to $Y_2{}^{**}$, the shift in the opportunity locus is even further rightward to RS. From assumption 6 we predict that if the household with opportunity locus AB consumed the combination represented by point J, it would begin to consume along the line *MN*. If when the opportunity locus was *FG* it chose the consumption combination represented by point *P*, the upward revision of the estimate of second period income will cause the household to choose along *VW*.

Clearly the increase in current consumption due to a rise in current income is larger, the larger the increase in expected future income it causes. But even in the limiting case in which future income is not at all affected by the rise in current income, a portion of the effect of the rise in current income will be felt in larger future consumption. This results from our view that an individual making his consumption decision does not plan one period at a time, but constructs a consumption plan for a number of future periods, taking into account the expected incomes in each of the future periods, as well as the rate at which it can exchange consumption in one period for consumption in another, as indicated by the rate of interest.

SAVING FOR RETIREMENT

Another way to view the household's saving–consumption decision is to think of the household as saving a portion of its income in each of the years of its productive life and using the proceeds of the savings program for living expenses during retirement. To make the illustration concrete, consider a household that wishes to accumulate an amount during its 40-year working life to provide $5000 annually for each of the 20 years of retirement. What is the effect of a change in the rate of interest on the consumption and saving of the household during its working years?

If the rate of interest is 5 percent per year, the household will have had to accumulate $62,300 by the time of its retirement to have $5000 to spend in each of its retirement years. Although the amount of the retirement fund is smaller than total consumption during retirement ($100,000), the fund will accumulate interest at 5 percent during retirement to account for the difference. The amount of the fund is calculated from

$$\frac{5000}{(1.1)} + \frac{5000}{(1.1)^2} + \cdots + \frac{5000}{(1.1)^{20}} = \$62,300$$

To accumulate $62,300 by retirement, the household will have to save $516 during each of the 40 years of working life. The needed amount X is calculated from

$$X(1.1)^{39} + X(1.1)^{38} + \cdots + X = \$62,300$$

The first term represents the amount to which the first contribution to the retirement fund will have grown by the time of retirement, assuming that it is made at the end of the first year of work. The other terms are calculated in a similar manner.

What happens if the rate of interest is 8 percent instead of 5 percent to the household's lifetime consumption and saving? First, at 8 percent the household will not need to have such a large sum saved by retirement, since the interest on the fund during retirement will be larger. In fact, the fund need be only $49,100. In addition, since the interest on the funds accumulated during the working life of the household will be larger, the annual payments into the fund can be smaller. In this case, they decline to only $190 per year.

In this special case, therefore, in which the household accumulated during its lifetime to have a fixed payment stream in the future, a rise in the rate of interest necessarily reduces current saving and increases current consumption. However, the household may increase its desired retirement consumption, since the amount of current consumption it must give up to do so has decreased, and current consumption might conceivably decline. For example, if the household saves $517 per year (the amount saved when the rate of interest was 5 percent plus $1), it will have accumulated $133,934 at retirement. This will permit consumption of $13,642 for the 20 years of retirement, and we cannot rule out this possibility.

THE INTEREST ELASTICITY OF SAVING

It is sometimes argued that the distribution of a household's current income between consumption and saving is unaffected by changes in the rate of interest, and occasionally empirical evidence is advanced to support this view. It is instructive in the context of the model developed here to ask what such behavior, if it exists, implies.

A change in the rate of interest necessarily shifts a household's lifetime consumption possibilities. Consider a household that is a net borrower both before and after the change. A rise in the rate of interest should lead to reduced consumption in both the present and the future (through the wealth effect) and to a reduction in present consumption and an increase in future consumption (through the substitution effect). If the household maintains its consumption plans for the present, we must conclude that the wealth effect produces an *increase* in present consumption sufficient to offset the substitution effect. Such a result seems to be highly implausible, and a household in this situation would be unlikely to react by keeping present consumption plans unchanged.

It is conceivable that the household saving for retirement will maintain its saving level during its working years at $516 in the face of an increase in the rate of interest from 5 to 8 percent. For this to occur, the substitution effect of the rise in the rate, which induces an increase in current saving, must be exactly offset by the wealth effect, which leads to a reduction in saving. Such an exact offset is highly unlikely, especially for all households.

There is another way of treating the insensitivity of household spending to the rate of interest, however. Suppose that variations in the rate of interest are "small" relative to variations in the other factors that affect consumption spending, as is likely to be the case. Statistical analyses may well show that the rate of interest is unimportant as a determinant of consumption, since its effects are swamped by other factors. Nevertheless, as our illustrative calculation of saving for retirement has shown, even small variations in the rate of interest can have large effects, especially if the effects are compounded over long periods. We are therefore inclined to conclude that interest rate changes are potentially important factors affecting some saving decisions.

NONHUMAN WEALTH

To this point we have assumed that the household entered the first period with no wealth other than its own earning capacity and that it planned to leave the second period with no residual wealth. Now we would like to consider the impact of abandoning the first assumption. If a household begins the first period with, say, a given amount of money, its opportunity locus is no longer bounded by what it will earn during the two periods: It can, in addition, draw on its money holdings to permit consumption in either of the two periods. Maximum consumption in the first period is now equal to the money with which the household entered the period, the income earned in the first period, and second period income divided by $1 + i$. Maximum second period consumption is now equal to (start-of-period money holdings plus first period income) times $1 + i$, plus second period income. Thus if a household were given a gift of money at the start of the first period, it would be able to increase its consumption in both periods, and this behavior would be represented by an outward parallel shift of the opportunity locus. Figure 5-7 compares the opportunity loci for a household before and after the receipt of the money. Once again, the opportunity locus AB represents the consumption possibilities for a household with first and second period incomes of Y_1^* and Y_2^* and an interest rate of i^*. If in addition to its labor income, the household also had M_1^* of money holdings at the start of the first period, it would face opportunity locus CD. The household can be ex-

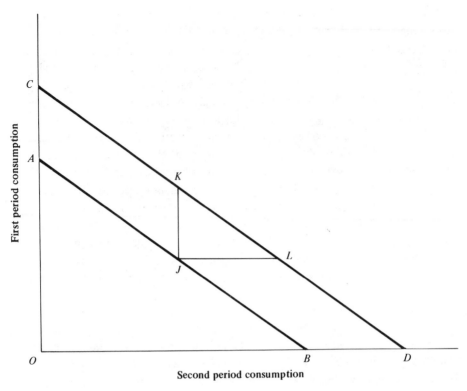

FIGURE 5-7

OA	$Y_1^* + \dfrac{Y_2^*}{1 + i^*}$	OB	$Y_1^*(1 + i^*) + Y_2^*$
OC	$Y_1^* + M_1^* + \dfrac{Y_2^*}{1 + i^*}$	OD	$(Y_1^* + M_1^*)(1 + i^*) + Y_2^*$

pected to increase its consumption spending in both the first and second periods. It should react to an increase in its nonhuman wealth in the same way it would react to an increase in its wealth occasioned by an increase in its current income, or in its expected future income. The effect should be to raise consumption spending in all periods.[9]

TAXES

Next we consider the role of taxes in determining consumption spending. We revert to our assumption that the household neither begins nor leaves the planning period with any accumulation of wealth. We want to know what effect the introduction of personal income taxes has on the opportunities available to, and the choices made by, a household. To simplify matters, we will assume that a constant proportion of personal income is paid as taxes. Thus we ignore the existence of personal exemptions and most deductions, as well as the existence of progressive tax rates. We further assume that taxes are paid on all interest income and that any interest payments made by a household can be deducted from taxable income.

The after-tax income the household will receive in the first period is now $Y_1^*(1-t)$ and in the second period it is now $Y_2^*(1-t)$, where t is the

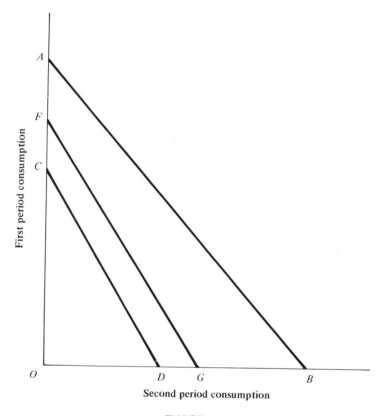

FIGURE 5-8

$$OC \quad Y_1^*(1-t) + Y_2^* \frac{1-t}{1+i^*(1-t)}$$

$$OF \quad Y_1^*(1-t) + \frac{Y_2^*}{1+i^*(1-t)}$$

$$OA \quad Y_1^* + \frac{Y_2^*}{1+i^*}$$

$$OD \quad [Y_1^*(1-t)][1+i^*(1-t)] + Y_2^*(1-t)$$

$$OG \quad [Y_1^*(1-t)][1+i^*(1-t)] + Y_2^*$$

$$OB \quad Y_1^*(1+i^*) + Y_2^*$$

tax rate. The rate of interest the household receives if it lends during the first period is $i^*(1 - t)$, and the rate it pays if it borrows is the same. There are thus two changes in the opportunity locus. First, the opportunity locus is shifted everywhere inward. For example, maximum first period consumption is now $Y_1^*(1 - t) + Y_2^*(1 - t)/[1 + i^*(1 - t)]$ and maximum second period consumption is $[Y_1^*(1 - t)][1 + i^*(1 - t)] + Y_2^*(1 - t)$. In addition, the slope of the opportunity locus steepens to $1/[1 + i^*(1 - t)]$. The impact on present and future consumption can be evaluated in terms of the substitution and wealth effects.

The change in the slope of the opportunity locus produces a substitution effect that involves an increase of first period consumption at the expense of consumption in the second period. The reward for refraining from first period consumption to increase second period consumption is now lower because of the introduction of the income tax. Since the opportunity locus shifts inward everywhere, the wealth effect clearly operates to reduce consumption in both the first and second periods. Overall, then, consumption in the second period must fall because of the introduction of the tax, but the impact of the introduction of the tax on first period consumption is ambiguous. If the substitution effect is sufficiently strong, the imposition of a tax on income may actually raise current consumption.

Suppose that instead of a permanent income tax, we introduce a tax believed by the household to be a temporary, applying only to income in the first period. What is the impact on consumption possibilities? Since interest is earned or paid only during the first period, the imposition of the temporary tax has the same impact on the slope of the opportunity locus as the imposition of the permanent tax. The slope steepens to $1 + i^*(1 - t)$. However, the wealth effect is not as large. Since only first period income is subject to the tax, maximum first period consumption is $Y_1^*(1 - t) + Y_2^*/[1 + i^*(1 - t)]$ and maximum second period consumption is $Y_1^*(1 - t)[1 + i^*(1 - t)] + Y_2^*$. The opportunity locus thus shifts inward but not as far as when the tax is a permanent one. Again, the substitution and wealth effects operate to produce an unambiguous decline in future consumption. The impact on first period consumption is again unclear.

CONSUMPTION AND INFLATION

To close this chapter, we discuss the role of the general level of prices in the consumption–saving decision of households. Thus far we have assumed implicitly that households are free of money illusion, that changing all prices and incomes by the same percentage does not alter their "real" behavior.

In effect, we have been assuming that all incomes are stated in real terms (i.e., are adjusted for changes in the general level of prices). Thus a household would make the same decision if its incomes in the first and second period were $100 and $200, respectively, and the index of the general level of prices stood at 100, as it would if incomes were $200 and $400, respectively, and the price index were 200. Since there is no difference in the real circumstances facing the household in the two situations, the decision makers involved are assumed to behave in the same manner.

The foregoing example pertains to different situations faced by the same household at different times. The situations help us to determine whether if the actual circumstances faced by the household are unchanged, behavior will be unchanged. Even if the household is free of money illusion, however, we cannot ignore the role of price expectations in the consumption decision. Suppose that a household knows that its money income will rise from the first to the second period but at least part of the increase is due to an increase in the general level of prices. In other words, the money income of the household rises by more than does its real income. The recognition by the household that prices will rise may change its consumption pattern from what it would have been if prices had been unchanging.

One can examine two possible situations here. In the first, potential lenders fail to recognize that prices will rise and do not adjust the interest rates at which they are willing to lend to reflect the forthcoming inflation. In addition, potential borrowers other than the household in question do not recognize that prices will rise, thus at the previous interest rate they do not change the amounts they wish to borrow. Since the household we are analyzing is a small participant in the market for funds, these assumptions assure that the interest rate faced by the household does not change because of the inflation. Let Y_1^* be the real income of the household in the first period and Y_2^* its real income in the second period. In addition, let P_1, the first period price level, be 1 and the second period price level be P_2. The rate of interest is i^*. Maximum first period real consumption is $Y_1^* + P_2 Y_2^* / (1 + i^*)$ and maximum second period real consumption is $[Y_1^*(1 + i^*) + P_2 Y_2^*]/P_2$. The slope of the opportunity locus is $P_2/(1 + i^*)$. The opportunity locus is thus made steeper by the existence of the inflation, which means that an inflation that is not reflected in a change in nominal interest rates has the same effect on consumption possibilities, therefore on consumption, as a decline in the rate of interest. The substitution effect of such a change is to induce the household to consume more in the first period and less in the second. The wealth effect can go either way. We have already analyzed such situations in detail.

In the second situation, all borrowers and lenders recognize that an inflation will occur, and the nominal rate of interest is adjusted upward to provide lenders with the same real return they would obtain if there were no inflation. For a lender to earn the same rate of return $i*$, the nominal interest rate must be $P_2(1 + i*)$. If in the absence of inflation, therefore, the rate of interest is .05 and the expected rate of inflation is .03 (i.e., $P_2 = 1.03$), the nominal interest rate must be .0815. Maximum first period real consumption is $Y_1 + P_2 Y_2 / P_2(1 + i*)$ and maximum second period real consumption is $Y_1 P_2(1 + i*) + P_2 Y_2 / P_2$. These can be seen to be the values of maximum first and second period consumption in the absence of inflation, and the slope of the opportunity locus is $1/(1 + i*)$, just as it was in the case of no inflation. An inflation that is fully anticipated and fully reflected in the nominal rate of interest leaves unchanged the opportunities facing the household, therefore, its real behavior.

SUMMARY

The savings–consumption decision results because a household need not consume at the same rate at which it earns its income. Within limits, it is free to adopt a consumption path different from its income path, to increase the satisfaction derived from the consumption from a given income stream. A household's consumption opportunities depend on its current and expected future incomes, the rate of interest, taxes, holdings of nonhuman wealth, and the anticipated rate of inflation. These opportunities, together with its preferences for current or future consumption, interact to determine a household's consumption plans.

NOTES

[1] To the extent that households acquire durable consumption goods such as houses, automobiles, and washing machines, the explanation of the acquisition of these assets, as opposed to their use, is treated as an aspect of investment behavior, which was discussed in Chapter 4.

[2] There are, of course, motives for saving other than to smooth out consumption patterns, the most important one being to provide a legacy for one's heirs. Such motives are not considered in the subsequent analysis.

[3] The case in which a household enters the first period with assets other than its human capital is considered below.

[4] Of course the description of a household as a lender or a borrower is not independent of the rate of interest. As the subsequent discussion indicates, a change in the rate of interest may cause a household to shift from one category to another.

[5] If a rise in the income of the first period increases the income expected in the second period, the shift in the opportunity locus is even greater, and the extent and nature of

the shift depend importantly on the response of expected second period income to a given change in first period income.

[6] All the results can be considered valid, with appropriate changes in signs, to a fall the rate of interest.

[7] The household may be on a higher or a lower indifference curve after the rise in the rate of interest.

[8] In an extreme case the household might maintain consumption in one of the periods at its initial level and accept the entire increase in wealth as an increase in consumption in the other period.

[9] An increase in wealth occasioned by a windfall gift can also be analyzed without considering the substitution effect, since no change in the rate of interest is involved.

6
Production and the market for labor

In previous chapters we have considered the demands for consumer and investment goods and the demands for financial assets. This chapter completes the discussions of the building blocks of our analysis by treating the market for labor and the supply of goods and services.

A chapter on the market for labor may seem a bit incongruous in a book on money and banking, but there is ample justification for its inclusion. A matter that has always concerned economists is the impact on the economy of a change in the quantity of money. In subsequent analysis of this question, we discover that the answer depends in part on what is assumed about the behavior of the participants in the market for labor. Under one, perhaps extreme, set of assumptions about the labor market, the effect of a change in the quantity of money is to change output and employment. Under other perhaps equally extreme assumptions, the effect is to change wages and prices. Without an understanding of the market for labor, therefore, it is impossible to analyze the effect of a change in the stock of money.

One more related justification is that a number of theories of the causes and consequences of inflation revolve around the supply of labor. Some theories argue that the principal source of inflation is the pushing up of wages by workers. In another theory, the supply of labor plays a decisive role in determining the effects on output and employment of attempting to stop on-going inflation. The analysis of inflation, which is carried out in detail in Chapter 15, requires a rudimentary understanding of the determinants of the demand and supply of labor.

In the first section of this chapter we describe the productive process that is assumed throughout this book. Next, we derive the demand for labor. Finally, we consider the supply of labor. The concluding Appendix examines some of the consquences of employing an aggregative analysis of the economy.

THE AGGREGATE PRODUCTION FUNCTION

At any moment, the capacity of an economy to produce goods and services depends on the quantities of productive resources it has inherited from the past and on the knowledge, also a legacy of the past, of ways to combine these resources to produce outputs. Among the productive resources are the labor force, including the skills its members possess; machinery, buildings, and other items of physical capital; land, and natural resources. The actual production undertaken in an economy over any period of time depends on the extent to which this productive capacity is utilized. Thus low output can be the result either of small capacity or of underutilization of a large one. This chapter examines the relationships among the various productive inputs and outputs during a given period of time. To simplify our discussion, we make the following assumptions:

1. We assume that it is possible to treat the economy as if a single homogeneous product, which serves as a consumption good and as an investment good, is the only commodity produced.
2. We assume that labor and capital are the only inputs to the productive process and that labor and capital are homogeneous.
3. We assume that technology (i.e., knowledge of the ways to combine inputs) is unchanged during the period being considered.[1]
4. We assume that the stock of capital, which is one of the determinants of the productive capacity of the economy, is the capital stock in place at the beginning of the period. Thus any investment occurring during the period will add to the productive capacity of the economy in future periods but will have no impact on current production levels.
5. We assume that all the existing stock of capital can be combined with whatever quantity of labor is employed. Thus even if some of the labor force is unemployed, there will be no idle capital.

These assumptions permit us to describe an aggregate production function of the form

$$Y = F(K, N) \tag{6-1}$$

where Y represents the rate of production of the homogeneous commodity during the period, K represents the capital stock in place at the beginning of the period, and N represents the number of laborers employed during the period. In the short run, with the stock of capital fixed, we can rewrite (6-1) as

$$Y = F^*(N) \tag{6-1'}$$

Equation (6-1') states that with the stock of capital fixed at K^*, the rate of output depends only on the quantity of labor employed. This relationship is plotted in Figure 6-1, which shows output increasing as the labor input increases along F^*. To show how the relationship between employment and output changes as the stock of capital changes, we have also plotted F^{**} in Figure 6-1, where F^{**} is drawn for the larger capital stock K^{**}. An improvement in technology is also represented by an upward shift.

In drawing Figure 6-1 we assumed that as the amount of labor employed increased while the stock of capital does not change, the rate of output would rise. At this point, we can be more explicit about the nature of this relationship, with the following assumption:

6. As the amount of labor employed increases while the stock of capital is fixed, each increment of labor adds less to output than did its predecessor (i.e., there are diminishing returns with respect to increases in the labor input).

As a result of assumption 6, we have the relationship between output and the labor input depicted in Figure 6-2.

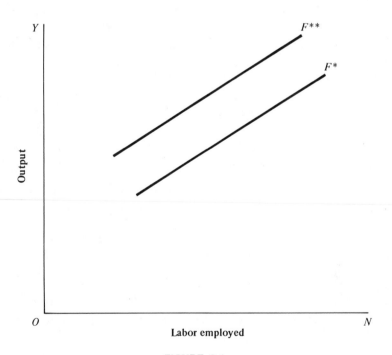

FIGURE 6-1

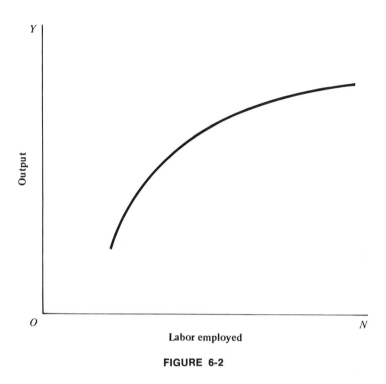

Y

Output

O

N

Labor employed

FIGURE 6-2

THE DEMAND FOR LABOR

What determines how much labor will be employed by business firms? Let us assume that each firm is such a small part of the markets in which it buys labor and in which it sells output that its own actions do not affect the prices in these markets (i.e., that these markets are perfectly competitive), and that business firms act to maximize their profits. Under these conditions, we can conclude that each firm will hire labor until the *marginal revenue product of labor*—the marginal physical product times the price of the product—equals the money wage. Since the marginal revenue product is the revenue the firm receives by hiring an additional unit of labor, and the money wage represents the cost of hiring that unit of labor, this policy will maximize the profit of the firm. We can also state the condition for profit maximization as follows: The marginal physical product of labor must equal the ratio of the money wage to the price of the product. The ratio of the money wage rate to the price level is called the *real wage rate,* since it measures the purchasing power of the income from supplying a unit of labor. Thus the equilibrium condition can be stated as the requirement for equality between the marginal physical product of labor and the real wage rate. Since for every

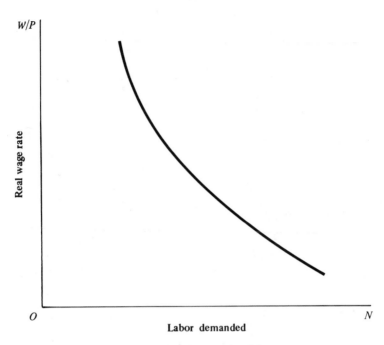

FIGURE 6-3   Demand for labor.

firm the real wage rate is fixed, each firm will adjust the quantity of labor it hires to ensure that the marginal physical product of labor is equal to that real wage.

We can employ the relationship between output and the labor input already developed, to determine the nature of the demand for labor. The slope of the curve in Figure 6-2 depicts the change in output that would accompany a small change in the labor input, the marginal productivity of labor. Since by assumption 6 the slope declines as the labor input rises, the demand for labor will be downward sloping. The demand for labor is constructed by calculating what the marginal product of labor is at each level of employment (i.e., the slope of the output–labor input relationship) and plotting the marginal product against the quantity of labor with which it is associated. The demand for labor associated with Figure 6-2 is plotted in Figure 6-3.

THE SUPPLY OF LABOR

In dealing with the supply of labor, we are close to the question considered in our discussion of the consumption–savings choice in relation to household behavior (Chapter 5). The problem for a worker is as follows: He has a given number of hours to allocate between working and leisure (168 hours per week, to be exact). Since he is assumed to be a price taker in the labor market—that is, the amount of labor he supplies has no influence on the wage he receives—the worker can calculate directly the amount of income he will receive for various quantities of labor supplied. But we must know what will happen to the quantity of labor the worker will supply if the wage rate changes. A rise in the wage rate alters the possibilities open to the worker. He can earn a higher income if he works the same number of hours as previously, or he can have greater leisure for the income previously earned. In addition, he can increase the number of hours worked, accepting less leisure for the sake of the higher wage rate. One cannot rule out any of these possibilities on theoretical grounds alone, and the empirical evidence is scanty. In the analysis that follows, however, we assume that an increase in the wage rate will be reacted to by at least some increase in the quantity of labor that workers wish to supply. Such a supply curve is illustrated in Figure 6-4.

We have been discussing the wage rate as if it were a well-defined concept. One question of great concern in much of our subsequent analysis is precisely which wage rate is the one to which workers respond. Suppose that the wage

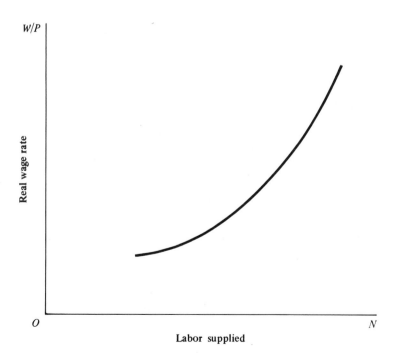

FIGURE 6-4 Supply of labor.

rate rises by 10 percent and at the same time the prices of the goods and services that workers wish to consume also rise by 10 percent. Under these circumstances, will laborers supply more labor in the face of the increase in the wage rate offered? Two alternative assumptions suggest themselves. The first is that workers respond only to changes in the real wage rate—the money wage rate divided by the price level; thus in the case in which wages and prices rise in the same proportion, the amount of labor supplied will be unchanged. In such a case laborers are said to be free of a money illusion. In other words, they recognize that the increase in the wage rate is illusory because it is accompanied by an increase in the prices of the goods they can buy, and they do not change the number of hours of labor they are willing to supply. At the other extreme, the workers fail to recognize, at least for a time, that although their wages have risen, the prices of the goods they buy have also increased; thus the workers' true circumstances are unchanged. Because of the money illusion, they may supply more labor in unchanged circumstances.

These alternative assumptions are significant in the analysis of the behavior of output, employment, and prices. In Chapter 15, which treats the inflationary process, we examine the effect of assuming that labor is at least temporarily led to believe that an increase in money wages is an increase in real wages, even though there is a proportionate increase in the price level.

APPENDIX ON THE INDEX NUMBER PROBLEM

When we speak about the behavior of national income we are considering a single index of the total output of the economy, a measuring rod that somehow permits us to combine into a single total such diverse items as automobiles, machine tools, haircuts, razor blades, and beer. Our discussion of production is greatly simplified if we can assume that such a measuring rod exists: If it does, we can ignore the impact on the market for labor of shifts of resources from, say, the production of haircuts to the production of beer. If we adopt the fiction that a single commodity is produced that can either be drunk or used to cut hair, then no shift in production is called for if people desire haircuts instead of beer. The product is simply directed to one use rather than to another.

The foregoing description is, of course, a fantasy. But need its failure to be true force us, in our analysis, to abandon the notion of national income as a meaningful aggregate? The answer to this question is: "It depends."

If one knew the physical quantities of each of the goods produced in an economy in two alternative situations, he would know the number of automobiles, machine tools, haircuts, razor blades, and gallons of beer produced in each situation. If one were lucky and the production of each good had changed by exactly the same percentage between the two positions (i.e., if the composition of total output had remained unchanged), he could state unambiguously that total output had changed by the percentage noted. Such a fortunate state of affairs is unlikely to occur, however. The composition of output tends to change, with the output of some goods rising, the output of others staying constant, and the output of still others declining. In such cases it is impossible to determine what is happening to total output by looking at physical production alone.

The failure of the physical outputs of all goods and services to change by the same percentage, however, need not prevent us from constructing a measure of total output. Suppose that while the physical outputs of various goods and services are changing by different percentages, prices of these goods and services continue to bear the same relationships to one another; that is, relative prices remain unchanged. Now if we know the market value of output in each of the two positions—the sums of the physical outputs times their respective prices—we can again determine the change in total output. We can see that this is so by means of an example.

Suppose that the economy makes two products: hamburgers and milkshakes. Suppose that in state I, 20 hamburgers and 50 milkshakes are produced and in state II, 60 hamburgers and 90 milkshakes are produced. (If the numbers bother you, think of these as millions of milkshakes and hamburgers.) Thus in moving from state I to state II the production of hamburgers increased by 200 percent and the production of milkshakes rose by 80 percent. In state I hamburgers sell for $1 and milkshakes for $2, whereas in state II milkshakes are $4 and hamburgers are $2. Since the prices of both hamburgers and milkshakes are twice as high in state II, their relative prices have remained unchanged. If we use these prices to evaluate output, the value of output in state I is

$$\$120 = \$1(20) + \$2(50)$$

and the value of output in state II is

$$\$480 = \$2(60) + \$4(90)$$

But since all prices have doubled, we know that total output has not risen by 300 percent, 360/120. In fact, the growth in total output must be less than 200 percent, since that is the amount by which hamburger production has risen, whereas the production of milkshakes has risen by even less. We can see what happened to total output in real terms—that is, removing the effects of the doubling of prices—by "deflating" the value of output in state II by the higher price level. If we do, we find that output has risen "in real terms" to only $240, $480/2, an increase of 100 percent. The increase can thus be seen to lie somewhere between the 200 percent increase in hamburger production and the 80 percent increase in milkshake production. It is, in fact, a weighted average of the two changes, the weights being the relative importance of each of the commodities in the original income, 1/6 for hamburgers and 5/6 for milkshakes. Thus when relative prices do not change, it is possible to determine the movement in total output by simply adjusting the money value of output to allow for changes in the general level of prices. As in the case discussed earlier, the treatment of total output as if it consisted of a single homogeneous commodity can be justified, provided one is willing to use relative prices to "weight" various items produced.[2]

Although unchanged relative prices permit one to describe precisely the behavior of real output, this situation resembles an unchanged composition of output in that it is an unlikely occurrence. When both relative prices and relative outputs are changing, it is impossible to characterize precisely the behavior of output. The best one can hope for is to place limits on this behavior, the range of these limits depending on changes in the composition of output and in relative prices.

Suppose that as previously, hamburger and milkshake production in states I and II are as follows:

Hamburger	I	20	Milkshake	I	50
Production	II	60	Production	II	90

However, relative prices in the two periods are different:

Hamburger	I	$1	Milkshake	I	$2
Prices	II	$2	Prices	II	$6

Since relative prices have changed, we must decide which set of relative prices to use as "weights." Let us proceed by evaluating each set of outputs by the relative prices prevailing in both periods. This gives us two estimates of the changes in output.

Using state I relative prices to evaluate the outputs, we find

$$\text{Value of state I output} = \$120 = \$1(20) + \$2(50)$$
$$\text{Value of state II output} = \$240 = \$1(60) + \$2(90)$$

Using state II relative prices, we find

$$\text{Value of state I output} = \$340 = \$2(20) + \$6(50)$$
$$\text{Value of state II output} = \$660 = \$2(60) + \$6(90)$$

If we measure the increase in output using state I relative prices, we see an increase of 100 percent, 120/120. If we measure the increase using state II relative prices, we obtain 94 percent, 320/340. Notice that the increases obtained, 100 percent and 94 percent, are narrower than the range of increases of each of the two products, 80 percent and 200 percent. The use of information about relative prices thus gives us more exact knowledge about the behavior of total output; but we cannot state with precision what is happening to total output unless either relative outputs or relative prices are unchanged. To return to the question that began this discussion, the treatment of national output as if it consists of a single homogeneous commodity that can serve a variety of uses is more easily justified, the closer are the assumptions of unchanged relative outputs and/or prices satisfied.[3]

The assumption that output consists of a single homogeneous commodity also permits us to speak unambiguously about movement in "the general price level," which is the price of the only good in our hypothetical economy. If we drop the assumption of a single good, we need to aggregate the prices of machine tools, automobiles, haircuts, razor blades, and beer into a single price index. An index that provides unambiguous information about movements in the general price level can be constructed only if (*a*) all prices change by the same percentage and/or (*b*) the composition of output does not change (i.e., all outputs change by the same percentage). Failure to meet either condition, or both of them, means that placing limits on the movements of prices is the best we can do. To avoid this difficulty, throughout this book we retain the assumption of a single homogeneous commodity, having national income as its output and the general level of prices as its price.

SUMMARY

It is a convenient fiction to assume that national income consists of a single commodity whose price is the general price level. Over any short period of time national output depends on the amount of labor employed. The supply and demand of labor are assumed to depend on the wage rate paid to labor.

NOTES

[1] Since we are concerned largely with alternative positions the economy might take at a point in time (rather than with the behavior of the economy over time), this assumption is a reasonable one.

[2] The fate of relative prices as shifts occur in the composition of output depends in part on how easily capital as well as labor can be shifted from producing one com-

modity to producing another. If such shifts can be accomplished easily, no capital need lie idle because it is poorly adapted to the production of the particular commodities being demanded. If, on the other hand, capital is rigidly tied to a particular productive process, shifts from production of one commodity to the other can have quite different effects (e.g., automobile assembly lines are ill designed for the production of beer and brewing vats are similarly useless for the production of automobiles). The total output that can be produced by a given quantity of the labor input will depend on the extent to which the particular form in which capital exists conforms to the demands for the various goods. In such cases, changes in relative product prices will occur in response to shifts in demand. The ability of capital to shift easily between productive processes is a necessary but not sufficient condition for unchanged relative prices.

[3] Note that the assumptions of homogeneity of capital and labor can be justified in a similar way. Even though we know that the labor force consists of nuclear physicists, bootblacks, neurosurgeons, barbers, and other dissimilar personnel, we can justify treating labor as if it consists of a single homogeneous input if the labor force always consists of the same proportions of various types of labor, or if relative wages of various types of labor remain unchanged. A similar argument holds for capital.

7
Income and price level determination

The preceding chapters have developed the building blocks of our analysis, the various behavioral and other functions that form the basis for our models of income and price level determination. This chapter completes one phase of our work by setting forth some simple models of the economy and demonstrating some of their features.

There are two significant omissions from the models considered in this chapter. First, there is no government spending and taxing activity. Such government activities are introduced in Chapter 9. Second, there are no financial institutions. The only existing financial assets are bonds, which are assumed to be homogeneous—the bonds are the debts of private economic units, firms or households—and money. The money in the system is the result of past government spending not financed by levying taxes. Thus we are assuming that government spending and taxing existed in the past but do not now exist; in the past, moreover, government tax receipts did not always match spending, with the result that the government was forced to issue money to meet its obligations. This is the stock of money with which the economy enters the period we are examining. Our rather strange set of assumptions permits us to defer until later a discussion the process by which money enters the economic system, but we can explore the effect on the economy of an existing stock of money, nevertheless. Chapter 9 begins a discussion of the sources of money in the American economy.

EQUILIBRIUM IN THE GOODS MARKET
If the economic system is to be in equilibrium, households and firms must be willing to purchase exactly the total of output that firms wish to produce. The significant word in the preceding sentence is "willing." If a given quantity

of output is produced during a period, at the end of the period that output must have been used up or it must be held by someone. However, if some of the holders are unwilling holders, or if some demanders receive a smaller quantity of output than they desire, we have to say that the economy was not in equilibrium during the period.

Here we are obliged to ask exactly how a person becomes an unwilling holder of goods or receives fewer goods than he desires. One possible source of this unwillingness, and one on which we will focus the most attention, is in the inventory holdings of business firms. Suppose that a firm wishes to keep its inventory holdings unchanged. It thus plans to produce the exact amount it expects to sell. So long as sales and production are equal, the firm ends each period with the inventory holdings that it desires. But if actual sales fall short of anticipated sales, the firm finishes with greater inventory holdings than it had planned. We can say that the firm experienced an unplanned inventory accumulation. Alternatively, sales might have exceeded planned sales and, in our example, production. If this happened, the firm would end the period with inventories smaller than desired and could be said to have experienced an unplanned inventory decumulation. How a firm reacts to such a discrepancy between its plans and its experience is a matter to be considered in greater detail below. The important point to note is that the firm must take some action if it is not to be frustrated in its plans during succeeding periods.

How can we express this equilibrium condition? There are two equivalent and alternative methods. The first is to state that equilibrium requires that planned consumption plus planned investment equal the quantity of output produced. If the sum of planned consumption and investment exceeds total output, someone's plans must be frustrated. In our example, there will be unplanned inventory decumulation by business firms that will adjust their behavior; thus the original situation cannot have been one of equilibrium. Alternatively, if the sum of planned spending falls short of output, there will be unplanned inventory accumulation, again causing business firms to adjust their behavior, revealing once more that equilibrium did not exist. The alternative statement of the equilibrium condition is to say that planned saving must equal planned investment.

Let us see why these two statements of the equilibrium condition are equivalent. Assume for the moment that there is no business saving.

The first condition states that

$$C + I = Y \tag{7-1}$$

where C is consumption, I is investment, and Y is national income. But we can define consumption as total income less saving $Y - S$. Substituting in (7-1) we obtain

$$Y - S + I = Y \qquad (7\text{-}2)$$

Subtracting Y from both sides and rearranging terms, we write

$$S = I \qquad (7\text{-}3)$$

Because it simplifies our exposition at a number of points, we will use the following version of this condition: Saving equals investment. However, we must remember that the condition is equivalent to the condition that demanders must be willing to purchase exactly the quantity of output that firms wish to produce.[1]

EQUILIBRIUM IN THE MONEY MARKET

A second condition required for equilibrium is that the economic system's stocks of assets of various kinds must be willingly held. Since there are no financial institutions in our hypothetical economy, the only kinds of asset we care about are money and bonds. The stock of money existing at any time is the result of past government spending financed by printing money. The stock of bonds in the system is the result of past decisions by business firms and households to spend more than their receipts (i.e., to become deficit spending units). The number of dollars and the number of bonds in the system are assumed fixed.

Assume that each bond is a promise to pay $1 per year in perpetuity. Even though the number of bonds is fixed at the beginning of the period, the total value of bonds in the system is not, since the value of a bond is $1/i$. As the rate of interest rises, the value of an individual bond, thus of the total stock of bonds, declines. Therefore, the total amount of wealth that must be held in monetary form is itself a variable, even though the number of bonds is not.

We can plot the total quantity of wealth to be held in monetary form as an inverse function of the rate of interest, as in Figure 7-1. The total stock of money is, of course, a constant independent of the interest rate. It is represented by OM. The value of bonds is a variable depending on the interest rate. It is $PQ = MR$ at interest rate i_0. The value of monetary wealth is OR at i_0. At a given interest rate there will thus be a given total of monetary wealth as well as a price, the interest rate, indicating the relative desirability of holding money and bonds. As the rate of interest falls, the stock of mone-

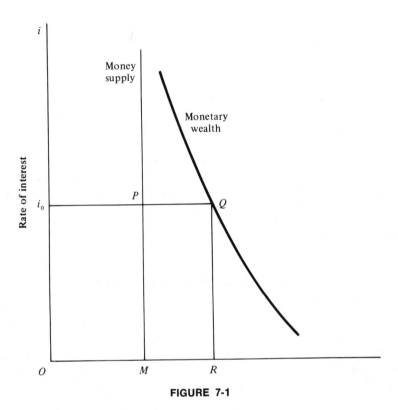

FIGURE 7-1

tary wealth will rise and the relative attractiveness of holding bonds will decline. Both these events will have the effect of increasing the amount of money demanded. The net effect on the quantity of bonds demanded is ambiguous, the larger wealth producing an increased demand while the lower interest rate produces a decreased demand.

The foregoing discussion makes clear that it is largely a matter of convenience whether one focuses on the demand for money or on the demand for bonds in analyzing equilibrium in asset markets. At any given interest rate, thus at any total of monetary wealth, a demand for money is the reciprocal of a demand for bonds. To say that the quantity of money demanded at a given interest rate rises is equivalent to saying that since the stock of wealth is constant, the quantity of bonds demanded at that interest rate has fallen. In the next sections we follow long historical precedent, focusing on the demand for money. This is a shorthand way of acknowledging that if the public holds the amount of money it wishes to hold, it also holds its desired quantity of bonds.

EQUILIBRIUM IN THE LABOR MARKET

There is a third condition to be satisfied if there is to be an overall equilibrium in the economic system, namely, the demand and supply of labor must be equal. If there is excess demand for labor, firms will be trying to employ more than is being offered at the going wage rate to increase output. They wish to increase output because the marginal revenue product of labor exceeds the wage rate being paid.[2] Alternatively, and this statement will be used more frequently in what follows, they wish to employ more labor because the marginal physical product of labor exceeds the real wage rate. If there is an excess supply of labor, there are more workers seeking work at the going real wage than there are positions available.

We can diagram the condition in the labor market by plotting the demand and the supply of labor, stated in man-years or man-hours of labor, against the real wage rate. Our previous assumptions were that the supply of labor is an increasing function of the real wage rate and, because of the assumption of diminishing returns to labor in the short run, the demand for labor is a decreasing function of the real wage rate.

PRICE LEVEL DETERMINATION AND THE REAL BALANCE EFFECT

We now wish to consider the behavior of a most important variable, the general level of prices. To do so we must consider one of the most significant relationships in our economic model, the real balance effect.

Recall that the quantity of money in the economic system has been determined entirely by the past actions of the government. Remember, too, that anything that increases the wealth of the private sector will increase consumption spending. What does the private sector's wealth consist of? The wealth of any individual household or firm consists of the difference between the assets it holds and its liabilities. The assets that a household or firm may possess in the hypothetical economy we are studying are money, bonds, and real capital goods. Its liabilities consist of debt to other individuals or firms. If we consolidate the balance sheets of the private sector, we can determine its net wealth position. All debts owed by one private economic unit to another are ignored. What remains? First, there is the real capital owned by the private sector: the buildings, inventories of goods, machines, automobiles, washing machines, and other property, owned by the private sector. And there is the money held by the private sector which was acquired from past financing of government deficits.

What can cause the value of the wealth of the private sector to change during any given short period? Given the fixed capacity of the capital goods to produce real output in the future, variations in the real value of the capital stock will change only because of changes in the rate of interest. In what follows we ignore this effect and treat the stock of real capital as fixed in value.

The value of money can also change if the general level of prices changes. A halving of the general price level results in a doubling of the value of money, thus an increase in the real wealth of the private sector. As we saw in Chapter 5, the larger a household's nonhuman wealth, the larger the share of its current income it is likely to consume. A rise in the value of the stock of money makes the public "richer" and creates the incentive and the ability for it to increase its consumption, hence to reduce its saving, out of current income.

GENERAL EQUILIBRIUM

We are now in a position to spell out our entire model and to investigate the determinants of the equilibrium values of the various variables which are determined within the model. All markets must be in equilibrium for the economy to be in equilibrium. We must specify what will happen in each of the markets—the money market, the labor market, and the goods market—if it is not in equilibrium. In the case of the labor market we assume that whenever there is excess demand for labor, the real wage rate will rise, and whenever there is excess supply of labor, the real wage rate will fall. Whenever there is excess demand for money, there is an excess supply of bonds; thus bond prices will fall (i.e., interest rate will rise). When there is an excess supply of money, interest rates will fall. Whenever there is an excess supply of goods, the price level will fall, and whenever there is an excess demand for goods, the price level will rise. Each variable in the system is assumed able to take on whatever value is required for the entire system to be in equilibrium.[3]

Since our model is meant to explain behavior in the short run, we assume that expectations about the future are affected only to the extent that they are influenced by current behavior. The following relationships describe the model:

Personal saving function	$S = f\left(Y, i, \dfrac{M}{P}\right)$	(7-4)
Business investment function	$I = g(i)$	(7-5)
Demand for money	$D_m = h(i, Y)$	(7-6)
Supply of money	$S_m = \dfrac{\bar{M}}{P}$	(7-7)

Supply of labor	$S_n = j\left(\dfrac{W}{P}\right)$	(7-8)
Demand for labor	$D_n = k\left(\dfrac{W}{P}\right)$	(7-9)
Aggregate production function	$Y = F^*(N)$	(7-10)
Goods market equilibrium	$S = I$	(7-11)
Money market equilibrium	$D_m = S_m$	(7-12)
Labor market equilibrium	$D_n = S_n$	(7-13)

Equation 7-4 describes household saving (or consumption) behavior. It states that current real saving is a function of current real income, the rate of interest, and the real value of the money stock, which is the nominal quantity of money divided by the price level. As our analysis of consumption behavior in Chapter 5 indicated, a household makes its consumption plans by considering the array of alternative consumption possibilities available to it in the current and succeeding periods, choosing that consumption combination which produces the greatest satisfaction. The factors constraining the choice are the level of wealth arising from nonlabor sources, current and future income, and the rate of interest. In the model we are studying, real wealth in nonmonetary form is not considered because the value of such wealth is not subject to change in the short period being examined. Expectations of future income may be included in the intercept of the function; or, to the extent that they are influenced by current developments, their effects are included in the effects of changes in current income.

As for the effect of the rate of interest on saving, as the discussion of Chapter 5 indicated, a change in the rate of interest produces a substitution effect and a wealth effect, and only the former effect has an unambiguous sign. However, in explaining aggregate behavior (i.e., the behavior of all households combined), it may be possible to assume that the gains in wealth to some due to a change in the rate of interest are exactly matched by the losses of wealth to others, and furthermore that the response in terms of savings to these equal and opposite changes in wealth are symmetric. Under these conditions, we can ignore the wealth effect of a change in the interest rate. The only effect is the substitution effect, whereby a rise in the rate of interest induces an increase in household saving. We assume that the substitution effect is the only effect operative for the aggregate of all consumers. Thus increases in the rate of interest are assumed to increase saving.

Equation 7-5, the investment function, shows that current real investment depends only on the rate of interest. Of course, this function is strictly correct only when expected future returns on all investment projects, as well as expected product and factor prices, are fixed. There is also the implicit assumption that there are always some investment projects not being undertaken because the rate of interest is too high.

Equation 7-6 represents the demand for money relationship. The real demand for money is a function of the interest rate both because of the transaction and precautionary motives and because of the uncertainty about the future course of interest rates, which works through the speculative motive.

Equation 7-7 states that the real supply of money is equal to the nominal supply of money $\bar{M}$, which has entered the system through past government spending (as opposed to being financed through taxes), divided by the price level.

Equations 7-8 and 7-9 state simply that the demand and supply of labor depend only on the real wage rate. Equation 7-10 describes the relationship between the quantity of labor employed by business firms and the level of output they produce. The relationship is conditioned by the level of technology that firms possess and the stock of physical capital with which they enter the period.

Equation 7-11 has been characterized as the goods market equilibrium: Given the level of output that firms are producing, consumers and firms are willing to purchase the quantity of output being produced. The equation does not say that firms wish to go on producing that level of output. The level of output that firms wish to produce is determined by the relationship among the product price, the wage rate, and the marginal productivity of labor. These relationships are described in (7-9), which states the condition for the amount of labor that firms wish to hire. Together with (7-10), the aggregate production function, this value determines the quantity of output that firms wish to produce. Even if households, firms, and governments wish to purchase the quantity of output currently being produced—that is, even if (7-11) is satisfied—there is no guarantee that firms will wish to continue producing that level of output. They will want to produce that level of output only if it maximizes their profits; that is, if (7-9) is satisfied.

Equations 7-12 and 7-13 set forth the conditions that both the money and the labor markets must also be in equilibrium.

THE WORKINGS OF THE MODEL

We are ready now to investigate the workings of our model. The first thing to recognize is that (7-8) through (7-10) and (7-13) represent a kind of closed system. For equilibrium to be achieved in the labor market, only one real wage can prevail, the real wage for which (*a*) the quantity of labor supplied (assumed to be an increasing function of the real wage rate) and (*b*) the quantity of labor demanded (assumed to be a decreasing function of the real wage rate), are equal. Let us call this real wage rate $(W/P)_e$, for equilibrium real wage rate. The quantity of labor employed is also determined in this market by the same process that determines the equilibrium real wage rate. Let us call the equilibrium level of employment N_e. Of course once the level of employment is determined, the level of output produced is also set, since the aggregate production function (7-10) determines this relationship.

These four equations have thus determined the values of four variables: the real wage rate, the quantity of labor demanded, the quantity of labor supplied, and total output (see Figures 7-2 and 7-3). The demand curve for labor in Figure 7-2 is (7-9) and the supply curve is (7-8). The equilibrium condition in this market is (7-13). Once the real wage and the level of employment have been established, we can calculate real income by projecting the level of employment against our output–labor relation, (7-10) plotted in Figure 7-3. If the economy is to be in general equilibrium, the rest of the system must somehow be made to adjust to the level of output determined by the equilibrium in the market for labor.

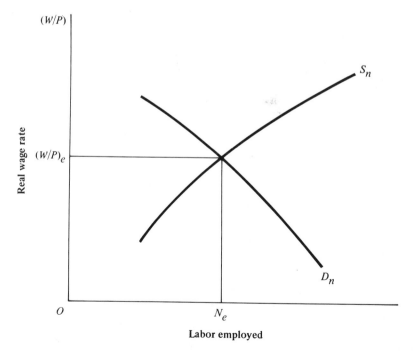

FIGURE 7-2

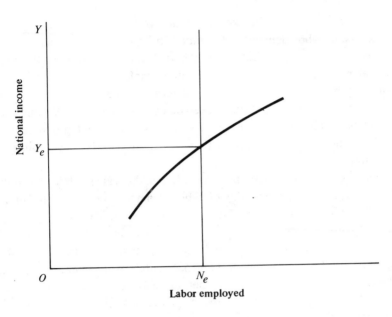

Y

National income

Y_e

O

N_e

Labor employed

FIGURE 7-3

From the point of view of the workings of the rest of the model, we can now treat the level of output as fixed at the equilibrium level of output Y_e. The remainder of the system is now required in its six equations to determine six unknowns, S, I, i, P, S_m, and D_m. There are two ways of approaching the determination of an equilibrium in this model, and it will be useful to consider both. First, since it is known that the level of real national income is unchanged no matter what happens in the money and goods markets, we can graph these markets in as follows: Consider the combinations of the price level and the rate of interest at which the goods market is in equilibrium. As the rate of interest rises, the volume of investment that firms wish to undertake declines. To produce a decline in saving, prices must fall, since a drop in price increases the value of wealth and increases the amount of consumption that a household wishes to undertake at every level of income. Thus curve GG in Figure 7-4 represents possible combination of i and P at which planned saving and planned investment are equal. This curve is drawn for given saving and investment schedules and for the given level of income, previously determined in the labor market.

Next consider the combinations of the price level and the rate of interest at which the money market is in equilibrium. As the rate of interest rises, the demand for money declines. To reduce the supply of money, the price level must rise, since the nominal supply of money is fixed. Curve MM in

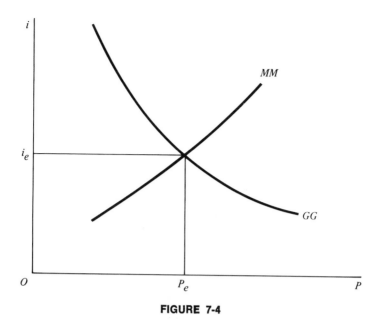

FIGURE 7-4

Figure 7-4 represents combinations of i and P at which the demand and the supply of money are equal.

Together, schedules MM and GG permit us to determine the equilibrium price and interest rate, P_e and i_e, in Figure 7-4. And we can now proceed to find the equilibrium values of the other variables in the system. Since the equilibrium price level has been ascertained, we also know the equilibrium money wage rate, the equilibrium real wage rate having been determined in the labor market. With the real income level, the interest rate, and the price level known, the volume of real saving and investment depending on these variables can be learned. And for the same reason, the quantity of money demanded and supplied is also known.

As any of equations (7-4) to (7-7) changes, either GG or MM shifts and a new price level and interest rate equilibrium combination is produced; but the equilibrium level of national income will be unchanged unless something is changed in (7-8) to (7-10).

SOME EXERCISES WITH THE MODEL

It is instructive to examine the effects of changes in some of the equations. Suppose that the saving schedule shifts so that, at every income level, people wish to save less than previously. The original GG curve is depicted, once again, in Figure 7-5. Although at point A planned saving once equaled

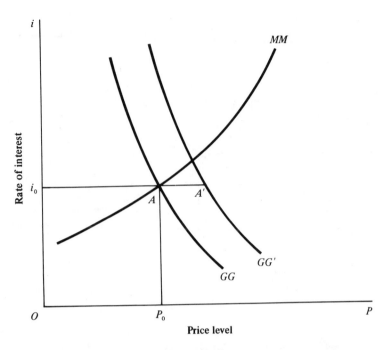

FIGURE 7-5

planned investment, this is no longer the case. At interest rate i_1 the volume of planned investment is the same as before, but the amount of planned saving is lower. How can we reduce planned saving to the level of investment planned at i_0? The answer is, of course, to raise the price level, since the effect of a rise in prices is to increase saving, through the real balance effect. Whereas point A was on the original GG curve, point A' is on the new curve GG'. Thus the downward shift in the saving schedule shifts the GG curve to the right. If we examine the effect of such a shift in Figure 7-5, we note that the price level and the rate of interest will rise. The equilibrium income level will not change because nothing has happened to change either the demand or the supply of labor. But the money wage rate will rise by the same percentage as the price level. This is required because the real wage rate must not change, if we are to preserve the equilibrium in the labor market. Furthermore, the new equilibrium will be characterized by lower investment, due to the higher interest rate, and higher consumption than in the original state. The rise in the price level serves to increase planned saving, but it does not fully offset the effect of the initial shift in the saving function.

What if the investment demand schedule shifts so that firms wish to invest more than previously, at every interest rate? Once again, look at point A

on curve *GG*. Now at i_0, P_0, planned investment exceeds planned saving. To increase planned saving without changing the rate of interest, the price level must rise. As a result, *GG* must shift to *GG'*. The effect on the equilibrium interest rate and price level of an upward shift in investment is the same as that of a downward shift in saving. But equilibrium investment and equilibrium saving will rise, unlike the case described earlier.

Suppose that the demand for money shifts so that at every interest rate, less money is demanded than previously. We have depicted the original *MM* curve in Figure 7-6. At point *B* on *MM*, where previously the demand for money equaled the supply of money, there is now an excess supply of money. To equate the demand and supply of money without changing the rate of interest, the price level must rise to reduce the real supply of money. Thus the *MM* curve must shift to *MM'*. Such a shift raises price and wage levels and lowers the rate of interest leaving the level of real income unchanged. The higher price level increases saving, through the real balance effect, and the lower interest rate increases investment.

What if the nominal supply of money *M*, instead of being at the level previously assumed, were instead twice as large? How would the observed equilibrium differ from that just described? Unlike the changes observed in Figure

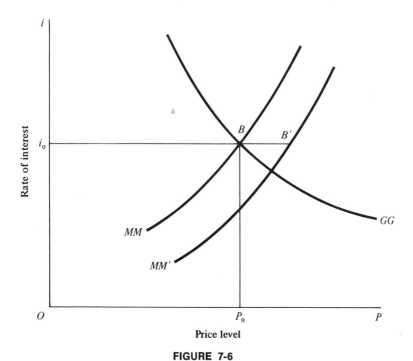

FIGURE 7-6

7-6, the higher money supply affects both the *MM* and the *GG* curves. The *MM* curve is shifted to the right because the price level must be higher or the interest rate lower for asset holders to be willing to hold the larger quantity of nominal money. The *GG* curve will shift to the right since at every previous price-level–interest-rate combination, real saving will be smaller than before because the public holds a larger money supply. Thus it might appear that although such shifts necessarily produce a higher price level, the effect on the rate of interest is uncertain. However, this is not the case. In fact we can show that the price level will have exactly doubled and the interest rate, and all other real variables will be unchanged in the face of a doubled money stock. Why is this so?

Suppose that the price level is less than doubled in the new equilibrium. Since we know that real income level is unchanged, the interest rate must rise if saving is to equal investment. Turning to the money market, where the real supply of money is increased, the interest rate must fall, to induce asset holders to willingly hold the larger real money supply. But of course the requirements with respect to the interest rate for equilibrium in the goods and money market are not consistent. Only if the price (and wage) level exactly doubles and the interest rate remains unchanged, can equilibrium be attained simultaneously in the two markets.

A doubled price level means an unchanged real supply of money. With the interest rate unchanged, real saving and real investment will remain unchanged. With the interest rate unchanged, the real demand for money will not change. The only effect of the nominal money supply being twice as large is a price and wage level that is twice as high. Real output, consumption, investment, and the interest rate are all unchanged. The result is illustrated in Figure 7-7.

We have obtained a result that has been asserted by students of economic affairs for perhaps 200 years. The result was obtained under somewhat specialized assumptions, however: (1) that the economy was in full employment equilibrium in the two positions compared, and (2) that none of the behavioral and technological relationships describing the economy had changed. Assumption 2 indicates that the price level is not uniquely determined once the money supply is known. The supply of money interacts with all the other relationships describing the economy to set the price level. But once these other relationships are fixed, changes in the price level are proportional to changes in the nominal supply of money. A doubling of the nominal money stock doubles the price level and leaves real national income unchanged. That is the essence of what might be called the "old-fashioned" quantity theory of money.

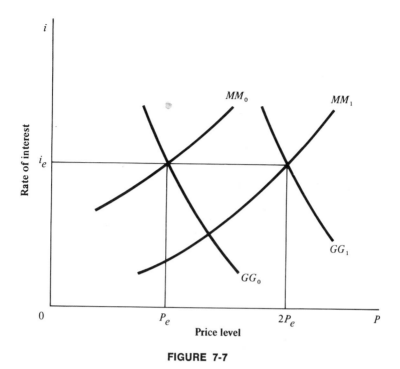

FIGURE 7-7

AN ALTERNATIVE VIEW

Our model can be displayed in another way that will be useful in making comparisons with the models to be developed later in this chapter. If we treat the price level and the nominal supply of money as fixed, we can determine the combinations of the level of national income and the rate of interest at which the money and goods markets are cleared. For a given price level, the higher the level of real national income, the higher must be the rate of interest, if the demand and supply of money are to be equal (i.e., if the money market is to be in equilibrium). If the real supply of money is fixed, a rise in the level of national income produces an increase in the quantity of money demanded. An increase in the rate of interest is required to counteract it. Curve LM_0 in Figure 7-8 represents, for a given P, possible combinations of the interest rate and the level of national income at which the demand and supply of money are equal. A lower price level implies an LM curve further to the right, since it involves a larger real money supply. The same holds for a larger nominal stock of money.

For a given price level, the higher the level of national income, the lower must be the rate of interest for planned saving to be equal to planned investment. As the level of national income rises, so does planned private saving. For investment to match the increase in private saving, the rate of interest must fall. A curve representing possible combinations of the interest rate and the level of national income at which planned saving is equal to planned investment is presented as IS_0 in Figure 7-8. The lower the price level and/or the larger the nominal money stock, the further to the right will lie each of the curves, since planned saving at every interest-rate–income-level combination will be lower, the larger is M/P.

If prices are completely flexible, whenever the IS and LM curves intersect at a level of real national income less than full employment output, the price level will fall. A decline in the price level will induce rightward shifts in both the LM and IS curves. In both cases the shifts are caused by a rise in M/P. The IS curve shifts because of the real balance effect and the LM curve because of an excess supply of money at the old equilibrium. Prices will continue to fall, and the IS and LM curves will continue to shift to the right until they intersect the full employment level of national income. Similarly, if the curves intersect to the right of full employment national income, the price level will rise until the curves are shifted left sufficiently to produce an intersection at full employment of national income. Since the LM and IS curves

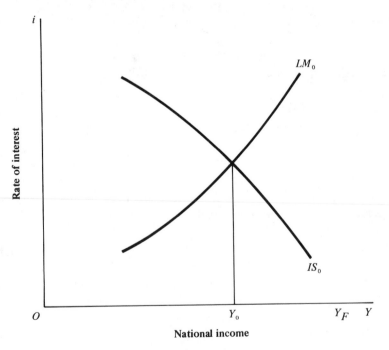

FIGURE 7-8

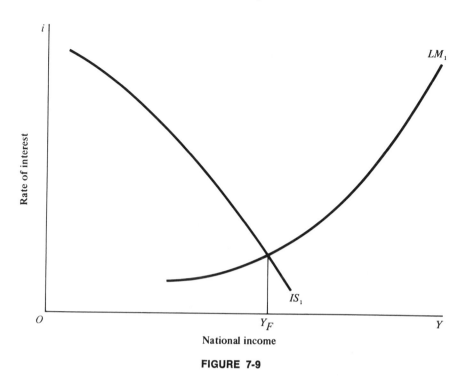

FIGURE 7-9

in Figure 7-8 intersect at an income level less than the full employment level, prices will fall and the curves will shift to the right until the intersection occurs at full employment. Such a situation is depicted in Figure 7-9.

The lesson to be learned from each of the foregoing exercises is that while wages and prices are completely flexible, there exists a price level at which full employment output will be demanded. If aggregate demand is less than full employment output, prices and wages will fall, causing the IS and LM curves to shift to the right, and full employment output will be demanded if prices fall far enough. If demand is excessive, prices will rise, and the IS and LM curves will shift to the left until the excessive aggregate demand is eliminated. In our model, there exists a price level at which full employment output will be exactly demanded, no more and no less. We leave until later the analysis of the process by which movement from one level of prices to another occurs. At this point we have established only that a price level consistent with full employment must exist.

SUMMARY

In this chapter it was assumed that prices and wages were completely flexible, that they would take on whatever values were required for full employment to be achieved. In an economy in equilibrium, all workers willing to work at the going wage are able to find employment. We called this situation full employment, since there is neither excess demand nor excess supply of labor. If more output is demanded than can be produced at full employment, the price level rises until the excessive demand for output is eliminated. If less than full employment output is demanded, prices fall until full employment is established.

NOTES

[1] If there is business saving S_b, the same result follows. If we call household saving S_h, consumption is total income less business saving, which is the part of total income not paid to households, less household saving. Substituting into (7-1), we obtain

$$Y - S_b - S_h + I = Y$$

Eliminating Y and rearranging terms gives

$$S_h + S_b = I$$

Throughout this chapter and the next we assume no business saving.

[2] We should try to keep in mind the distinction between this condition and the condition that planned saving must equal planned investment. The latter requires that the level of output that firms wish to sell (whatever it is) actually be sold to willing buyers. The former condition requires that the level of output that firms wish to produce be the one at which they maximize their profits.

[3] This assumption is crucial, and many of the controversies surrounding the behavior of the economy have centered on its validity. In the next chapter we explore the effect of relaxing the assumption by requiring some variables to be rigid.

8

Unemployment

In the model developed in the previous chapter, equilibrium in the economy involved full employment of labor. This was assured by our assumption that wages and prices were completely flexible and would take on whatever values were required to make the level of aggregate demand equal to full employment output. In such a model, unemployment can only exist during the movement from one equilibrium to another and is simply a transitory phenomenon, although the transition can take place over a considerable time.

Opposing the view that full employment is the "natural" state of an economy and unemployment is a "temporary" phenomenon, others have argued that rigidities can produce situations in which unemployment characterizes the equilibrium position of the economy. Table 8-1, which shows how unemployment in the United States has varied between 1929 and 1972, indicates that there have been periods of persistent and substantial unemployment. Between 1931 and 1940, the rate of unemployment was never less than about 15 percent of the labor force, and in 1933 it reached 25 percent. More recently, the rate of unemployment has been considerably lower, but it was almost 7 percent in both 1958 and 1961.

If, contrary to the assumptions made in the previous chapter, unemployment can be large and can continue for long periods of time, government action may be called for. Such policies are the subject of the next chapter. First however, let us examine some possible causes of unemployment.

RIGID WAGES

Suppose that we drop our assumption that wages are completely flexible. We assume instead that for any of a number of reasons, the money wage rate is rigid downward, and even if some laborers are unemployed, they do not respond by reducing the money wage they will accept.[1]

A great many reasons are offered for downward rigidities in the money wage level. Among the major ones are: (1) the existence of minimum wage laws; (2) the existence of trade unions that refuse to accept cuts in money wage rates, which they see as indicative of weakness in a union's ability to raise members' wages; (3) the preference of some workers to be laid off, using the time to seek a better job rather than accepting a reduced wage in the old job, and (4) the recognition by each laborer that a reduction in his wage only will do little to increase the likelihood of being employed, since overall demand is insufficient for all labor to be employed.

Suppose the economy is in equilibrium at full employment and an upward shift in the saving schedule occurs. Whereas in the previous case both the money wage rate and the price level declined proportionately, to induce a return to full employment, now the money wage rate is not permitted to decline. The foregoing analysis proceeded in the knowledge that the level of

Table 8-1 Unemployment as a percentage of the U.S. civilian labor force, 1929–1972

Year	Unemployment Rate	Year	Unemployment Rate
1929	3.2	1951	3.3
1930	8.7	1952	3.0
1931	15.9	1953	2.9
1932	23.6	1954	5.5
1933	24.9	1955	4.4
1934	21.7	1956	4.1
1935	20.1	1957	4.3
1936	16.9	1958	6.8
1937	14.3	1959	5.5
1938	19.0	1960	5.5
1939	17.2	1961	6.7
1940	14.6	1962	5.5
1941	9.9	1963	5.7
1942	4.7	1964	5.2
1943	1.9	1965	4.5
1944	1.2	1966	3.8
1945	1.9	1967	3.8
1946	3.9	1968	3.6
1947	3.9	1969	3.5
1948	3.8	1970	4.9
1949	5.9	1971	5.9
1950	5.3	1972	5.6

Source: Various issues of *Economic Report of the President.* Prior to 1947 the unemployment rate is the percentage of those 14 years of age and over who were looking for work but were unable to find it. After 1947 it is the percentage of those 16 years of age and over.

real national income could not change, but we can no longer be assured of such an outcome.

As before, the initial impact of the shift in the saving schedule is to reduce the level of national income and to reduce the rate of interest as the *IS* curve shifts to the left. The excess supply of goods that develops causes the general level of prices to decline. But if prices are reduced and the money wage rate is maintained, full employment cannot be maintained. Since firms are assumed to be attempting to maximize profits, they will hire labor until the marginal physical product of labor is equal to the real wage. But as prices fall while the money wage remains unchanged, the real wage will rise. Thus to equate the marginal physical product of labor and the real wage, it will be necessary to reduce employment.

The decline in the price level causes the *IS* and *LM* curves to shift to the right. But the increase in national income that is caused cannot be large enough to return to the original income level, since output will have fallen because of the rise in the real wage. In other words, the rightward shifts in *IS* and *LM* do not continue until the curves intersect at full employment output. Before that point is reached, the increase in demand due to these shifts reaches the point to which firms' desired output has fallen. By inducing an increase in aggregate demand and a reduction in aggregate supply, the reduction in the general level of prices eventually eliminates the excess supply in the goods market. This case differs from the one considered before, however, in that the new equilibrium occurs at a level of output below the full employment level.

In Figure 8-1, the curves LM_0 and IS_0 represent the situation before the shift in the saving schedule. The curves intersect at Y_0, which is full employment income. The shift in the saving schedule produces a leftward shift in the *IS* curve to IS_0'. If no further changes occurred, equilibrium income would be reduced to Y_0'. But at that level of demand there is an excess supply of goods, and prices therefore decline. The fall in prices produces rightward shifts in both *LM* and *IS*. The final equilibrium is depicted as Y_1, which is at the intersection of LM_1 and IS_1, which are drawn for the new, lower price level P_1.

At the new higher real wage rate, W_0/P_1, less labor is employed than previously. In addition, the real wage rate has increased, which means that the quantity of labor supplied has risen. Thus less labor is employed than initially, and the excess supply of labor is even larger than the difference between the current level of employment and the original full employment level. The situation in the labor market is depicted in Figure 8-2(a).

The original equilibrium real wage rate is (W_0/P_0) and the employment

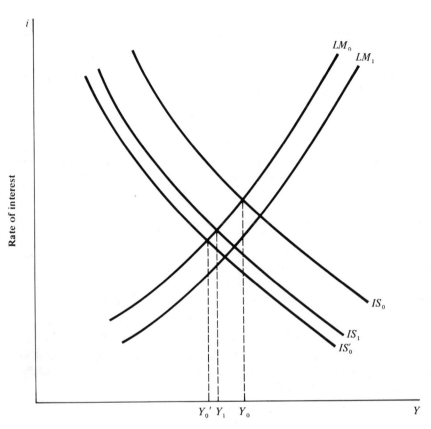

FIGURE 8-1

level is N_0. As prices fall with a rigid money wage rate, the real wage rises, the amount of labor demanded declines along D_n, and the amount of output supplied is reduced. Eventually the price decline eliminates the gap between aggregate demand and aggregate supply. At the new price level P_1, the equilibrium real wage rate, under the assumption of rigid money wages, is (W_0/P_1). Since employment has fallen from N_0 to N_1, $N_1 N_0$ might be considered to be one measure of the extent of unemployment induced by the rigidity of money wages. However, the rise in the real wage rate has induced an increase in the amount of labor supplied; thus another measure of unemployment, the one that would be obtained if all potential workers were asked whether they would be willing to work if they could find a job at the existing real wage rate, is $N_1 N_2$.

In Figure 8-2(b) we have projected the new employment level N_1 against the output–employment relation, indicating that the equilibrium output level

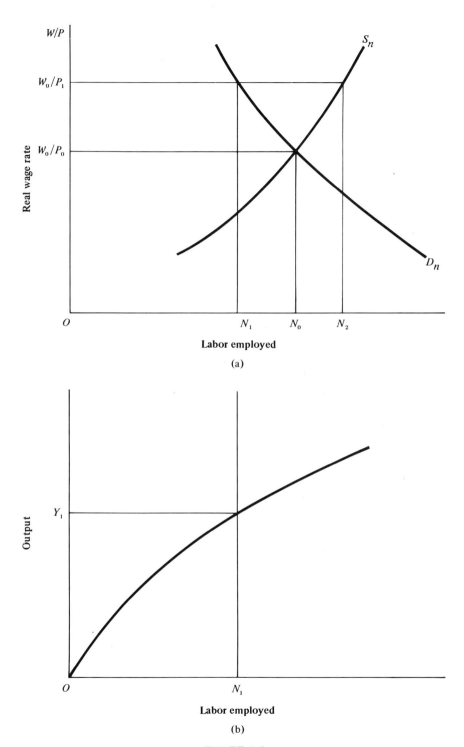

(a)

(b)

FIGURE 8-2

is Y_1. This corresponds, of course, to the equilibrium income level depicted in Figure 8-1.

But if workers are willing to offer more labor at a higher real wage, why would they be unwilling to offer an unchanged quantity of labor at an unchanged real wage (such as would occur if both prices and wages were reduced proportionately)? The answer lies in the laborer's lack of assurance that when he reduces the money wage he offers, the prices of the goods he buys will fall by the same percentage. Moreover, he may think he can obtain a job elsewhere at an unchanged money wage rather than retain the present job at lower money wage. These factors tend to induce laborers, at least for a time, to accept unemployment without a reduction in the money wage they are willing to accept. And so long as they do so, they prevent a decline in the price level large enough to restore aggregate demand to its full employment level.

RIGID PRICES

Let us assume that wages are flexible and that an excess supply in the labor market therefore produces a decline in the money wage rate, although factors exist to prevent declines in the price level, even in the face of an excess supply in the product market. This downward rigidity of prices in the product market may be the result of oligopolistic practices (although that condition would be inconsistent without construction of the demand for labor schedule), or it may have occurred simply because for a time at least, firms will respond to a reduction in the demand for their commodities at the old price level by laying off workers rather than by reducing prices, hoping that the decline in demand is temporary.[2]

Suppose that as unemployment develops from an increase in saving, the money wage is reduced but the price level does not change. The decline in the wage rate produces a reduction in the real wage rate and an increase in the quantity of labor demanded. At the same time, the quantity of labor supplied is reduced. Since prices are not falling, the *IS* and *LM* curves remain in their new positions, intersecting at a level of aggregate demand smaller than the full employment output level. As the real wage falls, the amount of labor that firms can hire is reduced, the output they can produce declines, and output eventually reaches the level of aggregate demand determined by the intersection of the *IS* and *LM* curves. When this position is reached, there is no longer an excess supply of goods, and the decline in the wage rate is ended. The new equilibrium involves a lower real wage, a lower money wage, and an unchanged price level. At the same time, there is excess demand for labor, but the wage rate is not bid up and additional laborers are not hired because firms realize that the additional output could not be sold. Again, rigidity in one variable in the system prevents the achievement of the full employment level of output as the equilibrium one.

SUMMARY

Given the assumption that wages or prices, or perhaps both, are rigid in a downward direction, full employment output as a rule will not be the level of output toward which the economic system tends. The economy may settle at a position in which labor is unemployed. As a result, if full employment output is to be achieved, active governmental intervention may be required.[3]

Chapters 7 and 8 have provided two contrasting models of the economy. In Chapter 7 the economy was assumed always to tend toward full employment of resources. Its ultimate arrival at that point was assured because wages and prices would continue to change until the goal was attained. In this chapter we assumed the opposite—that prices or wages are completely inflexible in the face of an excess supply of goods or labor, with the result that equilibrium at less than full employment is possible.

In Chapter 7 the full impact of a change in aggregate demand was on the price level. Total output did not change, given a change in aggregate demand. An increase in aggregate demand produced an increase in the general level of prices, which continued until the excess demand for goods was eliminated. Similarly, insufficient aggregate demand produced a decline in prices just large enough to assure that full employment was maintained. By contrast, in the models developed in this chapter, deficiencies in aggregate demand were at best partially offset by reductions in prices and wages. The other side of this coin is that variations in demand could affect output in such models.

The two models represent extreme versions of two widely held views concerning the economy. In one version, characterized in Chapter 7, the "natural forces" of the economy are always at work to restore full employment. Furthermore, the process is sufficiently strong and rapid that any deviations from full employment with stable prices are short-lived. Thus we have the implication that government need not take an active role in countercyclical policy. In one variant of this view, government policy is at least as likely to do harm as good, which leads one to conclude that passive government policy is called for.

In the other view, the forces leading to full employment are either non-existent or so weak that they cannot be relied on to restore full employment if unemployment develops. In addition, even if full employment would eventually be reached through downward wage and price flexibility, the process may be long enough to justify an attempt by government to bring about the desired result more quickly. Finally, those who hold this view also tend to believe that the effects of government policies will be felt rapidly enough to permit some improvement from an activist stabilization policy. In the next chapter we examine the workings of government policies. In Chapter 14 we analyze the effects of government policies and point to areas in which policy makers possess incomplete information.

Before concluding this chapter it should be noted that not everyone accepts the view that rigidities in wages and prices are the source of unemployment. According to some writers the large-scale unemployment that characterized the American economy during the 1930s resulted not from any inherent instability but rather from erroneous government policies, especially monetary policies.[4] In this view, unemployment may occasionally occur, but it is likely to be mild and temporary unless made worse by incorrect government actions. The stabilizing forces are the adjustments in wages and prices, which were considered in the previous chapter. Debate continues over which of these two views about the stability of the American economy is correct.

It is not the author's intention to argue here that government policies have always been wise. Nevertheless, he believes that a case can be made for government intervention to eliminate unemployment, although, as will be discussed later, the making of good government policy is not an easy task.

NOTES

[1] The view that wages are completely inflexible downward is often ascribed to John Maynard Keynes, *The General Theory of Employment Interest and Money,* Harcourt Brace Jovanovich, New York, 1935. However, Axel Leijonhufvud has argued in *On Keynesian Economics and the Economics of Keynes* (Oxford University Press, New York, 1968), that Keynes really believed that eventually wage demands would be reduced, but this result might take considerable time. For purposes of short-term analysis or public policy making, therefore, assuming downward rigidity of wages may be appropriate, especially for mild downturns in economic activity. Between 1929 and 1933 when unemployment in the United States increased substantially, hourly wages in manufacturing declined from 56 to 44 cents. Since then, however, with far lower rates of unemployment, there has been no year in which wage rates have declined in manufacturing.

[2] For a time they may even maintain their work force, either producing inventories or being partially idle, to avoid the costs of expanding their labor force when what is believed to be a temporary decline in demand is over.

[3] Downward rigidity in wages and/or prices is only one possible justification for an active government stabilization policy. There are several others. For example, even if full employment output will eventually be reached through downward price and wage flexibility, the process may be long enough to justify some intervention to hasten

the desired result. Moreover, the very process of price declines may generate expecta-tions of still further price declines, and this factor by itself may tend to make house-holds spend less rather than more, to be able to purchase goods at lower prices than currently exist. If this effect is sufficiently strong, it may offset the expansionary stimulus of the real balance effect, and *falling* prices, as opposed to lower prices, may actually reduce output. Finally, the decline in the level of prices can produce redistributions of wealth between creditors and debtors, increasing the wealth of the former by the amount that the wealth of the latter is being reduced. This assumes that the price decline is not correctly anticipated. We have been assuming, implicitly, that the amount by which the increase in wealth increased the spending of creditors is exactly the amount by which the spending of debtors has been reduced. In other words, we have been ignoring the effect of redistributions of wealth within the private sector. Unless we can ignore the effect of such wealth redistributions, we cannot make any overall judgment of the effect of a change in the general level of prices on spending. For example, if the amount by which debtors' spending decreases exceeds the amount by which creditors' spending increases, as a result of a redistribution of wealth occasioned by a fall in the price level, the decline in prices may *reduce* spending, even after allowing for the operation of the real balance effect.

⁴ This view is argued strongly by Milton Friedman in many of his writings.

9

Government
and national income

In Chapters 7 and 8 we developed the elements of a theory of national income and price level determination for an economy having no government and no financial institutions. This chapter remedies the former omission and retains the latter. We begin by considering the effect of a balanced budget government policy, in which the level of government spending and the level of government tax collections are always changed in the same direction and by the same amount. Next, we proceed to cases in which government spending increases (or tax decreases) are financed by printing new money. Then we examine open market operations, the exchange between the government and the private sector of money and bonds. This is followed by an investigation of the effects of government spending increases (or tax decreases) financed by issuing new bonds. Finally, we consider a government whose fiscal policy is accompanied by a monetary policy designed to maintain an "even keel" in money markets.

To avoid extensive repetition in this chapter, we consider only cases in which the economy is initially at less than full employment and the government is pursuing an expansionary policy to reduce unemployment. Consequently, we employ only the apparatus developed in Chapter 8, which permits unemployment of resources. The analysis would have to be modified only slightly, however, to deal with cases in which full employment of resources exists.

In addition, to avoid complicating the analysis, we assume that both prices and wages are rigid downward, the entire impact of any government policy being manifested in the form of higher real output and employment. In other words, only the IS and LM curves drawn for the existing price level need be considered. Since we are concerned primarily with comparing the impacts of alternative policies, failure to distinguish between the effects of the policies on output and the effects on prices is not important.

BALANCED BUDGET FISCAL POLICY

It is easiest to begin by examining government spending that is exactly matched by government tax receipts: In such cases the separation of the impact of government fiscal action from its monetary policy is drawn most clearly. This is not to say that the government will not engage in any monetary actions when its budget is balanced. The section of this chapter on open market operations reveals that a government with a balanced budget may be engaged simultaneously in exchanging money and bonds with the public. But when the government budget is balanced, it is possible to analyze separately the impact of changes in the level of government spending, financed by equal increases in taxation, without concerning oneself with any attendant financial transactions. Similarly, one can analyze the impact of monetary actions without worrying about the accompanying fiscal actions, so long as the government budget remains in balance.

We assume that the government determines the volume of its tax collections, either directly by legislation or by determining the level of tax rates it must set to obtain a given amount of revenue.[1]

We must make a number of modifications in the model developed in Chapter 7 before we can analyze the effect of this policy. First, the saving function must be changed, since all national income does not accrue to the household sector. National income differs from disposable income by the amount of taxes collected by the government. In symbols we have

$$Y_d = Y - T \tag{9-1}$$

where Y_d is disposable income and T is personal income taxes. The saving function now is

$$S = S(Y_d, i, M/P) \tag{9-2}$$

In addition, the equilibrium condition in the goods market must be changed to allow for the presence of government. For the goods market to be in equilibrium, consumers, business firms, and the government must be willing to acquire the output that firms wish to produce. In other words, the sum of planned consumption, planned investment, and planned government spending must equal the amount of national income produced. This is expressed symbolically as

$$C + I + G = Y$$

where G is real government expenditures on goods and services. Since consumption is equal to national income minus personal saving and taxes, we can rewrite this as

$$Y - S - T + I + G = Y$$

where T is government tax collections in real terms. Subtracting Y from both sides and rearranging terms, the equation can be rewritten as

$$S + (T - G) = I$$

The term $(T - G)$, the government budget surplus, is often referred to as *government saving*, the difference between what the government receives and what it spends. Therefore, for equilibrium to exist in the goods market, planned saving must still equal planned investment, with saving now defined to include government as well as private saving.

Curves LM_0 and IS_0 in Figure 9-1 are drawn on the assumption of no government spending and no taxes; these curves represent the combinations of the interest rate and the income level at which equilibrium exists in the money and the goods market, respectively. The equilibrium rate of interest is i_0 and the equilibrium income level is Y_0 and, by assumption, this represents a situation of less than full employment.

Into this situation we introduce government spending exactly matched by tax collections.[2] Since the government policy produces no change in the stock of money, the LM curve is unchanged. However, as a result of the introduction of income taxes, disposable income is smaller at every level of national

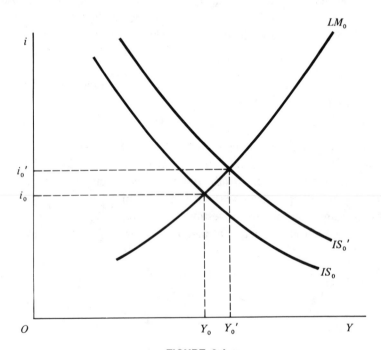

FIGURE 9-1

income than it was previously. Therefore, at any combination of the interest rate and national income at which saving previously equaled investment (i.e., at every point along *IS*), there is now an excess of planned investment over planned saving. Since the government budget is balanced, the amount of government saving is unchanged: It is still zero. But private saving will be smaller at every income-level–interest-rate combination, since disposable income is now smaller than national income due to the taxes.[3] Therefore, at every point along IS_0 there is an excess of planned investment over planned saving. To eliminate this disequilibrium in the goods market, the rate of interest must rise, to reduce planned investment and to increase planned saving, and/or national income must increase, to increase private saving. In other words, the *IS* curve must shift to the right, as to IS_0' in Figure 9-1.

The result of the balanced increase in government spending and taxes is, therefore, expansionary. National income and employment will rise. Private investment will fall because of the higher rate of interest, which is also attributable to the policy. But consumption spending will rise. This somewhat unexpected result—namely, that a balanced change in government spending and taxation is expansionary—is referred to as the *balanced budget theorem*. The new equilibrium thus involves a higher real output level than initially. As a result of the higher interest rate, private investment is reduced. But the net effect of the balanced budget policy is expansionary, and this reduces unemployment. If the policy is carried far enough, unemployment can be eliminated.

GOVERNMENT SPENDING FINANCED BY PRINTING MONEY

Government spending exactly matched by tax collections is a rare event. Often the government runs a deficit and, more rarely, a surplus. What is the impact of government spending financed entirely by printing money?

In Figure 9-2 we illustrate the introduction of government spending financed by printing money into an economy in which unemployment exists. In the absence of government, the intersection of IS_0 and LM_0 indicates the equilibrium level of national income, Y_0. The additional government spending shifts the *IS* curve to the right for two reasons. First, government spending not financed by tax collections reduces government saving. Second, the larger nominal money stock combined with the rigid price level yields an increase in the real money stock, therefore reduces private saving. Consequently, at every point along IS_0 there is now an excess of planned investment over planned saving, and the curve must therefore shift to IS_0'. The shift in the *IS* curve is larger than in the case of the balanced increase in government

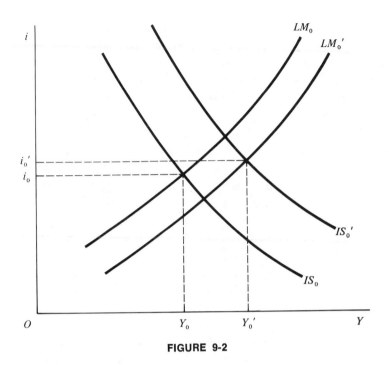

FIGURE 9-2

spending and taxes, both because of the larger money stock and because of the absence of taxes.

At the same time, the *LM* curve shifts to the right. This occurs because with a larger money stock, at every interest-rate-income combination along LM_0 there is now an excess supply of money. To eliminate this excess, the level of income must rise, the interest rate must fall, or both.

The result of the policy of increasing government spending and financing the increase with newly printed money is expansionary and is more expansionary than the balanced budget policy. The rightward shift in *IS* is larger in this case, and it is accompanied by a shift in the same direction in *LM*. The rise in national income is larger and unemployment is reduced more in this case. The interest rate may rise or fall, depending on the relative sizes of the shifts in *LM* and *IS*. If the interest rate rises, as in Figure 9-2, the government policy reduces private investment. If the interest rate falls, an increase in private investment will accompany the increase in government spending.[4]

We can also consider what will happen if after government spending has been increased for one period, it is returned to its previous level. The *LM* curve is not affected, since it is drawn for the new, larger stock of money. The additional money created during the period in which government spending was financed by printing money does not disappear when the government budget is once again brought into balance. At the same time, the *IS* curve shifts to the left, although it does not return to its original position. Again, the additional money created during the period in which the government ran a deficit still affects the volume of household saving. At the same time, of course, government spending is reduced; thus the curve does not remain at IS_0'. Because the government has once run a deficit, equilibrium income is made permanently higher, even after government spending has returned to its original level.

OPEN MARKET OPERATIONS

Not all government deficits are financed by printing money. Some are financed by the sale of government bonds to the public. Before turning to the analysis of such policies, it is instructive to consider another kind of activity in which the government can engage. The government can exchange bonds for the money holdings of the public. It can buy bonds held by the public with newly printed money, or it can sell bonds to the public for money.[5]

Let us consider the sale of government bonds to the public. Recall that the demand for money can be thought of as the counterpart of the demand for bonds. Once an individual has decided how large a portion of his portfolio he wishes to hold in the form of monetary assets, an increase in the amount of money he holds must mean a decrease in the amount he wishes to hold in bonds. When the public is asked to hold a larger quantity of bonds and a smaller quantity of money, it must be induced to do so.

Figure 9-3 illustrates this point. The distance *OM* represents the quantity of money in the system, and the distance from *OM* to *WW* represents the value of bonds. If the *number* of bonds the public holds at any given time is fixed, the *value* of bond holdings varies inversely with the rate of interest. A reduction in the rate of interest increases the value of each bond, thus the total value of bonds.

The curve *DD* represents the demand for money. The quantity of money demanded increases as the rate of interest declines, for the reasons discussed at length in Chapter 3. The curve *DD* can also be thought of as showing how the public would wish to distribute its holdings of monetary assets between money and bonds at various rates of interest.

The equilibrium rate of interest is i_0, where the quantity of money demanded and the quantity of money supplied are equal. Alternatively, at i_0 the distribution of monetary assets (*OM* of money and *MN* of bonds) is the same as that which the public wishes to hold. At interest rates in excess

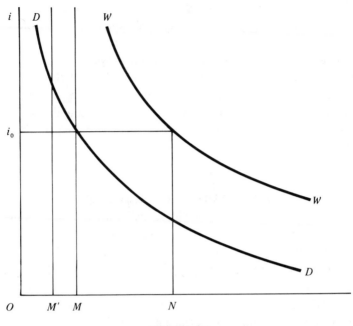

FIGURE 9-3

of i_0, there is an excess supply of money. Another way of saying the same thing is that at interest rates above i_0, the way in which the public wishes to distribute its holdings between money and bonds requires more bonds than exist. As a result, the public will attempt to acquire bonds for money. In the process, however, the value of bonds in existence is increased and the quantity of money demanded increases. The process continues until the rate of interest reaches i_0.

A numerical example will help illustrate this point (see Figure 9-4). Suppose that there are 10 bonds in the system, each representing a promise to pay $1 per year in perpetuity, and the amount of money in the system is $100. At an interest rate of 20 percent the total value of bonds is $50, since each bond is worth $5. Total monetary assets have a value of $150. At an interest rate of 10 percent total monetary assets are worth $200, and at an interest rate of 5 percent they are worth $300.

If the quantity of money demanded at a 10 percent rate of interest is $100, 10 percent is the equilibrium rate. At an interest rate of 20 percent, where the quantity of money demanded is, say, $80, there is an excess demand for bonds, since bonds are worth $50 and the value of bonds demanded is $70

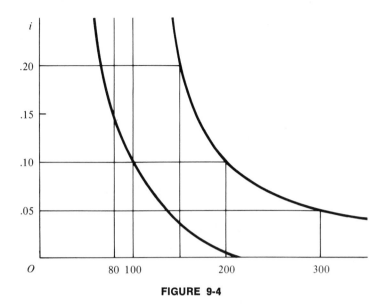

FIGURE 9-4

(which is the difference between the total value of monetary assets, $150, and the quantity of money demanded, $80).

The disparity between asset holdings desired and assets supplied leads to an attempt on the part of the public to increase their bond holdings and to decrease their money holdings. This attempt is only partially successful because the value of money in the system is fixed. But the initial disequilibrium is overcome, since by the attempt to exchange money for bonds, bond prices are raised (i.e., interest rates are reduced), and the increase in bond prices raises the value of all bonds and increases the quantity of money demanded. As assumed, equilibrium is finally reached at an interest rate of 10 percent, where the quantity of money demanded is $100.

Now suppose that the government wishes to exchange bonds for the public's holdings of money. Since this is to be a voluntary transaction, the return from bond holdings must be made attractive enough to induce the public to part with a portion of its money holdings.

Suppose that the government wishes to reduce the public's money holdings to *OM'*. The larger the rise in the interest rate the public requires to willingly reduce its money holdings by *M'M*, the greater the number of bonds the government must purchase to bring about the reduction. To continue the foregoing example, if the government wished to reduce the private sector's money holdings by $20, it would have to allow the rate of interest to rise to 20 percent. At that rate of interest the public would be willing to hold $80 in money. Since bonds are worth $5, the public would have to receive 4 bonds before it would give up the $20. But monetary assets are still worth a total of $150 at an interest rate of 20 percent, since the public now holds $80 in money and 14 bonds, each worth $5.

Suppose, instead, that the government wished to purchase enough bonds to increase the public's holdings of money by $20 (from $100) and that the interest rate would have to decline to 5 percent to induce the public to hold $120 in money. Since at a 5 percent rate of interest the price of a bond is $20, the government would have to purchase only one bond. The public now holds $120 in money and 9 bonds, which have a combined value of $180. Total monetary assets at an interest rate of 5 percent are thus still $300, as they were when the public held $100 in money and 10 bonds.

A change in the composition of monetary assets thus results in a shift in the *LM* schedules. An increase in the stock of bonds and a reduction in the stock of money creates an excess demand for money. Thus the open market operation described shifts the *LM* curve to the left.

What is the effect of the open market operation on the *IS* curve? Since the stock of money is reduced, it would appear that the amount of saving people wish to engage in should be increased for every price level. But this result needs further analysis. While the stock of money held by the public is reduced, the stock of government bonds held by them is larger. Should we not allow for the larger holdings of government bonds in determining the wealth of the public? The value of these bonds represents the present value of the interest payments that bond holders expect. But these interest payments must be satisfied by future taxes, and the present value of future taxes that the public owes because of its holdings of bonds is exactly equal to the value of its bond holdings. Thus the government bonds do not represent net wealth of the public. The money stock is included as wealth because there is no need to collect future taxes or to engage in any other actions to satisfy any liability that accompanies the issuance of the money. Thus the open market sale also serves to reduce the wealth of the public. This shifts the *IS* curve to the left. Since both *IS* and *LM* are shifted leftward, the result of the open market sale of securities is deflationary, leading to lower national income and employment. This case is illustrated in Figure 9-5.

GOVERNMENT SPENDING FINANCED BY SELLING BONDS

We are now in a position to consider the effects of an increase in government spending financed by selling bonds. Such a transaction can be thought

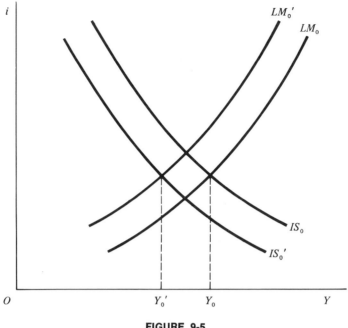

FIGURE 9-5

of as composed of two parts, both previously analyzed. First, government spending financed by printing money occurs. Next, there is an open market sale of bonds equal to the amount of the newly issued money. The former act is expansionary. The latter is deflationary. The overall effect of the transaction is the sum of the effects of the two transactions comprising it.

The effect of the policy is to shift the *IS* curve to the right and the *LM* curve to the left. The *IS* curve shifts rightward because government spending is larger and the nominal money stock is unchanged. The *LM* curve shifts leftward because the nominal stock of money is unchanged and the stock of bonds is larger. This is illustrated in Figure 9-6.

The curve $M + B/i$ represents the value of the initial amounts of bonds and money as a function of the rate of interest. The curve D_m, designating the initial demand for money schedule, shows how the public would like to distribute its holdings between money and bonds at various rates of interest. The equilibrium rate of interest is initially i_0.

The curve $M + B'/i$ represents the value of the larger amount of bonds and the original money stock. The number of bonds is larger because of the additional bonds sold to finance the increase in government spending. However, the interest rate will not remain constant at i_0 because the public will not be willing to absorb the additional bonds at the old rate of interest. In-

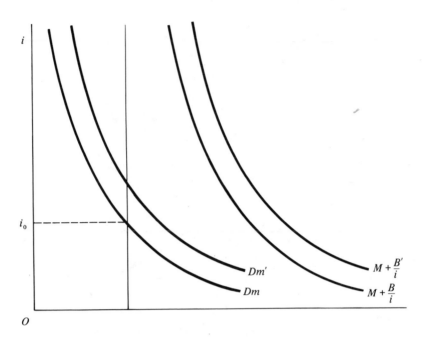

FIGURE 9-6

stead, they will attempt to exchange a portion of the additional bonds for money. In the diagram, this effect is demonstrated as a rightward shift in the demand for money to D_m'. The equilibrium rate of interest is therefore increased. The interpretation of this for the LM curve is as follows: The increase in the number of bonds that the public is asked to absorb creates an excess supply of bonds (i.e., an excess demand for money) at the interest-rate–income-level combinations along LM_0. The result is a leftward shift to LM_0'.

The net effect of the policy is indeterminate. The combination of a rightward shift in IS and a leftward shift in LM can either reduce real output or increase it. The policy is more likely to lead to an increase in output, the smaller the increase in the rate of interest the public demands to hold the additional bonds and the less sensitive is private spending to changes in the rate of interest. In the example illustrated in Figure 9-7, the net effect of the policy is expansionary.[6]

EVEN-KEEL POLICY

We have been assuming that the government began by planning to finance its spending in one of three ways, by taxation, by the issuance of newly printed

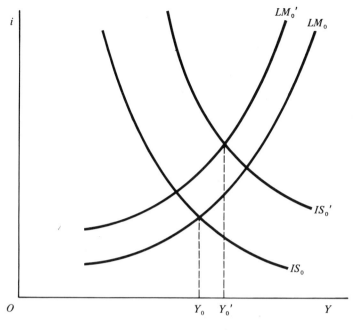

FIGURE 9-7

money, or through the sale of bonds. The method of finance was presumed to have been decided in advance of the spending. There is, however, an alternative assumption. Suppose that the government decides to increase its spending and to choose the combination of money and bond finance that prevents the interest rate from changing. This is often referred to as *even-keel policy*. The financing policy is carried out to keep the money market steady (i.e., to prevent the equilibrium rate of interest from being affected by the government spending program). Sometimes the additional amount of money that must be issued even exceeds the government spending increase (i.e., additional open market purchases are called for), since, as we have already seen, the interest rate may rise even when an increase in government spending is financed entirely by printing money.

Since the equilibrium interest rate will be unaffected by the policy pursued, we can draw the *LM* curve as a horizontal line. An increase in government spending produces a rightward shift in the *IS* curve (see Figure 9-8). The effect of an increase in government spending is clearly expansionary, producing an increase in real income and employment. If government spending and taxation changes are always accompanied by even-keel policy, we can unambiguously determine the direction of the effects of these policies.

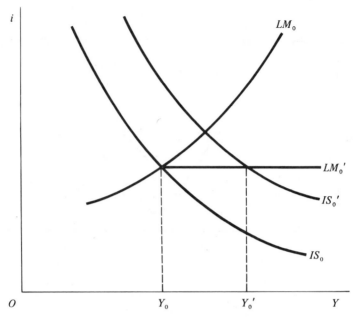

FIGURE 9-8

WHAT IS FISCAL POLICY?

As the foregoing discussion makes clear, there are a number of policies that can be pursued to eliminate any shortfall between the demand for goods and services and the capacity of the economy to produce them. Increases in government spending financed by the issue of new money and open market security purchases are clearly expansionary, and an increase in government spending financed by the issue of bonds may be. Nevertheless, there is considerable disagreement over the relative effectiveness of monetary and fiscal policy as a stabilization tool. As the next chapter reveals, part of this controversy has a substantive character and can be resolved by improvements in our understanding of how the economy functions. However, a more disturbing problem is that participants in the debate do not always mean the same things when they refer to monetary and fiscal policy. Proponents of monetary policy tend to *define* fiscal policy as the case of all deficits financed by issuing bonds.[7] As we have seen, increases in government spending financed in this manner are less expansionary than are those financed by printing money. They may, in fact, be deflationary. On the other hand, some supporters of fiscal policy tend to *define* fiscal policy to involve an even-keel policy.[8] Yet we also know that such policies may involve substantial issue of new money to keep interest rates from rising as government spending is increased.

Opponents of fiscal policy might argue that the expansionary impact of the government policy would not have occurred in the absence of the issue of new money. Its proponents may reply, however, that the additional money would not have been created if government spending had not increased. But clearly much of this debate is merely semantic. "Fiscal policy" will have a smaller effect if it is defined to involve bond finance than if it is defined to involve money finance. The definition chosen is a matter of convention. But some convention must be adopted. One cannot answer the question, What is the effect of an increase in government spending? without knowing how the increase will be financed.

A classic case illustrating the importance of asking this question properly involves the assessment of the impact of the tax cut of 1964. Personal income tax rates were reduced in 1964 to stimulate demand and to reduce unemployment, which had exceeded 5 percent of the labor force since 1958. Unemployment subsequently declined to less than 4 percent by 1966, and this was claimed as an important victory for the view that taxes and government spending could be manipulated to maintain the economy at or close to full employment. However, many monetarists criticized this view, arguing that the expansion that followed the tax cut should be credited to the increase in the money supply due to the financing of the government deficit. One retort to this was that the increase in the money supply resulted from the government deficit and would not have occurred if taxes had not been cut.

Clearly, the resolution of this debate would require us to know what the money supply would have been if taxes had *not* been cut. But even without this knowledge, we may be able to reach an agreement about how the effect of the tax cut would have differed if the growth in the money stock had been smaller than it was. By now most economists believe that if the government deficit that resulted from the tax cut had been financed by the issuance of bonds, the impact of unemployment would have been smaller than it actually was. And this consensus is more important than the assignment of credit for the resulting gain in output to either monetary or fiscal policy.

SUMMARY

Actions taken by the government with respect to spending, taxation, and the stock of money can effect the levels of output and employment. Increases in government spending can have different effects depending on whether they are financed by additional taxes, by the sale of bonds, or by the issuance of new money. Similarly, increases in the stock of money can have different effects depending on whether they result from the financing of government spending or from the purchase of bonds from the public.

NOTES

[1] This assumption is clearly at odds with reality, since governments can do no more than determine tax rates with precision, actual tax collections being dependent on the interaction between these rates and the tax base. Nevertheless, we will retain the assumption in this chapter because it considerably simplifies our discussion.

[2] The assumptions made here are unnecessarily restrictive. The following analysis holds for any case in which there is a balanced increase of government spending and taxes, regardless of the state of the government budget before the increase occurs.

[3] This assumes that a portion of the reduction in disposable income affects saving and a portion affects consumption.

[4] The same analysis could have been employed for the case of a reduction in taxes with the resulting deficit financed by issuing money.

[5] In this chapter we do not distinguish between the administrative branch of the government and the central bank. Both are included in "government." In the United States, open market operations are conducted almost exclusively by the central bank, the Federal Reserve.

[6] A similar analysis would hold for a decrease in taxes, with the resulting revenue deficiency being financed by selling bonds.

[7] This is the view of Michael Keran, "Monetary and Fiscal Influences on Economic Activity—The Historical Evidence," *Federal Reserve Bank of St. Louis Review,* November 1969, p. 10.

[8] A clear statement of this view can be found in Arthur M. Okun, *The Political Economy of Prosperity,* Norton, New York, 1970, pp. 53–59.

10

The effect of government policy: Some special cases

This chapter deals with some potential sources of failure of government policies. In our previous discussions, government policy always "worked" in the sense that if pursued with sufficient vigor, it succeeded in bringing about full employment. But some economists have argued that there are situations in which government policies will not be successful. We now examine some of these arguments, assuming as in the previous chapter that both wages and prices are inflexible downward and that the government is attempting to move the economy toward full employment.

INTEREST INELASTIC SPENDING

Some writers have argued that investment spending by business firms is unresponsive to changes in the rate of interest.[1] Similarly, arguments have been advanced that personal saving is also interest inelastic. If private spending does not respond to variations in the rate of interest, we obtain the vertical IS curve depicted as IS_0 in Figure 10-1. If saving depends on national income, there is only one income level at which planned saving and planned investment are equal. This is shown as Y_0. Movements in the rate of interest cannot be used to close a gap between saving and investment. The only role that the rate of interest plays is to assure equality between the demand for and the supply of money. If LM_0 represents combinations of the rate of interest and national income at which there is equilibrium in the money market, the equilibrium rate of interest is i_0 and the equilibrium income level is Y_0.

If the government wishes to employ open market operations to increase

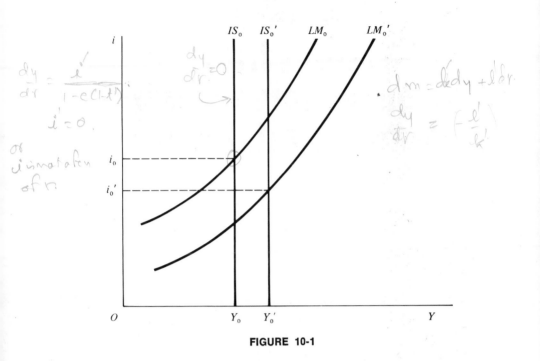

FIGURE 10-1

employment, it buys bonds. As our previous analysis has shown, this shifts
the *LM* curve rightward, as to LM_0' in Figure 10-1, and also shifts the *IS*
curve rightward, as to IS_0'. The shift of *LM* occurs because the open market
operation produces an excess supply of money at the original equilibrium.
The shift of *IS* occurs because the real stock of money is one of the determinants of private saving.

The result of the open market operation is that national income increases
to Y_0'. The rate of interest may rise or fall, depending on the relative magnitudes of the shifts in *LM* and *IS*. In Figure 10-1 the shifts produce a decline
in the rate of interest, an outcome we believe to be the more plausible one.

With a decline in the rate of interest produced by the open market security
purchase, we might expect private spending, particularly investment spending,
to increase; but this is ruled out by our assumption that such spending is
interest inelastic. Consequently, the increase in national income is smaller
than if we had assumed that spending would respond to variations in the
rate of interest. In fact, if one denies the significance of the stock of money
as a determinant of saving behavior, so that the *IS* curve does not shift, the
policy pursued by the government fails to increase national income at all.[2]
Those who believe that spending is interest inelastic assign a relatively minor
role to monetary policy as a stabilization tool and argue that fiscal policy,

which directly shifts the *IS* curve by changing government spending and taxes, must be relied on if full employment is to be achieved.

There is, however, an alternative view, even if one believes that spending is interest inelastic. Some suggest that the impact of monetary policy on spending occurs primarily through the direct effect of the larger money supply rather than through the indirect effect of changes in the rate of interest on spending. In the case we are considering, this means that they expect the shift in the *IS* curve produced by the open market operation to be the principal way in which monetary policy affects national income. Monetary policy can be effective even if spending is interest inelastic, so long as private spending responds directly to changes in the stock of money.

INTEREST INELASTIC DEMAND FOR MONEY

Certain economists believe that the demand for money is not very sensitive to the rate of interest. If we assume, in the extreme, that the demand for money is completely interest inelastic, we obtain the vertical *LM* curve depicted as LM_0 in Figure 10-2. Given the real supply of money, there is only one income level, Y_0, at which the demand for and the supply of money are equal. Variations in the rate of interest affect investment and consumption

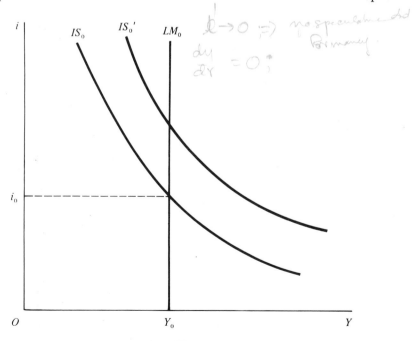

FIGURE 10-2

spending, but they do not change the quantity of money demanded. The equilibrium rate of interest is i_0 and the equilibrium income level is Y_0.

Into this situation we introduce government spending financed by taxes. The balanced increase in government spending and taxes shifts the *IS* curve rightward to IS_0'. But since there is only one income level at which the demand for money and the (fixed) supply of money are equal, the *LM* curve does not change. The impact of the government policy is thus to raise the rate of interest and to leave the income level unchanged. As the rate of interest rises, those elements of private spending which are sensitive to the rate of interest decline. Equilibrium is reached when the reduction in private spending just matches the increase in government spending.[3]

If the increase in government spending is financed by issuing bonds, a similar result follows. The *IS* curve shifts to the right but the *LM* curve is unchanged, since the public's demand for money is assumed to be interest inelastic. Bond-financed government spending is more expansionary when the demand for money is interest inelastic than when it is not. In the latter case, the increase in bonds held by the private sector must be accompanied by an increase in the rate of interest; that is, the *LM* curve must shift to the left. In the former case, the *LM* curve remains unchanged, since the public's demand for money depends only on income. Only if the increase in spending is financed by the issuance of money will national income rise. The printing of new money produces a rightward shift in the *LM* curve, although its slope remains unchanged. The intersection of the new *LM* and *IS* curves is, of course, at a higher level of national income. But it is the increase in the stock of money that has produced the rise in income, not the change in government spending. If the increase in the stock of money had been produced by an open market operation, the same change in national income would have occurred.

Not surprisingly, those who hold to the view that the demand for money is interest inelastic tend to argue that the stock of money, not government spending and taxation, must be employed by the government as a tool of stabilization. Increases in government spending, they insist, are unlikely to produce an increase in income unless accompanied by an increase in the stock of money.

THE LIQUIDITY TRAP

Some economists believe that there is a floor to the rate of interest. At some very low interest rate, people are willing to increase their holdings of money without any further decline in the rate of interest because they fear a capital loss on any additional bond holdings. As the rate of interest declines, an increasing number of people believe that the next movement of the interest rate must be upward. At a sufficiently low rate of interest, the feeling is held by everyone. Thus if the stock of money is increased through open market operations, where ordinarily we would expect the public to demand a lower rate of interest (to be willing to hold the smaller quantity of bonds and the larger stock of money), such demands are no longer heard. The public is, in effect, "saturated" with bond holdings and is willing to give up some of them without waiting for a decline in the rate of interest. The result is that open market purchases leave the rate of interest unchanged.

A liquidity trap is designated as the horizontal portion of the LM curve depicted as LM_0 in Figure 10-3. If the economy is in such a trap, as shown by the intersection of IS_0 and LM_0, an increase in the money supply produced by an open market bond purchase shifts the IS curve but leaves a portion of the LM curve unaffected. The effect of the open market purchase is to raise national income, because of the shift in the IS curve, although the rate of interest remains unchanged. The size of the increase in income is smaller than it would have been if the interest rate had declined, so long as private spending is elastic. Since the policy fails to reduce the rate of interest, it

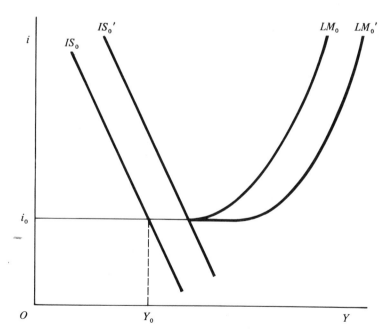

FIGURE 10-3

does not stimulate that portion of private spending which is responsive to changes in the rate of interest. As in the case considered earlier, if the open market operation leaves the *IS* curve unaffected, the open market purchase produces no change in national income. The only effect is to alter the composition of the private sector's portfolio. Spending is not affected.

Naturally, those who believe that the economy can fall into a liquidity trap argue that monetary policy may be very ineffective in bringing about a change in national income once the rate of interest has reached a level so low that open market operations produce little change in the rate of interest. They say that fiscal policy, which directly shifts the *IS* curves through changes in government spending and taxes, must be relied on to reduce unemployment under such conditions.

As in the case described earlier, however, there is an alternative interpretation. Even if one concedes the existence of a liquidity trap, monetary policy need not be ineffective. If one believes that the principal force of monetary policy is felt through the direct impact of changes in the money supply on spending, rather than indirectly through the effect of changes in the rate of interest, then the failure of an open market operation to reduce the rate of interest need not cause concern. Even in a liquidity trap, this direct effect can be relied on. It is through the shift in the *IS* curve rather than the change in the rate of interest that changes in the money stock are expected to produce the desired increase in national income.

HOW PLAUSIBLE ARE THESE SPECIAL CASES?

Hardly anyone nowadays believes that the extreme cases just analyzed adequately describe the real world. The evidence that the demand for money and private spending are interest elastic has been documented in previous chapters. Furthermore, the notion that a liquidity trap exists, or at least that we have ever reached it, is questioned by many economists. What then is the purpose of the present chapter if the cases it describes are implausible?

First, the chapter provides an additional test of our understanding of the model of the economy developed in this book. By providing a set of exercises, the chapter should demonstrate whether the reader's understanding of the analysis of the previous few chapters is complete. If you have had difficulty following the brief explanations provided in this chapter, it would be advisable to reread the more extensive discussions in previous chapters.

Second, although most economists do not believe that the extreme versions of the model presented here are correct, it is nevertheless true that there is a range of opinion regarding the magnitudes of the parameters considered here. And monetarists and other economists can still be distinguished by the belief of the former that the demand for money has a smaller interest elasticity than the latter assign to it. Furthermore, the monetarists believe that spending is highly responsive both to changes in the rate of interest and, especially, directly to changes in the stock of money. With this in mind, it is possible to rationalize the attention spent on the special cases considered in this chapter.

SUMMARY

The interest elasticity of private spending and the interest elasticity of the demand for money are among the factors that determine the effect of changes in government spending and changes in the stock of money. The smaller is the interest elasticity of spending, the smaller is the effect we can expect from a reduction in the rate of interest caused by an open market purchase of bonds. The smaller is the interest elasticity of the demand for money, the smaller is the effect we can expect from an increase in government spending or a reduction in taxes unless it is accomplished by an increase in the stock of money.

NOTES

[1] In Chapter 4 we examined some of the possible reasons for this.

[2] Another possible reason for the failure of the *IS* curve to shift is that the public may not regard a substitution of money for bonds in its portfolio as an increase in wealth.

[3] For a discussion of this point see R. W. Spencer and W. P. Yohe, "The 'Crowding Out' of Private Expenditures by Fiscal Actions," *Federal Reserve Bank of St. Louis Review,* October 1970.

11

Commercial banking and national income determination

In this chapter we remedy the second omission in the models employed in Chapter 7, the absence of financial institutions. Here we analyze an economy in which there are commercial banks. We defer until Chapter 12 an analysis of the role of other financial institutions. In the first section we show that the models employed in previous chapters are unaffected if banks are required to hold currency reserves equal to 100 percent of their deposit liabilities. Next we examine the effect of introducing a fractional reserve banking system. We place particular emphasis on bank holdings of excess and borrowed reserves and on the public's choice between currency and bank deposits. Then we develop a supply of money function, which we incorporate into the models of income determination previously presented. Finally we apply the model to a variety of real world situations.

100 PERCENT RESERVE BANKING

The introduction of commercial banks into an economy permits members of the public to choose between holding their money as currency or as bank deposits. The holder of a deposit is assumed to be able to convert it to currency on demand by presenting a check drawn against his account at his bank. If he gives such a check to someone else in payment of an obligation, that party can also obtain currency on demand. Because of this feature, the deposits are called *demand deposits*. Since both currency and demand deposits are means of payment, they are generally acceptable in payment of obligations, and both are considered to be money. It is not, however, a matter of indifference to an individual or a firm whether money is held in one or another of these forms. For various reasons, including greater ease of transfer and greater safety against loss or theft, households and firms tend to keep the bulk of their money holdings in the form of demand deposits.[1] But currency holdings cannot be reduced to zero, since it is generally impossible to use checks to pay for such low-cost items as bus rides, soft drinks, newspapers, and shoeshines.[2]

The simplest kind of banking system to analyze is one in which, by law, banks are required to hold currency equal to 100 percent of their deposit liabilities.[3] Thus if a member of the public deposits $100 in currency in his bank, the changes in the respective balance sheets are as follows:

Nonbank Public		Banking System		
Currency	−$100	Currency	+$100	Deposits +$100
Deposits	+$100			

The nonbank public has succeeded in changing the form of its money holdings, reducing its currency holdings, and increasing its holdings of demand deposits. The banking system has increased its currency holdings and increased its deposit liabilities. Since banks are required to hold currency reserves equal to their deposits, the process stops here. The amount of money held by the public is not changed by the conversion of currency to deposits.[4]

We can now see that there are two possible interpretations of the monetary system assumed in our previous analysis. Under the first interpretation there are no financial institutions: The entire money supply consists of currency issued by the government, and the public does not have the option of holding bank deposits. Under the alternative interpretations, there exist commercial banks which are subject to a 100 percent reserve requirement. In either case, the nominal money supply arises from government spending not financed either by taxation or by the issue of bonds. Thus the size of the money supply is determined completely by government. If the public wishes to place some of its currency holdings on deposit at banks, the money supply is unaffected.

FRACTIONAL RESERVE BANKING

In the banking system of the United States, banks that are members of the Federal Reserve system are required to hold reserves equal to only a fraction of their deposit liabilities.[5] The Federal Reserve Act sets limits within which the Board of Governors of the Federal Reserve may place these requirements.

As of July 1972, legal reserve requirements against demand deposits were made to depend only on the volume of deposits at a bank and not, as previously, on the location of the bank, as well. The legal reserve requirements currently in effect are as follows:[6]

Amount of Demand Deposits	Reserve Percentage Applicable
First $2 million or less	8 percent
$2–10 million	10 percent
$10–100 million	12 percent
$100–400 million	13 percent
Over $400 million	$17\frac{1}{2}$ percent

Thus a small bank with $10 million of deposits would face a legal reserve requirement of 9.6 percent, a bank with $100 million in deposits would have a legal reserve requirement of 11.8 percent, and a large bank with $1 billion in deposits would have a legal reserve requirement of 15.6 percent of deposits. In effect, the graduated legal reserve requirement subsidizes small banks by permitting them to lend out a larger proportion of their deposits than can large banks.

In a world of fractional reserves, banks must hold reserves in excess of required reserves, or have highly liquid assets, if they are to be able to meet deposit outflows without forced liquidation of assets at less than full value or the need to borrow reserves. Required reserves do not fill this need as they do in a system of 100 percent reserves. Consider a bank that holds no excess reserves in a situation in which the reserve requirement is, say, 20 percent. The balance sheet is as follows:

Currency	$200,000	Deposits	$1 million
Bonds	$800,000		

The bank has loaned out all its currency holdings in excess of required reserves. If someone now demands that the bank redeem $50,000 of his deposits for currency, the bank's balance sheet would be as follows:

Currency	$150,000	Deposits	$950,000
Bonds	$800,000		

But the bank is no longer satisfying the legal reserve requirement. Its currency reserves are $150,000, but its deposits are $950,0000, a ratio of 16 percent. To once again satisfy the legal reserve requirement, the bank must sell $40,000 of its holdings of bonds or borrow that amount.

The bank could have avoided both these actions if it had held reserves in excess of legally required reserves. Suppose that its balance sheet had initially been:

Currency	$240,000	Deposits	$1 million
Bonds	$760,000		

The bank is thus holding reserves equal to 24 percent of its deposits. A deposit outflow of $50,000 would leave the bank still satisfying the legal reserve requirement. Its reserves would be $190,000 and its deposits $950,000, a ratio of 20 percent. Thus it is clear that legally required reserves of less than 100 percent do not fully protect the bank against deposit drains. To sustain these drains without being forced either to liquidate assets or to borrow, the bank must hold reserves in excess of legal requirements. Thus even if reserves were not required by law, banks would still hold them.

Instead of liquidating a portion of its portfolio or holding excess reserves, the bank could choose to borrow reserves when it is unable to meet the legal reserve requirement. Banks that belong to the Federal Reserve system are permitted to borrow reserves at their regional Federal Reserve Bank and to pay interest (at the discount rate) for the amount borrowed. The bank we have been considering, if it holds no excess reserves and chooses to borrow at the discount rate in the face of a decline in deposits, will have the following balance sheet:

Currency	$190,000	Deposits	$950,000
Bonds	800,000	Borrowed reserves	40,000

With deposits of $950,000, the bank has required reserves of $190,000 and therefore must borrow $40,000 in reserves from the Federal Reserve. The amount of borrowing is smaller than the deposit outflow, since the decline in deposits has reduced required reserves by $10,000. The quantity of borrowing necessary to satisfy the legal reserve requirement is equal to the amount of bonds the bank would have to liquidate if it chose that method of offsetting the effects of deposit drain.

Our discussion of 100 percent banking indicates that in such a world, a shift of the public's holdings between currency and bank deposits leaves the supply of money unaffected. In the case of a fractional reserve system, however, such shifts can change the supply. Suppose that banks hold neither excess nor borrowed reserves, bank reserves thus exactly equaling required reserves. The reserves held by the banking system consist of currency deposited by members of the public who prefer to have at least part of their money holdings in that form. Suppose that a member of the public withdraws a portion of his deposits from his bank, to increase the proportion of his money held in currency. This action reduces the capacity of his bank to hold earning assets, and it is forced to sell a portion of its bond holdings. If the purchaser of the bonds that the bank sells withdraws deposits from his bank, that bank, too, is forced to liquidate some of its assets. The process continues until the legal reserve ratio for the banking system as a whole is restored. But this can only be accomplished by a reduction in total bank deposits, and therefore in the supply of money. A rise in desired holdings of currency thus reduces the money supply. This is because, in effect, currency has a reserve ratio of 100 percent, whereas deposits require only fractional reserves. Given the quantity of reserves, the supply of money that can be supported declines as the proportion of the money supply held as currency increases. If the reserve requirement on deposits is 100 percent, such shifts do not affect the supply of money.[7]

THE PROCESS OF MONEY "CREATION"

The process by which the monetary base becomes "multiplied" into a larger money supply is easiest to describe if we assume that banks hold no excess reserves and the public holds no currency. Suppose that because the monetary base is increased as the government engages in expenditures that are not financed either by taxes or by borrowing from the public, new money must be printed. If the increase in the monetary base is $100, the legal reserve requirement is 20 percent, and the person who sold the goods to the government deposits the proceeds into his bank, bank A, the latter's balance sheet becomes

Bank A			
Currency	$100	Deposits	$100

Since the bank has excess reserves of $80, it will purchase bonds in this amount. The seller of the bonds will now have $80 which, we assume, he will wish to deposit in his bank, say bank B. The balance sheets of the two banks are now

Bank A				Bank B			
Currency	$20	Deposits	$100	Currency	$80	Deposits	$80
Bonds	80						

Bank A no longer has excess reserves, but bank B holds excess reserves of $64, which it will wish to lend. If the seller of the bond purchased by bank B places the proceeds of the sale in bank C, the situation becomes

Bank A		Bank B		Bank C	
Currency $20	Deposits $100	Currency $16	Deposits $80	Currency $64	Deposits $64
Bonds 80		Bonds 64			

Bank C now holds approximately $51 in excess reserves, which it will desire to lend. At each "stage" a portion of the monetary base is absorbed as required reserves. The process will continue until the entire monetary base is employed in this fashion. The $100 will ultimately "support" $500 in deposits if the reserve requirement is 20 percent. If there are no currency holdings and no excess reserves, the stock of money will equal the monetary base divided by the reserve requirement. On the other hand, if banks do hold excess reserves or if the public holds currency, the stock of money will be smaller.

SOME MONEY SUPPLY IDENTITIES

Before turning to a theory of money supply determination, it is useful to develop some definitions and identities that link the monetary aggregates discussed below.

First, we define the money supply M as equal to currency Z plus deposits D:

$$M = Z + D \tag{11-1}$$

The quantity of reserves in the system R consists of unborrowed reserves R_u, which entered the system through government action, and borrowed reserves R_b, which entered the system through bank borrowing at the Federal Reserve:

$$R = R_u + R_b \tag{11-2}$$

Total reserves are eventually used either as currency Z, legally required reserves R_r, or excess reserves R_e.

$$R = Z + R_r + R_e \tag{11-3}$$

If we define the proportion of money holdings that people wish to keep in the form of currency as z, we have

$$Z = zM \quad \text{and} \quad D = (1 - z)M \tag{11-4}$$

If we define the legal reserve requirement as q, we have

$$R_r = qD \qquad (11\text{-}5)$$

and if we define the ratio of excess reserves to deposits as e we write

$$R_e = eD \qquad (11\text{-}6)$$

We are now in a position to display the proximate determinants of the money supply.

Substituting (11-4), (11-5), and (11-6) into (11-3), we have

$$R = zM + q(1 - z)M + e(1 - z)M \qquad (11\text{-}7)$$

But since reserves can also be defined as in (11-2), we obtain

$$R_u + R_b = zM + q(1 - z)M + e(1 - z)M \qquad (11\text{-}8)$$

Now we find the following definition of the money supply:

$$M = (R_u + R_b) \frac{1}{z + q(1 - z) + e(1 - z)} \qquad (11\text{-}9)$$

Thus the money supply can be defined as the product of the *monetary base,* unborrowed plus borrowed reserves, times the *money multiplier,* which can be seen to depend on the currency ratio z, the legal reserve ratio q, and the excess reserve ratio e. (The monetary base is also referred to as *high-powered money.*) For a given monetary base, the money supply will be larger, the smaller are z, q, and e. And other things equal, a rise in either borrowed or unborrowed reserves will increase the money supply.

We can use (11-9) to illustrate a number of points just made. Suppose that $q = 1$.[8] Then we get

$$M = (R_u + R_b) \frac{1}{z + 1(1 - z)} = R_u + R_b$$

This means that with 100 percent reserves, the stock of money is equal to the monetary base, and the public's choice between currency and deposits, as given by z, does not affect M.

If the currency ratio z is zero and there are no excess reserves, we have

$$M = (R_u + R_b) \frac{1}{q}$$

Thus we learn that if there are neither currency holdings nor excess reserves, the money supply equals the reserve base divided by the legal reserve ratio.

If there are currency holdings but neither borrowed nor excess reserves, we get

$$M = R_u \frac{1}{z + q(1 - z)}$$

Thus the larger is the currency ratio z, the smaller the supply of money.

AN ILLUSTRATIVE CALCULATION

To have an idea of the magnitude of the money multiplier for the United States economy, the currency ratio z, is approximately one-quarter and the legal reserve ratio for demand deposits q is about 15 percent. Both borrowed reserves and excess reserves tend to be small, and we ignore them in the following calculation. If unborrowed reserves are \$90 billion, we write

$$M = (90) \frac{1}{(.25) + .15(.75)} = 250$$

This calculation suggests that the stock of money—currency plus demand deposits—is about 2.8 times the volume of reserves. The actual multiplier is somewhat smaller, about 2.6, because a portion of reserves is held as legal reserve requirements against time deposits, which are not included in the foregoing definition of the money stock. Furthermore, although borrowed and excess reserves are not considered in the calculation because they are small, they may be important sources of short-run variations of the stock of money.

ELEMENTS OF A THEORY OF MONEY
SUPPLY DETERMINATION

Our discussion thus far has focused on the proximate determinants of the money supply, providing an identity that links the money supply to its determinants, the amounts of borrowed and unborrowed reserves, the currency ratio, the legal reserve requirement, and the ratio of excess reserves to deposits. The quantity of unborrowed reserves as well as the size of the legal reserve requirement and the discount rate are largely under the control of the government.[9] But the other factors—the volume of borrowed and excess reserves and the currency ratio—are determined by the public, and we need a theory to explain how these are arrived at.

Banks hold excess reserves for essentially the same reasons that members of the public hold precautionary money balances. They do not wish to be forced to sell illiquid assets or to borrow reserves. A bank is in the business of receiving deposits, making payments on demand as claims are made on these deposits, and holding earning assets. Banks are subject to day-to-day fluctuations in their deposits as paychecks are received, many common transactions take place—for example, as disbursements for living expenses are made, business firms receive payments for goods sold and make disbursements for wages, and dividend payments are made. If, on a given day, a bank receives deposits equal to the payments it must make against deposits, there is no need to rearrange its portfolio. It can continue to hold the volume of earning assets that it previously held, and it has no need to borrow funds. The likelihood of receipts and disbursements being exactly equal on any given day, or even for any short period, is very small.

There is a positive probability attached to a number of possible deposit inflows or outflows. In Figure 11-1 we illustrate a hypothetical distribution of deposit gains or losses for a period. The probability of a deposit loss larger than X or of a gain above Y is assumed to be zero. The probability of a loss greater than Z is the area of the distribution between Z and X. If, on balance, deposits flow in during a given period, the bank need not rearrange its portfolio. But if there is a deposit outflow, the bank will have to either liquidate a portion of its portfolio or borrow reserves, unless its excess reserves exceed the deposit drain less the reduction in required re-

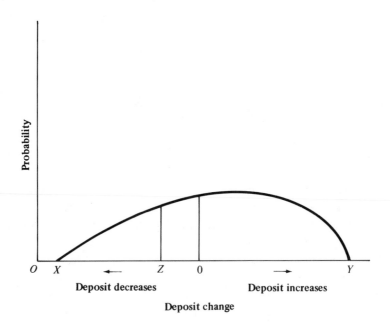

Deposit decreases   Deposit increases

Deposit change

FIGURE 11-1

serves. A bank can completely avoid one of these eventualities only by holding excess reserves equal to the largest possible deposit drain (X in Figure 11-1), minus the reduction in required reserves associated with that drain. To hold excess reserves of less than this amount is to risk the occurrence of a deposit drain that will force asset liquidation or borrowing. But a bank's earnings would be needlessly impaired if the institution held reserves so large that it was never required to liquidate assets.

A bank can calculate the volume of excess reserves it should hold if it is to maximize "expected profits." By in fact holding this volume of excess reserves over long periods, the bank can maximize its profits. Under this policy, the bank will be forced at times to liquidate assets or to borrow. The factors determining the optimum volume of excess reserves are (1) the degree of liquidity of the assets in the bank's portfolio, (2) the interest rate on these assets, (3) the interest rate at which the bank can borrow, and (4) the probability distribution of deposit changes. The more liquid the assets in the bank's portfolio, the higher the interest rate on these assets, the lower the interest rate at which the bank can borrow, and the more the probability distribution is skewed toward deposit inflows, the smaller will be the bank's optimum holdings of excess reserves.[10] If we assume that factors 1 and 4 are unchanged during the period being considered, the amount of excess reserves held—thus the frequency with which banks borrow reserves—depends only on the interest rate on bank assets and on the rate of interest at which the bank can borrow reserves.

Under the American banking system, banks that are members of the Federal Reserve system can borrow reserves at the *discount rate,* an interest rate set by the various Federal Reserve banks. The Federal Reserve banks exercise a degree of surveillance on the borrowing and at times discourage prolonged borrowing by member banks. The effectiveness of this surveillance is subject of some dispute. Here we assume that banks can borrow as much as they wish at the discount rate, the amount of borrowing being dependent on the profitability of the action contemplated. The higher the discount rate is set, other things equal, the larger will be the quantity of excess reserves held and the smaller will be the volume of bank borrowing at the discount window.

We assume throughout this discussion that the discount rate exceeds the interest rate on bonds; otherwise, there would be no reason for banks not to borrow unlimited reserves for investment in higher yielding assets. Knowing that the discount rate in the United States is often less than the interest rate on the assets held by banks, we can understand one of the reasons for the Federal Reserve banks' need to exercise surveillance on member bank borrowing. In the model being considered, banks do not "plan" to borrow; but if banks hold portfolios for which expected profits are maximized, they are occasionally "forced" to borrow. Thus if banks enter a period in which they hold relatively few excess reserves, bank borrowing will be large. It will have paid the banks to run the risk of having to borrow, since the expected return from such a policy is large.

We are now in a position to present a theory of money supply determination. Since there is no very good theory explaining the forces that determine the proportion of money holdings that people wish to keep as currency, we assume simply that this proportion is fixed in the short run; that is, we retain (11-4)

$$Z = zM \tag{11-4}$$

Recall that no bank ever "plans" to borrow reserves in this model. But banks will risk having to borrow reserves if there exists a sufficient reward for doing so. Suppose that during a period the total deposits of the banking system do not change, but some banks lose deposits while others gain them. Suppose further that some of the banks that lose deposits are forced to borrow reserves and the banks that gain deposits simply build up their holdings of excess reserves. Because of this reallocation of deposits among banks, excess reserves are smaller than those with which the banking system began the period, and borrowed reserves are positive. But actual excess reserves will be larger and actual borrowed reserves smaller, the larger are initial excess reserves.

These points can be illustrated by means of an example. Consider two situations in which the reserve requirement is 20 percent and bank A loses $200 of deposits to bank B during the period. In the first situation both banks initially held excess reserves equal to 10 percent of their deposits. Their balance sheets are as follows:

Bank A					Bank B			
Reserves	$300	Deposits	$1000		Reserves	$300	Deposits	$1000
Bonds	$700				Bonds	$700		

After the reallocation of deposits and bank A's borrowing to meet the reserve requirements, the balance sheets are as follows:

Bank A					Bank B			
Reserves	$160	Deposits	$800		Reserves	$500	Deposits	$1200
Bonds	$700	Borrowed			Bonds	$700		
		reserves	$ 60					

Total excess reserves are now $260, all held by bank B, and borrowed reserves equal $60.

In the second situation, the banks initially held excess reserves equal to 20 percent of their deposits. The balance sheets are thus:

Bank A					Bank B			
Reserves	$400	Deposits	$1000		Reserves	$400	Deposits	$1000
Bonds	$600				Bonds	$600		

After the reallocation of deposits the balance sheets are:

Bank A					Bank B			
Reserves	$200	Deposits	$800		Reserves	$600	Deposits	$1200
Bonds	$600				Bonds	$600		

Excess reserves are now $400, and there are no borrowed reserves. Thus for a given reallocation of deposits, the larger initial excess reserves, the larger will be actual excess reserves and the smaller actual borrowed reserves. Therefore, any factor that raises initial excess reserves also raises actual excess reserves and reduces actual borrowed reserves. Thus we obtain

$$R_e = E(i, d) \tag{11-10}$$

and

$$R_b = B(i, d) \tag{11-11}$$

where R_e and R_b are actual excess and borrowed reserves, respectively, d is the discount rate, and i is the interest rate on bonds, the only asset that banks are assumed able to hold.

If we substitute (11-4), (11-10), and (11-11) into (11-3), we have

$$R = zM + q(1 - z)M + E(i, d) \tag{11-12}$$

But since reserves can also be defined as in (11-2), we write

$$R_u + B(i, d) = zM + q(1 - z)M + E(i, d) \tag{11-13}$$

From this we can derive the money supply function as

$$M = \frac{R_u + B(i, d) - E(i, d)}{z + q(1 - z)} \tag{11-14}$$

Government policy thus consists of setting R_u through open market operations, and q and d directly. Suppose that these values are fixed:

$$R_u = \bar{R}_u \qquad (11\text{-}15)$$
$$q = \bar{q} \qquad (11\text{-}16)$$

and

$$d = \bar{d} \qquad (11\text{-}17)$$

The supply of money can now be seen to depend on the rate of interest on bonds. The higher this rate, the smaller the quantity of excess reserves held, and the larger the volume of borrowed reserves. This is because a higher interest rate on bonds induces banks to economize on their initial holdings of excess reserves. As a result, they have smaller excess reserves and larger borrowed reserves than would have been held if the interest rate on bonds were lower and there were larger initial holdings of excess reserves. In Figure 11-2 a money supply function is drawn for given values of R_u, q, d, and for given functions for excess reserves, borrowed reserves, and currency demanded. The higher the rate of interest i, the larger the quantity of money supplied.

It is instructive to see how the money supply function shifts in response to changes in each of its determinants. Suppose that the quantity of unbor-

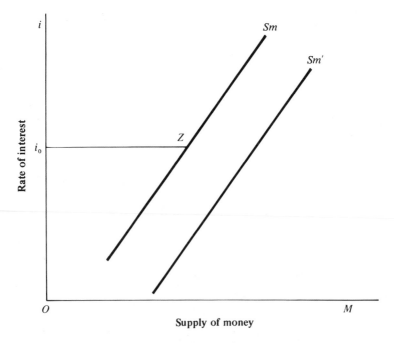

FIGURE 11-2

rowed reserves R_u is increased through open market purchases of bonds. Take point Z on S_m in Figure 11-2. Whereas previously the quantity of excess reserves held at i_0 was the amount that banks desired to hold, they now hold more excess reserves than they desire. For the same interest rate to prevail, the money supply must be larger than before. As the money supply increases, a portion of the additional reserves are absorbed in a larger demand for currency and a portion in larger required reserves. Only if the money supply grows, can the same interest rate prevail.[11] Thus the result of an increase in unborrowed reserves is to shift the money supply function to the right to, say, S_m', increasing the amount of money that is supplied at any rate of interest.

If the reserve requirement q is reduced, the effect is similar to that of an increase in the quantity of unborrowed reserves. Whereas initially banks held the amount of excess reserves that they desired, a reduction in the reserve requirement makes their excess reserve holdings excessive. The result is to shift the supply of money to the right.

Consider a reduction in the discount rate d. For each interest rate on bonds, the amount of initial excess reserves is now larger than desired. Banks thus attempt to reduce the excess reserves. A given interest rate on bonds can only be maintained if the money supply rises.

Suppose that the public decides to reduce the proportion of its money balances held in the form of currency. As a result, banks hold more excess reserves than they desire, and the supply of money shifts to the right.

Suppose that banks wish to hold fewer excess reserves than previously. The only way to maintain the rate of interest is to increase the supply of money. If this is done, the public's desired holdings of currency will increase and the process will continue until banks hold only the volume of excess reserves that they desire. Once again, the result is a rightward shift in the money supply.

Each of these changes—the increase in the supply of unborrowed reserves, the reduction in the legal reserve ratio, the reduction in the discount rate, the reduction in currency holdings, and the decline in the amount of excess reserves that banks wish to hold—serves to increase the amount of money that will be supplied at every rate of interest.

THE MONEY SUPPLY FUNCTION AND NATIONAL INCOME AND PRICE LEVEL DETERMINATION

In the models of income and price level determination presented in Chapters 7 and 8, the nominal supply of money was determined directly by the actions of the government. In an economy with fractional reserve banking, however, the nominal stock of money in existence results from the interaction of the behavior of the government, the banking system, and the public.

Suppose, for example, that the government engages in an open market security purchase. As we have just seen, the result of this policy is to shift the supply of money function to the right. Since there is now a larger quantity of unborrowed reserves in the system, the banking system will be willing to supply more money at every rate of interest. The modification in the supply of money function shifts the *IS* and *LM* curves (or the *MM* and *GG* curves, if there is full employment) to the right. Since for every rate of interest the quantity of money supplied is now greater than before, at every point along the *LM* curve there is now an excess supply of money. Similarly, since a larger stock of money means more consumption spending, at every point along the *IS* curve there is now an excess demand for goods. For the money market to return to equilibrium, the rate of interest must fall and the income level must rise (i.e., the *LM* curve must shift to the right). For the goods market to return to equilibrium, income and the rate of interest must rise (i.e., *IS* must shift to the right).

The original equilibrium is depicted as the intersection of LM_0 and IS_0 in Figure 11-3. The new equilibrium occurs at the intersection of LM_0' and

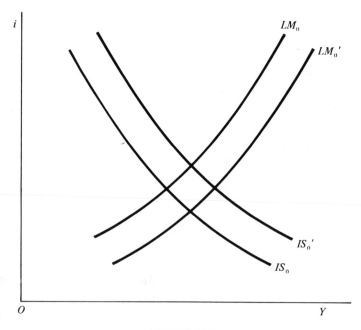

FIGURE 11-3

IS_0'. The two situations differ only in that the supply of unborrowed reserves is larger in one than in the other. The open market operation has resulted in an increase in income. The impact on the rate of interest is ambiguous, depending on the relative magnitudes of the shifts in the *LM* and *IS* curves.

The effect of the open market purchase is clearly expansionary, and the same kind of effect could have been achieved if other determinants of the supply of money had changed. For example, a reduction in the discount rate or in the level of legal reserve requirements would also have shifted the supply of money function to the right and would, therefore, have had a qualitatively similar effect on *IS* and *LM*. The existence of a fractional reserve banking system has made us look behind the money stock to its determinants, the behavior of the monetary authorities, commercial bank portfolio policies, and the public's deposit-currency choice. The analysis developed in Chapters 7 and 8 is still useful, but this chapter has forced us to recognize that changes in the money supply are produced jointly by the monetary authorities and the public, and we must understand this interaction.

IMPLICATIONS OF AN INTEREST ELASTIC MONEY SUPPLY

The most significant difference between the model developed in this chapter and those discussed previously is that here the money supply varies with the rate of interest. With the discount rate, reserve requirements, and unborrowed reserves unchanged, if the demand for goods and services increases and the interest rate is driven up, the quantity of money supplied will grow. The growth is spurred because banks are induced by the higher interest rate to hold fewer excess reserves and to borrow more frequently from the Federal Reserve. This section traces the implications of an interest elastic supply of money for some of the questions considered in Chapters 7 and 8. First we examine the full employment model, then turning to the underemployment case.

Whereas both the *MM* and *GG* curves in Chapter 7 were drawn for a stock of money fixed in nominal terms, the *MM* and *GG* curves must now be drawn for a given set of government policy variables: the nominal supply of unborrowed reserves, the legal reserve requirement, and the discount rate.[12] In Chapter 7 the upward slope of the *MM* curve was ascribed to the higher price level that is required to equate the demand and supply of money as the interest rate rises. Now as the interest rate rises, not only does the real amount of money demanded decrease but the nominal amount supplied increases. As a result, the price level must rise by even more than would be required if the nominal stock of money were fixed, if equilibrium in the money market is to be maintained. The *MM* curve is thus flatter than it would be if the nominal money stock were fixed by the government.

The analysis of the effect on the *GG* curve is somewhat more complex. As the rate of interest declines, the demand for consumption and investment goods increases. In addition, as the interest rate declines, the nominal stock of money declines. The question is whether the decline in the amount of bank deposits, hence in the stock of money, should be regarded as a decline in wealth.

In Chapters 7 and 8 there was only one type of money, the obligation of the government. If we allow for the existence of commercial banking, however, a portion of the stock of money consists of deposits held at banks. And if we further allow for fractional reserve banking, the supply of money will exceed the non-interest-bearing obligations of the government.[13] Should this excess be included in the wealth of the public? It is to this question that we now turn.

Suppose that entry into banking is free and banks are free to compete for depositors' business and for the assets they wish to hold in their portfolios. In such a world, so long as economies of large-scale operation do not permit a few banks to dominate markets, competition will force the earnings of banks to the same level that would be earned in other competitive industries. The differential interest rate between that on bank deposits and that on bank loans would be just sufficient to pay for the use of the resources other than deposits used in the banking business.

At the other extreme, suppose that only a small number of banks are permitted to engage in the business of banking and a restriction, which can be readily enforced, prohibits banks from competing for deposits. If this is the case, the banks that are lucky enough to be permitted to operate can expect to earn profits in excess of those earned elsewhere. The rate the banks can earn on bonds will exceed the rate (assumed to be restricted to zero) they pay on deposits. In such a case, if the licenses to operate banks are granted at no charge, those persons receiving the licenses experience an increase in wealth. How large is this increase? Suppose that in the presence of banks, members of the public hold no currency and banks hold required and excess reserves equal to a fraction, say, g, of their deposits. Assume further that there are no borrowed reserves. Then if the supply of unborrowed reserves is T, the stock of money will equal T/g and the banking system will have "created" $T/g - T$ of new money. And, their holdings of bonds will also equal that amount. Their earnings will equal the rate of interest on bonds times *either* the amount of money they have created *or* their bond holdings. If the rate of interest is i, their annual earnings will be $i(T/g - T)$. But a stream of earnings of $i(T/g - T)$ in perpetuity is worth $T/g - T$ when discounted at an interest rate of i. The granting of a limited number of franchises to operate banks has thus increased the wealth of the private sector by $T/g - T$.[14]

At what point between these two extremes does the real world lie? Entry into the business of banking is clearly limited in most countries, including the United States, where a charter to operate a bank must be obtained either from the federal government or from one of the states. In addition, there is a restriction that forbids the payment of interest on demand deposits. On the other hand, banks do compete with one another for deposits through such devices as the provision of free or below-cost checking services, the construction of many branch offices to offer more convenient banking services to their customers, and the provision of financial and other advice to their customers at no cost. Thus even though entry into banking is limited and interest payments on deposits are prohibited, it is possible that competition by banks for deposits in ways other than by interest payments serves to reduce the return that can be earned in the banking business to that which can be earned in other industries. It is also possible that the granting of a limited number of licenses to banks does not produce any increase in the wealth of the private sector. In what follows, we shall assume that there is *some* gain in the wealth of the private sector as a result of limiting entry into banking, although the increase in wealth is less than the amount of money created by the banking system.

We can now return to the analysis of the effect of assuming that the supply of money varies directly with the rate of interest along the *GG* curve. A decline in the rate of interest increases private spending through its effect on both saving and investment. It also produces a decline in the wealth of the private sector through its effect on the nominal supply of money. As a result, the rise in the price level that must take place, if equilibrium in the goods market is to be preserved, is smaller than it would be if the money supply, thus private wealth, were unaffected by the decline in the rate of interest. The effect of assuming that the money supply varies directly with the rate of interest is thus to make the *GG* curve steeper.

In Figure 11-4 we have *GG* and *MM* curves drawn under the assumption of a fixed supply of money. In contrast, the *GG* and *MM* curves in Figure 11-5 are drawn for the assumption that the supply of money is responsive to changes in the rate of interest. Consequently *MM* is flatter and *GG* steeper, than in Figure 11-4.

If now there is, for example, an increase in the amount that business firms wish to invest at every rate of interest, the *GG* shifts to the right. As before, the rate of interest is increased. However, in Figure 11-5 this serves to increase the supply of money and private wealth. Since both effects are expansionary, the price level must rise by more than it would rise if the supply of money were unchanged. An upward shift in the investment demand func-

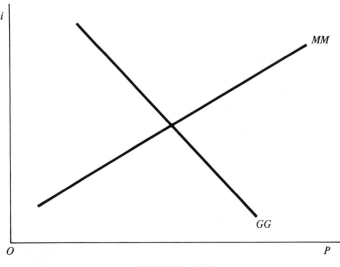

FIGURE   11-4

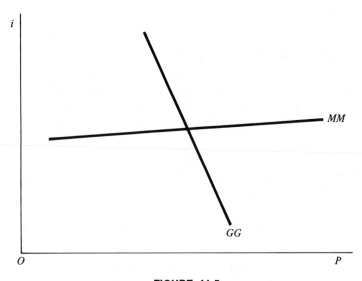

FIGURE   11-5

tion is thus more expansionary when the supply of money is interest sensitive than when it is not.

Next, consider a decline in the demand for money, which serves to shift the *MM* curve to the right. In Figure 11-5 this reduces the stock of money and the amount of private wealth. To preserve general equilibrium, a smaller rise in the price level is required than would be called for if the nominal money stock were constant. In effect, a portion of the reduction in the demand for money is satisfied by a reduction in the nominal amount supplied, leaving a smaller portion to be satisfied by the rise in the price level. A decline in the demand for money is thus less expansionary when the supply of money is interest sensitive than when it is not.

Now let us consider the less than full employment case. Assuming that the supply of money is responsive to the rate of interest has the effect of flattening the *LM* curve. As the interest rate rises, the nominal stock of money also rises. Therefore, as the income level rises, increasing the quantity of money demanded, a part of this increase is satisfied by an increase in the nominal supply. As a result, the interest rate does not have to rise by enough to equate the demand for money with a fixed supply. The *IS* curve is now steeper than before. As the rate of interest declines, the amount of private wealth also declines, reducing the size of the increase in income required to maintain equilibrium in the goods markets. In Figures 11-6 and 11-7 we present *IS* and *LM* curves drawn on the assumptions of fixed and interest sensitive money supply, respectively.

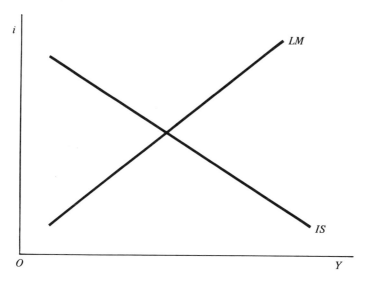

FIGURE 11-6

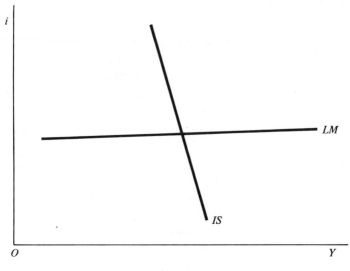

FIGURE 11-7

Let us analyze the implications of assuming an interest sensitive money supply in the less than full employment case. Suppose that the investment demand schedule shifts and business firms now wish to invest more than they previously did at every interest rate. The result is to shift the *IS* curve rightward and to raise the rate of interest. In the case described in Figure 11-6, the nominal money supply remains constant in the face of the rise in the interest rate. The increased demand for money occasioned by the higher real income level must be completely satisfied by raising the interest rate enough to reduce the total demand for money to the fixed supply.[15] This serves to offset the expansionary stimulus due to the shift in the investment demand function.

Next, consider the case of an interest sensitive money supply. By raising the rate of interest, the shift in the investment demand schedule increases the nominal stock of money. As a result, the wealth of the private sector increases and this is expansionary. In addition, the increase in the money stock enables a portion of the increased demand for money to be satisfied by a rise in the supply. As a consequence, the increase in real income, and probably in prices as well, is larger when the money supply is interest sensitive than when it is fixed.

Finally, consider the case of a decline in the demand for money, which shifts the *LM* curve to the right. With the nominal money stock fixed, the interest rate declines, investment and consumption spending are stimulated, and real income and possibly the price level increase. With the supply of money interest sensitive, one effect of the decrease in the demand for money is to reduce the nominal supply. As a result, the reduction in the rate of interest is smaller than it would have been if the money supply had been fixed. Therefore, the increase in private spending and the subsequent increase in real income are less. An interest sensitive supply of money thus lessens the expansionary effect of a decline in the demand for money.

WHO MAKES MONETARY POLICY?

As we have seen, the principal instruments of monetary policy are open market operations, which change the monetary base, reserve requirements, which determine the portion of the base held by commercial banks, and the discount rate, which affects the willingness of banks to hold excess reserves and to borrow reserves. These instruments of monetary policy are determined in the United States by the Federal Reserve system. The "Fed" has two main components. The first is the Board of Governors, which consists of seven members who serve staggered terms of 14 years and are appointed by the President. The second consists of the 12 regional Federal Reserve banks; six of the directors of these institutions are elected by member banks in their districts, the remaining three directors being appointed by the Board of Governors.

The Board of Governors establishes legal reserve requirements within limits prescribed in the Banking Act of 1935. Each Federal Reserve Bank sets its own discount rate, subject to the approval of the Board of Governors. In recent times the discount rate has almost always been identical in the 12 Federal Reserve districts. Open market policy is determined by the Federal Open Market Committee, which consists of the Board of Governors and the presidents of five of the regional banks. The policy is carried out by the Federal Reserve Bank of New York.

USES OF THE MONEY SUPPLY MODEL: SOME EXAMPLES

To demonstrate the usefulness of the model of money supply determination developed in this chapter, this section applies the model to some real-world situations. The applications presented are not intended to be exhaustive but to show how the model can be employed. As the Introduction to this book stressed, it is not possible for a textbook writer to anticipate all the developments in the institutions he is trying to analyze, but the framework provided to the student should still be useful in this analysis. The student and the instructor are urged to see whether the model developed in this chapter can usefully be applied to developments more current than those reported here.

A floating discount rate

In the United States, where the discount rate tends to stay constant for fairly long periods, the profitability to a bank of holding excess reserves varies with changes in the rate of interest on earning assets. Rises in the rate of interest induce banks to hold fewer excess reserves, consequently, to be forced to discount more frequently. The money stock therefore tends to be higher when interest rates are high than when they are low. If the government wishes to maintain the stock of money as the interest rate changes, it may thus be obliged to embark on offsetting open market operations. Another alternative, one that is employed by the Federal Reserve, is to watch over member bank borrowing, to discourage banks from being continuously in debt to the Fed. Banks are told that borrowing is to be temporary and that they are to seek other means, primarily the sale of assets, to meet any long-term reserve deficiencies. Thus although the discount rate is frequently thought of as a tool of monetary policy being manipulated to encourage or discourage borrowing, banks are not free to borrow as much as they wish, and the amounts available are determined by notions of good banking practice rather than by considerations of monetary policy.

To avoid the need either for continuous open market operations or surveillance of bank borrowing, Canada has adopted a *floating discount rate*. Under this arrangement, the discount rate is set at a fixed differential above some market rate of interest. As that rate rises, so does the discount rate, thus removing the incentive for banks to reduce their holdings of excess reserves. Banks are free to borrow as much as they wish, but they are discouraged from "excessive" borrowing by its unprofitability. Here, of course, the discount rate is not a tool of monetary policy. But neither is it under the American system, if the volume borrowing is limited by the monetary authorities. The discount rate can be used as an instrument of monetary policy, being raised to discourage borrowing and lowered to encourage it. But if this is its role, banks must be free to borrow as much as they wish. Alternatively, the discount rate may be a penalty rate, designed to make available reserves to banks temporarily requiring them. If this is the case, care must be taken that the discount rate remains above the interest rate on other assets. Unfortunately, the American system tries to have the discount rate assume both roles, making it difficult for the system to perform either well. The virtue of the Canadian system is that it unambiguously adopts the penalty rate role for the discount rate.

The absence of a floating discount rate in the United States means the Federal Reserve may have to raise the discount rate frequently as the rate of interest on other assets rises, to prevent banks from holding smaller excess reserves and borrowing more reserves, thus leading to an undesired expansion in the stock of money. In 1973, under such conditions, the discount rate was changed no less than seven times, beginning the year at $4\frac{1}{2}$ percent and ending it at $7\frac{1}{2}$ percent. However, if policy does not respond quickly to changes in other interest rates, the Fed may find that the discount rate is "out of touch" and that banks are engaging in more borrowing at the discount window than the Fed would like.

The federal funds market

At any given time, some banks are likely to be holding excess reserves while the reserves of other banks are beneath the legal minimum. This is the natural outcome of the process of check payment and collection under which it is difficult for a bank to forecast precisely the magnitude of its deposit inflows and outflows over short periods. Although banks with deficient reserves can borrow at the discount rate, a market has developed in which they can tap the excess reserves of other banks. Since there are no interest payments on excess reserves, it is in the interest of banks that hold them to make loans to banks in need of reserves. The *federal funds market* provides for the short-term exchange of reserves among banks. When the rate of interest on federal funds is less than the discount rate, borrowing federal funds is clearly an attractive way to meet a reserve deficiency. But the rate on federal funds occasionally rises above the discount rate, which suggests that banks are sometimes reluctant to borrow at the discount window even if they would have to pay a higher rate of interest to obtain reserves elsewhere.

These available federal funds, by providing an alternative source of reserve to banks temporarily "caught short," permit the banking system to utilize its reserves more efficiently. That is, the alternative source makes it possible to place reserves in the banks in which the funds are most needed. Furthermore, the existence of the market permits a bank to hold fewer excess reserves because it furnishes an accessible and low-cost source of reserves if a deposit outflow is experienced. Thus the introduction and development of the federal funds market shifts the supply of money function to the right.

Excess reserves during the 1930s

During the Depression of the 1930s, excess reserves held by commercial banks in the United States rose dramatically. Reserves in excess of legal reserve requirements, which were about 2 percent of deposits in 1933, rose

to almost 8 percent of deposits by mid-1936. They declined as reserve requirements were increased in 1936 and 1937, but by the beginning of 1941 they
had grown to more than 14 percent of deposits. By the mid-1940s, however,
excess reserves had returned to their previous low levels, where they have
remained ever since.

Two explanations have been advanced for the unusual behavior of excess
reserves during the 1930s. The first is that with low interest rates prevailing
during the period, the expected profit-maximizing behavior of banks caused
them to want more excess reserves. In an extreme version of this theory,
banks were believed to wish to hold any increase in deposits in the form
of excess reserves because the return from holding earning assets was so low.

The view that banks will wish to hold larger quantities of excess reserves
as the rate of return on earning assets declines, is consistent with the theory
developed in this chapter, but the magnitude of the increase in excess reserves
appears to be too large to be explained by this factor alone. Morrison has
suggested a complementary explanation, which he views as far more important.[16] With almost 9000 banks failing in the early 1930s, with runs on banks
becoming common, and with doubts growing about the willingness of the Federal Reserve to make sufficient loans to banks with deficient reserves, Morrison argues that banks increased the amount of excess reserves they wished
to hold at any interest rate. In effect, he says that the demand function for
excess reserves shifted greatly because of the financial panic of the early
1930s, and it was not until more than a decade later that the effect of the
experience ceased to be reflected in the management of bank portfolios.

The two explanations of the large increase in excess reserves during the
1930s are easily understood within the context of the model developed in
this chapter. Under the first explanation, the decline in economic activity
served to lower the rate of interest. This event induced a movement along
the supply of money schedule. Excess reserves rose and the stock of money
declined in response to a decline in the rate of interest. According to Morrison, however, another force was at work which produced a leftward shift
in the supply of money function. This force was the increasing caution of
commercial banks, an attitude stemming from the large-scale bank failures
during the early 1930s and the fact that the Federal Reserve did not prevent
such failures from occurring.

Float

The Federal Reserve handles a major portion of the nation's check collection process. When a customer deposits into his bank a check drawn on
another bank, the receiving bank often deposits the check in its account at

the Federal Reserve. If the banks are in the same geographic area, the check is quickly presented for payment at the paying bank. More or less simultaneously, the account of the receiving bank is credited and that of the paying bank is debited at the Federal Reserve.

By contrast, when the paying and receiving banks are in different parts of the country, the receiving bank's account may be credited before the account of the paying bank is debited. This is because crediting of the receiving bank's account takes place according to a prearranged schedule. When one bank receives credit for a check before another bank has had its account at the Fed reduced, this gives rise to an additional source of reserves of the banking system called *float*. Although fairly predictable, the float tends to rise in periods of poor weather, which slows the collection process.

A recent change in Federal Reserve policy has altered the magnitude of the float. Beginning September 21, 1972, all member banks of the Federal Reserve system must pay for checks on the same day the instruments are presented. Previously, banks often took a day or more in making payment. The Fed estimated that the change would reduce the magnitude of the float by about $2 billion. Unless the Fed undertakes offsetting policies, therefore, the effect of the change in check clearing practices would be to shift the supply of money schedule to the left, reducing the quantity of money that would be supplied at any rate of interest.

Gold and the stock of money

Among the goods and services the government may acquire and not pay for through taxes is gold: either newly mined domestically produced gold (in which case its production appears as part of the current output of the nation), or gold previously produced or produced in other countries (in which case it would not). Sales of gold from the existing stock serve to reduce the volume of unborrowed reserves, and purchases of gold serve to increase it. But purchases or sales of any other existing asset or newly produced good would have similar effects. The principal difference is that the United States government previously stood ready to buy and sell gold at a previously determined price to selected parties. As a consequence, the initiative for such purchases or sales did not come from the government. However, the government could, and did, offset the effect on the money stock of a purchase of gold by selling an equivalent amount of securities on the open market.

SUMMARY

In a world of 100 percent banking, it is appropriate to regard the nominal stock of money as being set by the government. However, where fractional reserve banking exists, the stock of money is determined by the interaction of the behavior of the government, the banking system, and the nonbank public. Therefore, these factors should be included in any theory of the determination of the supply of money contained in a complete model of income determination.

NOTES

[1] In the United States more than three-quarters of the money stock is held in the form of demand deposits. In mid-1972 the public held $54 billion of currency and $178 billion of demand deposits.

[2] An increase in the use of credit cards for small purchases will probably reduce both the demand for money and the proportion of money holdings that people will keep in the form of currency.

[3] In the United States the bulk of bank reserves are held on deposit at the central bank, the Federal Reserve; but it does no harm, and greatly simplifies matters, to assume that banks hold all their reserves in the form of currency. To be more realistic, we could have assumed that banks always convert these currency holdings to deposits at the Federal Reserve. These deposits are payable in currency on demand to the banks that hold them.

[4] One may wonder just how banks are able to earn incomes under this arrangement, since they cannot make loans on the basis of their deposits. The answer is that they must charge for the safekeeping and fund transfer services they provide to their depositors. Something like this occurs in the form of service charges even under the fractional reserve banking system in existence in the United States. But such charges would undoubtedly be much larger if we were to shift to a 100 percent banking system.

[5] Banks that are not member banks are usually subject to reserve requirements imposed by the states from which they received their charters. All banks with national charters must be members of the Federal Reserve system. State-chartered banks need not join the system.

[6] *Federal Reserve Bulletin.*

[7] The money supply need not fall as a result of a currency shift if banks are willing and able to hold fewer excess reserves or to borrow more reserves.

[8] In such cases, of course, e will be zero.

[9] Changes in unborrowed reserves that occur through government purchases or sales of gold can occur at the initiative of parties other than the government, but these are usually offset by other government actions designed to keep unborrowed reserves unchanged.

[10] Another factor is the legal reserve requirement. The higher the legal reserve requirement, the smaller the amount of bonds that will have to be sold to meet any given deposit drain. In the example considered earlier, the bank was forced to sell $40,000 of bonds to meet the 20 percent reserve requirement. If reserves equal to 50 percent of deposits were required, a bank holding reserves just equal to legal requirements, $500,000, would have had to sell only $25,000 of bonds to continue to meet the requirement in the face of a $50,000 deposit drain.

[11] Alternatively, we could have inquired about the change in the rate of interest required to keep the supply of money from changing. By increasing excess reserves and reducing

borrowed reserves, a reduction in the rate of interest will permit the increase in unborrowed reserves to be absorbed.

[12] In addition, equations describing the demands for excess and borrowed reserves and the public's demand for currency are presumed to be given in drawing MM and GG.

[13] With 100 percent reserves, banks are merely acting as depositary institutions and do not affect the amount of money in the system. Their existence merely changes the form in which money is held, not its amount.

[14] This assumes that there are no costs other than interest payments on deposits.

[15] If the price level rises, the real stock of money will actually decline.

[16] George R. Morrison, *Liquidity Preferences of Commercial Banks,* Chicago, University of Chicago Press, 1966.

12

The role of nonbank financial institutions

In our analysis to this point, we have assumed the existence of only one kind of financial institution, the commercial bank. But in any developed economy, as well as in many underdeveloped ones, other financial institutions provide services similar to those offered by banks. These institutions permit wealth to be held in forms other than currency, bonds, physical capital, and commercial bank deposits. In the United States, for example, wealth owners can choose among shares of savings and loan associations (S&Ls), deposits at mutual savings banks, shares in credit unions, cash surrender values of life insurance policies, the liabilities of consumer finance companies, and many other alternatives. At the same time, the existence of these institutions provides to would-be borrowers sources of loans alternative to commercial banks. In this chapter we wish to analyze the effects of the existence of these financial institutions.

ASSUMPTIONS

For convenience, we assume that the only kind of nonbank financial institutions are S&Ls, whose liabilities are called *shares*. S&L shares supply services similar to those provided by bank deposits. Shares, like deposits, possess smaller risk of loss or theft than currency. Shares, like deposits, constitute a place in which precautionary balances held to meet unforeseen contingencies, can be kept. As with deposits, wealth owners can place their funds in shares if they fear a decline in the value of bonds. But there are important differences between deposits and shares. Unlike deposits, shares cannot be transferred by means of check. To transfer these funds, the wealth owner must first convert them to currency or to a check drawn on the deposits of the S&L at a commercial bank. And unlike deposits, shares earn explicit interest payments.[1]

When S&Ls begin operations they must offer a return on shares sufficiently large to induce wealth owners to shift from other assets to shares.[2] As funds are shifted to S&Ls, the capacity of the latter to acquire earning assets is increased. However, they cannot hold earning assets equal to the amount of funds that they acquire for two reasons. First, the institutions may be subject to legal reserve requirements of a type similar to those imposed on commercial banks. Second, just as commercial banks hold excess reserves to be able to meet some loss of deposits without having to liquidate their assets, S&Ls pursue similar policies. For both reasons, then, the capacity of S&Ls to acquire earning assets as funds are shifted to them rises less than does the volume of funds acquired.[3]

In Chapter 11 we analyzed the factors that determine the volume of reserves commercial banks will wish to hold for every dollar of their deposits. In addition to the legal reserve requirements, these factors include the discount rate and the rate of interest that banks can earn on the assets they hold. Similar factors explain the ratio of reserves to shares held by S&Ls. But in this chapter, to focus on the wealth owners' choice of the assets they wish to hold, we assume that banks and nonbanks hold reserves equal to fixed ratios of their deposits and shares, respectively. In other words, we are assuming that the reserve policies of financial institutions are unresponsive to the rate of interest.

Moreover, we depart from the conditions set forth in Chapter 11 by assuming that there is no demand for currency by wealth owners. By omitting this manner of wealth holding, we are able to concentrate on other alternatives to shares which wealth owners might wish to hold. To include currency as an alternative asset would complicate our analysis without affecting the conclusions reached.

We also assume that when wealth owners do shift a portion of their holdings to shares, the entire shift occurs at the expense of deposits. In other words, the impact of the introduction of the S&L industry is on commercial banks. For the reasons just outlined, wealth owners regard shares as a substitute for deposits. The extent of the shift will depend on how close a substitute shares are for deposits and on the rate of interest paid on shares.[4]

Finally, we assume that the reserves of S&Ls are held either in the form of deposits at commercial banks or in the form of vault cash at the S&Ls themselves. Before we explore the implications of these alternative assumptions, let us summarize them.

1. The only kind of nonbank financial institution is the S&L.
2. Commercial banks hold reserves equal to a fixed proportion of their deposits, call it q, and S&Ls hold reserves equal to a fixed proportion t of their shares.
3. There are no demands for currency from the public.
4. Shares are a substitute for deposits and for no other assets.
5. S&Ls hold reserves as either (a) deposits at commercial banks, or (b) vault cash.

If we call the nonbank public's deposits at commercial banks D, shares S, and high-powered money H, we find

$$H = q(D + tS) \qquad (12\text{-}1)$$

if we adopt assumption 5a, and we have

$$H = qD + tS \qquad (12\text{-}2)$$

if we adopt assumption 5b. High-powered money is equivalent to the monetary base discussed in Chapter 11.

To analyze the effect of introducing S&Ls where none previously existed, we begin with a situation in which only commercial banks exist (see Figure 12-1). The right-hand panel of the diagram shows the public's demand for money, consisting only of deposits (see assumption 3), as a function of the rate of interest on bonds. More deposits are demanded as the rate of interest on bonds declines, for the reasons explored in detail in Chapter 3.[5] The left-hand panel of Figure 12-1 shows the demand for high-powered money, also drawn as a decreasing function of the rate of interest. In this model high-powered money is demanded only because commercial banks wish to hold reserves equal to a proportion of their deposits. The larger the volume of deposits, the larger the demand for high-powered money to serve as reserves against these deposits. The demand for high-powered money is equal to q times the volume of deposits from assumption 2. There is no increase in the demand for reserves caused by the decline in the interest rate on bonds. (See assumption 2.)

In the situation depicted in Figure 12-1, the equilibrium rate of interest on bonds is i_1. At i_1, the quantity of high-powered money demanded for reserves against deposit level D_1 is just equal to the amount of high-powered money supplied by the government, H. At interest rates above i_1 the amount of deposits demanded produces a demand for high-powered money less than H. Banks will therefore wish to hold more bonds, and this will drive down

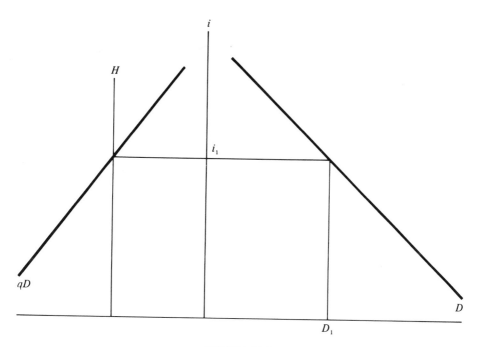

FIGURE 12-1

the rate of interest on bonds. At interest rates below i_1, there will be an excess demand for high-powered money and banks will sell some of their bond holdings, thus raising the rate of interest.

If we now introduce a savings and loan industry, we have the situations depicted in Figures 12-2 and 12-3. The situations are identical in that the entire shift in the demand for shares comes at the expense of deposits, following assumption 4. They differ in that Figure 12-2 assumes that S&Ls hold their reserves as deposits at commercial banks (assumption 5a), whereas in Figure 12-3 we assume that reserves are held at vault cash (5b). The implications of these alternative assumptions are explored in turn.

The situation depicted in Figure 12-2 is drawn for a fixed rate of interest on shares as well as a fixed level of national income. The curve D^* in Figure 12-2 lies to the left of D in Figure 12-1, since a portion of the demand for deposits has been replaced by a demand for shares. We now introduce the curve S, which in Figure 12-2 represents the demand for shares as a function

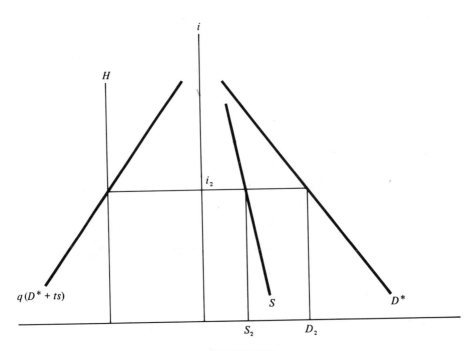

FIGURE 12-2

of the rate of interest on bonds. Like the demand for deposits, it is downward sloping. In addition, because of the assumption that the entire increase in shares of S&Ls comes at the expense of deposits, its distance from the vertical axis is exactly equal, at every rate of interest, to the amount by which the demand for deposits has shifted to the left. In the left-hand panel of Figure 12-2 the demand for high-powered money, assumed fixed at H, is now $q(D^* + tS)$. Since S&Ls hold reserves equal to t times their shares and commercial banks hold reserves equal to q times both the public's deposits and S&L's reserves, this point lies to the right of the demand for high-powered money in Figure 21-1, t being less than 1. In other words, at every rate of interest on bonds a smaller amount of high-powered money is demanded than previously because a shift of \$1 from deposits releases q of high-powered money and the shift of \$1 to shares increases the demand for high-powered money by only qt. The equilibrium interest rate on bonds implied in Figure 12-2 is i_2.

However, we cannot be sure that Figure 12-2 depicts an equilibrium situation unless we explore the relationship between i_2 and the interest rate on shares on which the figure is based. Our model must contain a relationship between the rate S&Ls pay on shares and the amount they earn on their earning assets, bonds. We assume that competition among S&Ls drives the gap between these rates to the point at which S&Ls earn normal profits, indicating that a direct relationship exists between these rates. If the interest rate on shares on which Figure 12-2 is based turns out to involve below-normal profits at an interest rate on bonds of i_2, the interest rate on shares will be reduced. This shifts the demand for deposits to the right and that for shares to the left, the shifts being of equal absolute amounts. The result is an increase in the demand for high-powered money, which raises the interest rate on bonds and closes the gap between the interest rate on shares and that on bonds. The process continues until S&Ls are earning normal profits. In equilibrium, the rate of interest on bonds will be lower than it was in the absence of commercial banks. This is because there has been some shift from deposits to shares, thus reducing the demand for high-powered money and creating an excess supply of high-powered money at i_1. The result must be to reduce the interest rate on bonds. The equilibrium volume of deposits plus shares is larger than the equilibrium volume of deposits in Figure 12-1 (i.e., $S_2 + D_2 > D_1$), since a decline in the interest rate on bonds raises the demand for alternatives to bonds. However, D_2 must be smaller than D_1; otherwise the demand for high-powered money would exceed the supply.

The case depicted in Figure 12-3 is identical to that in Figure 12-2 except that the demand for high-powered reserves is $qD + tS$. For each dollar of deposits held, q of high-powered money is absorbed as reserves. For each dollar of shares held, t of high-powered money is absorbed in vault cash held as reserves. Thus the demand for high-powered money declines by q for each dollar of funds shifted from deposits and increases by t for each dollar shifted to shares. Whether such shifts result in a reduction or an increase in the demand for high-powered money depends on the relationship between q and t. In general, t will be smaller than q; thus the demand for high-powered money is reduced by the introduction of S&L.[6] But the reduction will be smaller than in Figure 12-2. Consequently, although the interest rate on bonds declines, the fall is smaller and the equilibrium interest rate on shares is higher than it is when reserves of S&Ls are held at commercial banks. In other words, although i_3 is less than i_1 it is greater than i_2.

The expansionary effect of introducing S&Ls is therefore smaller than it is when S&Ls reserves are held in commercial banks. We know that this is true because in Figure 12-2 the capacity of commercial banks to absorb bonds is not permanently reduced by the introduction of S&Ls, since the latter hold their reserves at the banks. When S&Ls hold reserves as vault cash, their

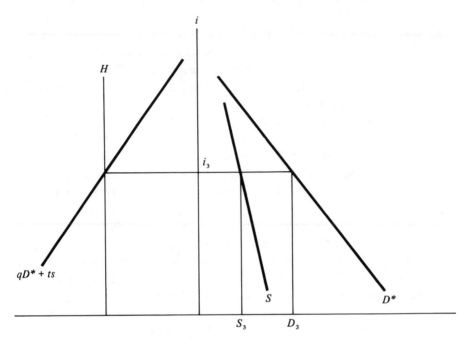

FIGURE 12-3

growth is at the expense of the capacity of the banks to absorb bonds. The increase in the bonds absorbed by S&Ls is larger than the amount released by commercial banks in this case because of the higher reserve requirements to which commercial banks are subject.

Since the fall in the rate of interest on bonds is less than in Figure 12-2, the sum of S_3 and D_3 is less than the sum of S_3 and D_2. And since the rate of interest on shares is greater than in Figure 12-2, S_3 is greater than S_2. In Figure 12-3, consequently, the equilibrium quantity of money, bank deposits, D_3, is less than that in Figure 12-2, D_2.

SOME ILLUSTRATIVE NUMERICAL EXAMPLES

It may be useful to demonstrate the points developed previously by means of some numerical examples. Suppose that no savings and loan associations exist, that there is 100 in high-powered money, and that commercial banks hold reserves equal to 20 percent of their deposits. In this case, the balance sheet of the commercial banking system is as follows:

Banks			
Reserves	100	Deposits	500
Loans	400		

The banking system has "created" 400 of money by making loans of 400.

If we introduce S&Ls holding reserves equal to 5 percent of their deposits as deposits at commercial banks, and if the public wishes to hold S&Ls shares in the ratio of one share to three bank deposits, we obtain

Banks				S&Ls			
Reserves	100	Deposits	492	Reserves (Deposits at banks)	8	S&L shares	164
Loans	400	Reserves of S&Ls	8	Loans	156		

The volume of loans outstanding is greater than previously. All high-powered money eventually comes into the hands of commercial banks, since S&Ls hold their reserves in the form of bank deposits. Thus the lending capacity of the banking system is unchanged. But S&Ls are able to make loans to the extent that the public desires to hold shares instead of bank deposits. Whatever the amount of reserves held by S&Ls, the total amount of loans will increase so long as there is some shift from deposits to shares. Note, too, that the stock money has declined. However, the interest rate will decline because the combined demand for bonds from banks and S&Ls is greater than the demand for bonds when there were only banks. The same phenomenon also suggests that the amount of money substitutes, savings and loan shares, has increased, more than offsetting the reduction in money.

If we now examine the case in which S&Ls hold their reserves in the form of vault cash but retain the assumptions that they hold reserves equal to 5 percent of shares and that the public wishes to hold shares and bank deposits in the ratio 3:1, we have

Banks				S&Ls			
Reserves	92	Deposits	462	Reserves (Vault cash)	8	S&L shares	154
Loans	370			Loans	146		

Here, the volume of loans made by the banking system and the stock of money decline because a portion of high-powered money, 8, goes into the vaults of savings and loan associations. However, because of our assumption that the reserves held against shares are smaller than the reserves held against deposits, the volume of lending increases from 400 in the initial example to 516 in the present one. The increase, however, is smaller than it is when S&Ls hold their reserves in commercial banks, where total lending is 556. And, of course, the interest rate will be higher than in the second example but smaller than in the first.

Case	Public's Holdings		Loans Outstanding	
No S&Ls	Money	500	Banks	400
S&Ls hold reserves at	Money	492	Banks	400
commercial banks	Shares	164	S&Ls	156
S&Ls hold reserves as	Money	462	Banks	370
vault cash	Shares	154	S&Ls	146

The introduction of S&Ls is clearly expansionary. The magnitude of the expansionary effect depends first on where S&Ls hold their reserves; second, on the amount of reserves held by S&Ls; and finally, on the extent to which the public substitutes against deposits and in favor of shares.

SHARES AS A SUBSTITUTE FOR BONDS

If we drop the extreme assumption that the entire volume of funds shifted into S&Ls comes at the expense of deposits, supposing instead that a portion comes at the expense of bonds, the leftward shift in the demand for deposits at every interest rate on bonds is less than the rightward shift of the demand for shares. As a result, the reduction in the demand for high-powered money as funds are shifted into S&Ls is smaller than in the cases outlined previously. This reduces the decline in the rate of interest on bonds caused by the introduction of the S&L industry.[7]

THE EFFECT OF INTRODUCING S&LS

How has the introduction of S&Ls affected the conclusions previously reached? In general, introducing S&Ls has made the equilibrium rate of interest on bonds smaller than before; thus the new feature is expansionary. The extent of the expansionary effect depends on the degree of substitutability between deposits and shares and on the amount and manner of the reserves held by S&Ls. The expansionary impulse will be larger, the larger the degree of substitutability between deposits and shares, the smaller the volume of reserves held by S&Ls per dollar of shares, and the greater the amount of the reserves that S&Ls hold at commercial banks rather than as vault cash.

Figures 12-1 through 12-3 have been drawn for a fixed level of national income. But we have seen that the rate of interest consistent with a given level of income is lower after the introduction of nonbank intermediaries than before. The result is to shift the *LM* curve to the right and to increase the equilibrium level of national income.[8] The extent of the increase depends, of course, on the interest elasticity of the demand for investment spending.[9]

IMPLICATIONS FOR THE CONDUCT OF MONETARY POLICY

What is the impact of introducing nonbank intermediaries for the effectiveness of monetary policy? Consider Figure 12-1, where only commercial banks exist. Suppose that in an attempt to pursue a contractionary policy, the monetary authorities reduce the supply of high-powered money through open market sales of securities. This action raises the rate of interest and reduces the equilibrium volume of bank deposits. The *LM* curve is thus shifted to the left, reducing the equilibrium level of national income.

Now suppose that there are nonbanks, as in Figure 12-2. The initial effect of the reduction in the volume of high-powered money is to raise the rate of interest on bonds, as in Figure 12-1. But the process does not stop there. The rise in the rate of interest on bonds results in S&Ls earning above-normal profits. Competition among S&Ls for shares increases the rate of interest paid to holders of these shares. As a result, the demand for deposits is shifted to the left and that for shares moves to the right. This lowers the quantity of high-powered money demanded at every rate of interest and serves to reduce the increase in the interest rate on bonds that would otherwise take place. The process continues until the rate of interest on bonds and the rate of interest on shares yield normal profits for S&Ls. The increase produced in the interest rate on bonds is smaller than it would be in the absence of nonbank intermediaries. Thus monetary policy is less effective, in the sense that the volume of open market sales needed to produce any given increase in the rate of interest on bonds is now larger than it was when banks were the only financial institution.[10] The reason is that the increasing tightness in the money market produces a shift in funds from banks to other intermediaries. Since such shifts are expansionary, the contractionary impact of the reduction in high-powered money is lessened. The leftward shift in the *LM* curve is smaller than it is when there are no nonbank intermediaries.

SUMMARY

The presence of financial institutions other than commercial banks can effect the rate of interest and, hence, the behavior of the economy as a whole. The impact of these institutions depends on the extent to which asset-holders are willing to hold their liabilities, on the assets which are substitutes for these liabilities, and on the amount and nature of the reserves these institutions hold.

NOTES

[1] In focusing on S&Ls we do not intend to minimize the importance of other nonbank intermediaries. Since the qualitative impact of the introduction of such an intermediary is the same whether the intermediary is a savings and loan association, a credit union, or a life insurance company, it makes little difference which one we focus on. We might as well have assumed that the only intermediary was a life insurance company, which issued a liability called the cash surrender value of life insurance policies. The choice would not have affected the analysis of this chapter.

[2] The rate that S&Ls can pay is related to the rate that they can earn on the assets they hold, and this connection is explored shortly.

[3] Although S&Ls are subject to legal reserve requirements, many other nonbank intermediaries are not. These intermediaries nevertheless hold reserves, to avoid the need to liquidate other assets to satisfy claims against liabilities. For example, if policy loans at life insurance companies grow rapidly and life insurance companies do not hold some reserves, they will be forced to liquidate earning assets, with some risk of failing to obtain the full market value of these assets. The amount of such "precautionary balances" held in the form of money depends, of course, on the return from holding these balances in alternative form. In fact, most such reserves of life insurance companies are held in the form of short-term interest-bearing securities.

[4] We examine briefly below the effect of assuming that a portion of the funds shifted to shares comes at the expense of the bond holdings of wealth owners.

[5] The level of income was assumed constant in drawing Figure 12-1. If we were to raise the level of income, the demand for deposits would shift to the right.

[6] One of the reasons for this is the relatively high legal reserve requirement against commercial bank deposits. In addition, there is the greater instability of bank deposits, compared with the liabilities of other financial institutions.

[7] Theoretically, if the substitution against bonds is sufficiently large, the introduction of S&Ls can actually raise the rate of interest. We are inclined to dismiss such a possibility as unlikely, in practice.

[8] Notice that the *LM* curve is drawn for a fixed quantity of high-powered money rather than for a fixed stock of money.

[9] Recall that the size of the rightward shift in the *LM* curve as a result of the introduction of S&Ls depended on the substitutability of shares and bonds for money.

[10] This analysis proceeds on the assumption that S&Ls are able to compete freely for shares. But in fact certain restrictions on their ability to alter the rate they pay are similar in effect to the ban on interest payment on demand deposits. Thus if there is a ceiling to the rate of interest payable on shares and the rate is at that ceiling, S&Ls cannot compete for new shares even if there is an increase in the rate of interest on bonds that produces above-normal profits. The result is that there is no shift from deposits to shares to partially offset the contractionary policy. In fact, to the extent that people are induced to shift from shares to bonds, the contractionary effects of the policy may be reinforced.

13
American financial institutions

In this chapter we begin a detailed description of American financial institutions. In previous chapters concerned with the behavior of national income and the price level, we facilitated our analysis by making a number of simplifying assumptions about the operations of financial institutions. Thus in Chapter 11 we assumed that commercial banks were in the business of accepting demand deposits and of buying bonds. In Chapter 12, where nonbank financial institutions were introduced, we assumed the only such institution to be a savings and loan association that issued shares and purchased bonds. The links between banks and S&Ls consisted of the competition of demand deposits and shares for a place in asset holders' portfolios and the competition for bonds that each financial institution desired to hold in its portfolio.

In practice, of course, there are many types of financial institutions, and the liability of each is somewhat differentiated from the liabilities of competitors. Financial institutions moreover, may hold a wide variety of financial assets. In exploring many differences among institutions and assets, however, we should not lose sight of the fundamental point made in previous chapters: that all such institutions issue liabilities that are to some extent competitors for a place in asset holders' portfolios and that they compete with one another for earning assets. This chapter stresses the differences among the institutions, but the similarities should not be minimized.

These institutions share one very significant characteristic, however. They all serve as intermediaries between those who hold their liabilities and those to whom they lend. For example, household savers might conceivably be willing to make mortgage loans directly to persons wishing to purchase houses. But the assets thus acquired by households would have many undesirable properties. Mortgage loans are not liquid, divisible, or easily reversible.

Contrast these properties of mortgage loans with those of savings and loan shares. Shares are perfectly liquid and divisible and are reversible at little or no cost. Therefore, we would expect savers to accept a lower rate of return on shares than they would require as an inducement to hold mortgages directly. As a result, S&Ls can make mortgage loans at an interest rate lower than households would accept for holding mortgages.

The undesirable characteristics of mortgage loans are not as important to S&Ls as they are to households because S&Ls hold a large number of mortgages and have a large number of depositors. On the same day that some depositors wish to withdraw funds, a savings and loan association need not liquidate its loan portfolio if other depositors are adding funds to their accounts. In any event, S&Ls will be able to hold relatively small quantities of cash reserves and still satisfy the liquidity needs of their depositors. In addition, S&Ls are able to spread default risk over a large number of mortgages. Whereas the holder of a single mortgage would suffer a large loss in the event of default, such a loss would be small for the holder of a large number of mortgages, such as a savings and loan association.

The institutions described in this chapter have in common the function of serving as intermediaries between lenders and borrowers. They provide lenders with assets having characteristics superior to those which could have been obtained if they had made direct loans. As a result, the individual institution may be able to offer better terms to borrowers.

COMMERCIAL BANKS

There were almost 14,000 commercial banks in the United States, and at the end of 1972 almost 6,000 were members of the Federal Reserve system. Representing only about 40 percent of all commercial banks, member banks nevertheless had about 80 percent of all deposits in commercial banks and held similar percentages of the loans and securities held by the commercial banking system. Whereas the average member banks owed $78 million in deposits, the figure for nonmembers was only about $16 million.

Commercial banks that have national charters—about one-third of all banks—are required to become members of the Federal Reserve system. This subjects them to reserve requirements against their deposits established by the Fed and allows them to borrow at the Federal Reserve. Banks with state charters can elect Federal Reserve membership. Only about one-seventh of them do so, but state members owe approximately as many deposits as do nonmembers, since they are much larger banks than the nonmembers (see Table 13-1).

Table 13-2 illustrates the balance sheet of the typical member bank at the end of 1972. Loans represented about 55 percent of its assets, and securities about one-quarter. Cash assets, which include reserves held at the Federal Reserve as well as vault cash, were about 16 percent of all assets. Demand deposits accounted for about 35 percent of total liabilities, and capital and time deposits represented about 41 percent. Demand deposits were about 86 percent of time deposits.

Not only are commercial banks the sole financial institutions able to issue demand deposits, they are also differentiated by virtue of being the dominant lender to businesses. At the end of 1972 more than one-third of all commercial bank loans were for commercial and industrial purposes, with real estate loans (one-quarter) and loans to individuals (one-fifth) being other principal lending activities. The securities portfolio consisted primarily of obligations of state and local governments (almost one-half) and the United States government (more than one-third).

The composition of commercial bank balance sheets does not remain constant over time but is sensitive to economic conditions. We have argued in

Table 13-1 Deposits of commercial banks by class, December 31, 1972 (millions of dollars)

	Average Deposits Excluding Interbank[a]	Number of Banks
All commercial banks	$41.5	13,927
Federal Reserve members	78.3	5,704
National members	73.3	4,612
State members	99.7	1,092
Nonmembers	16.0	8,017

[a] Interbank deposits are those owned by other banks.
Source: Federal Reserve Bulletin.

Table 13-2 Typical member bank, December 31, 1972 (millions of dollars)

Cash assets	$ 16.9	Deposits	
Securities	23.9	Interbank	$ 6.2
Loans	57.8	Demand	36.3
Other assets	4.0	Time	42.0
		Borrowings	6.4
		Other liabilities	4.4
		Capital	7.3
	$102.6		$102.6

Source: Federal Reserve Bulletin.

Chapter 11 that the volume of excess and borrowed reserves will depend on the discount rate and the rate of interest that banks can obtain on earning assets, among other factors. In addition, the distribution of bank assets between loans and securities will depend on the interest rates on these respective assets as well as on bank size and on the relative importance of time and demand deposits. At the end of 1960, for example, loans represented only about 45 percent of total bank assets as compared with the 55 percent at the end of 1972. In addition, the composition of bank liabilities depends on the interest rate paid on time deposits and on the rates of return that can be obtained on assets that are substitues for bank deposits. At the end of 1960, time deposits were less than half as large as demand deposits, but time deposits exceeded demand deposits at the end of 1972.

Competition for bank deposits

In the United States commercial banks are forbidden by law to pay explicit interest on demand deposits. In spite of this restriction, however, there are ways for a bank to provide payments to depositors. Since there are costs of accepting deposits and clearing checks, if the charges to a customer for servicing his account are less than these costs, a bank is in effect paying the depositor for maintaining his deposit. Most banks have service charges geared to the average or minimum amounts a depositor maintains, but if the customer's deposit is large enough, he can obtain "free" checking services. In addition, a bank can provide other services to its customers at less than cost, to attract deposits. These services include giving financial advice, executing purchases and sales of securities, and making loans in periods of credit stringency.

Although banks are not permitted to make explicit interest payments on demand deposits, they can do so on time deposits. However, they are not completely free to set these rates at the level they might wish. The rate of interest the bank is permitted to pay has a ceiling set by the Federal Reserve system if the bank is a member[1] and by the states for nonmember banks. This rate is usually at or below the rate banks would be willing to pay in a free market. Currently, these regulations permit different rates to be paid on different types of deposit. The rates differ according to whether the deposit is of the passbook type, for which withdrawal can occur at any time, or whether it involves a certificate of deposit (CD), for which there can be no repayment until a specific maturity date. Higher interest rates are permitted on the latter. Even within the category of CDs, higher rates are permitted, the longer the period of the deposit and the larger the amount. Thus passbook deposits can only receive 5 percent, but for CDs in amounts greater than $100,000 there is no maximum interest rate.[2]

Obviously, the $100,000 CD is not likely to be held by the small investor. Rather, it is the type of asset that a business firm might employ to hold temporarily idle cash.[3] However, firms have many alternative forms in which they can hold this cash, and if the rate payable on CDs is not sufficiently high relative to rates on these other instruments, there will be shifts of funds from time deposits at commercial banks. This is exactly what happened between 1968 and 1969, when the maximum interest rate payable by commercial banks was restrained by regulation to a level well below that which potential depositors could earn on other instruments. The result was a decline in CDs exceeding 50 percent. Only after rates on the other instruments declined did banks restore their CD business.[4]

Deposit insurance

All banks belonging to the Federal Reserve system, and many others as well, insure their depositors against the possibility that the bank will fail.[5] In the event of a failure, the Federal Deposit Insurance Corporation, an agency of the United States government, will reimburse the insured bank's depositors for any losses suffered up to a previously stated maximum.[6] This arrangement removes one of the reasons for preferring currency to bank deposits—namely, the possibility that the latter, in the absence of insurance, will be lost if the bank fails. It also reduces the possibility of large shifts from deposits to currency as wealth holders begin to fear bank failures. During the early 1930s, before the introduction of deposit insurance, many banks failed and customers of other banks shifted their holdings of deposits to currency. This shift severely complicated the problem of executing monetary policy, since a large shift in the currency–deposit ratio produces a large change in the relationship between unborrowed reserves and the stock of money. Thus even if reserves had been increased, which they were not, the money stock, and banks credit, might have fallen, since the ratio of currency to deposits rose as much as it did.[7]

Branch banking, bank holding companies, and banking competition

Banks are subject to regulation by the states in which they reside and by the federal government. Federal law forbids the maintenance by a single bank of branches in more than one state. Thus a bank can accept deposits from customers in several states and make loans to borrowers in several states, but it must confine its branch locations to a single state. In some states (California is a prominent example), banks are free to have as many branches as they desire, located in any part of the state. In other states, particularly

New York, a bank's branches are restricted to certain parts of the state.[8] In a number of states (e.g., Illinois and Texas) banks are forbidden to maintain branches at all. Many states in which branching is forbidden have developed group banking, whereby a single entity, usually a holding company, has control over a number of legally independent banks. A number of bank holding companies control banks in several states.[9] Another important institution is the *one-bank holding company,* which holds shares in a single bank and is permitted to engage in nonbanking activities. The Chase-Manhattan Corporation, which controls the Chase-Manhattan Bank, is one such company. Recent challenges from other industries to prohibit one-bank holding companies from extending their activities into these industries have yet to be resolved.

States usually prohibit branch banking because of a fear that if multiple branches are allowed, a few large banks will dominate banking in a state and will be able to engage in monopolistic or oligopolistic banking practices, paying less for deposits and charging more for loans than would competitive banks. Some of the same anticompetitive effects would undoubtedly also be felt if a number of banks were linked through a group rather than being legally a single entity; thus most states that prohibit branching also limit group banking.[10] Those favoring branch banking stress that economies of scale in banking are such that if banks are restricted to a given area, they will be too small to exploit these potential advantages and bank costs will be too high. At the same time, they argue, unit banking often results in one monopolizing bank in many small towns, or no banks at all, whereas, if branching were permitted, there might be a number of competing branches of large banks.

In addition to establishing regulations with respect to branch or group banking, state and federal governments also are concerned with mergers between existing banks. Where two banks in a given market combine, the result is the elimination of a potential source of borrowed funds for loan customers and a potential place in which to deposit funds for asset holders. Nevertheless, state and federal regulatory agencies have permitted many mergers, particularly during the past few years, often on the grounds that the mergers permit the surviving institution to provide better banking services than either merging bank could have supplied alone. Furthermore, it is often felt that the improvement in service is large enough to overcome any anticompetitive effects due to the merger. The seriousness of the anticompetitive effects is presumably dependent on two principal factors. First, the number of banks in a market: There would likely be a smaller effect in the event of the merger of two banks in a market having fifty banks than if the only two banks in a market merged. Second, there is the size of the banks involved: It is more significant if the two banks that control a majority of the banking assets in a market combine than if two relatively small institutions take this action.[11]

MUTUAL SAVINGS BANKS

Another important kind of financial institution in the United States is the mutual savings bank. The liabilities of mutual savings banks are similar to the time deposits of commercial banks. Deposits at mutual savings banks are primarily those of households. The deposits earn interest and, in principle, require notice in writing before withdrawals can be made. In practice, this requirement is virtually always waived. The assets of mutual savings banks consist of loans, which are primarily home mortgage loans, and corporate securities. Together these comprise about 90 percent of all mutual savings bank assets, with mortgage loans accounting for almost 70 percent. Thus the main business of these institutions is to accept time deposits from households and to make mortgage loans, providing an alternative asset for wealth holders to hold and an alternative source of funds for borrowers, primarily mortgage borrowers. They also compete with commercial banks as suppliers of funds for installment loan purposes. At the end of 1972 deposit liabilities of mutual savings banks were $95 billion. Mortgage loans totaled $71 billion.

SAVINGS AND LOAN ASSOCIATIONS

The business of savings and loan associations is almost identical to that of mutual savings banks, but the S&L industry is somewhat larger. At the end of 1972 savings and loan associations held about $206 billion of mortgages, and their deposit liabilities, variously called savings capital or savings and loan shares, amounted to about $207 billion. Like mutual savings banks, S&Ls are largely in the business of providing an alternative source of funds to mortgage borrowers and an alternative asset to be held by households that are wealth owners. About 85 percent of total S&L assets were held in the form of mortgage loans, a somewhat higher percentage than that held by mutual savings banks.

MUTUAL SAVINGS BANKS VERSUS
SAVINGS AND LOAN ASSOCIATIONS

Due to a combination of historical accident and differences in legal regulations, mutual savings banks are the dominant retail savings institution in some parts of the country and lagging, or not existing, in others. Of the 500-odd mutual savings banks in the United States, more than 450 are in New York, Massachusetts, Connecticut, New Jersey, New Hampshire, and Maine. More than 300 are in New York and Massachusetts, but 32 states have none at all. Almost half of all mutual savings bank deposits are held by banks in New York City, and about three-fourths of all such deposits are in banks in New York State and Massachusetts.

There are about 6000 savings and loan associations in the United States, but less than one-quarter are located in New England or in the Middle Atlantic states. In the Midwest, the South, and the West, S&Ls are the predominant retail savings institution. About 60 percent of all deposits at S&Ls are in states having no mutual savings banks.

The deposits of all mutual savings banks and most S&Ls are insured against the failure of the institution. Savings bank deposits are insured either by the Federal Deposit Insurance Corporation or by the Mutual Savings Bank Central Fund of Massachusetts. Savings and loan association deposits are insured by the Federal Savings and Loan Insurance Corporation.[12] All savings banks are chartered by the states, but there is a dual (federal-state) chartering system for S&Ls, and many are federally chartered. No savings bank or association, even if federally chartered, can maintain branches in more than one state.

For a variety of reasons, the growth rates of mutual savings banks and S&Ls have differed markedly in recent years.[13] In 1953 both institutions had deposits of about $27 billion. Since then, deposits of mutual savings banks have gone up about $3\frac{1}{2}$ times and those of S&Ls have risen almost 8 times; thus savings bank deposits were $95 billion and deposits in S&Ls were $207 billion at the end of 1972.[14]

Interest ceilings on savings institutions

Like commercial banks, savings and loan associations and mutual savings banks are restricted in the interest they can pay on their deposits. This is said to be because if there were unfettered competition for funds, savings and loan associations would be vulnerable to the effects of large swings in the rate of interest. Since mortgage loans, which are the principal holdings of S&Ls, are made for long periods, the portfolios of these institutions tend to turn over relatively slowly. If interest rates are stable for long periods, the yields on mortgage loans and interest payments on deposits will adjust, permitting S&Ls to earn a profit. But suppose that interest rates rise. A large proportion of the portfolio of S&Ls will be invested in relatively low-yielding mortgages. If S&Ls must raise the rate they pay on deposits, they will be operating at a loss. If they fail to raise the rate, however, they will lose funds to other institutions and will be forced to liquidate their portfolios. But the value of a low-yielding mortgage will have declined, like the value of a low-yielding bond when interest rates rise. Furthermore, because of the illiquidity of mortgages, S&Ls may fail to realize the full value of these instruments.

For all these reasons, it has been a matter of policy to restrict the interest rate that various financial institutions may pay on their deposits. By preventing competition, it is thought that the danger to savings institutions due to fluctuating interest rates can be avoided. The rate of interest on commercial bank time deposits is typically kept below the permitted rate on S&L shares. This does not result in all small deposits going to S&Ls, presumably because some households value the convenience of having saving and checking deposits in the same institution.

But savings and loan associations cannot be completely shielded from competition by restricting the rate of interest that other financial institutions can pay. Asset holders can always purchase marketable bonds if the yield on bonds is high enough. Thus consideration is being given to allowing S&Ls to increase the flexibility of yields on their assets—for example, by permitting them to make more short-term loans for purchases of household durable goods. But the leading proposal is to sanction the offering of variable interest rate mortgages. Under this arrangement, the interest charges paid by a borrower would vary with other market interest rates, rising when they increase and declining when they decline. Thus even though their loan portfolios do not turn over rapidly, S&Ls would be better able to compete for funds with commercial banks.

LIFE INSURANCE COMPANIES

Life insurance companies are a fourth major financial institution. The total assets of life insurance companies amounted to more than $239 billion at the end of 1971. When a person "buys" an ordinary life insurance policy, he is in effect purchasing insurance and beginning a saving program. His premiums are employed both to meet the claims against the company for current deaths and to build up the cash surrender value of his insurance policy. As a person accumulates cash surrender value, the insurance company is able to buy earning assets. A portion of the return on these assets is used to defray insurance premiums. A policyholder has the right to borrow, at a previously established interest rate, against his policy's cash surrender value. He must pay interest to borrow his "own" money because as described previously, a portion of the investment earnings on the insurance company are used to defray insurance premiums, and the funds loaned to a policyholder are not available to be placed in other assets.

Table 13-3 indicates the breakdown of life insurance company assets at the end of 1972. Clearly, the largest items are the bonds of business firms and mortgage loans. The principal liability of life insurance companies is, of course, the accumulated savings of policyholders, the cash surrender values of life insurance policies.[15]

OTHER PRIVATE FINANCIAL INSTITUTIONS

In addition to commercial banks, mutual savings banks, saving and loan associations, and life insurance companies, other private financial institutions engage in similar activities. They issue a distinctive kind of liability that competes for a place in wealth holders' portfolios, and they employ the proceeds of the sale of their liabilities to acquire earning assets.

Credit unions

Credit unions are nonprofit organizations that accept deposits and make loans. The principal difference between credit unions and retail savings institutions of other kinds is that loans can only be made to members of the union.[16] Credit unions typically make installment loans to their members, mainly for the purchase of automobiles or other durable goods.

Consumer loan and sales finance companies

Consumer loan and sales finance companies differ from credit unions in two ways. First, their resources are obtained not from retail deposits but through the issuance of marketable liabilities. Second, their loans are not restricted to any group of potential borrowers. However, their loan business

Table 13-3   Distribution of assets of life insurance companies
————————————December 31, 1972————————

Asset	Percentage
Government securities	5%
Business securities	
Bonds	36%
Stocks	9%
Mortgages	34%
Policy loans	8%
Other assets	8%

Source: Federal Reserve Bulletin.

is also of the installment type, the loans of sales finance companies being principally for the purchase of consumer durables, whereas loans of consumer loan companies are not tied directly to the purchase of a particular item.

FEDERALLY SPONSORED INSTITUTIONS

Besides private financial institutions, there exist a number of institutions that originated through government initiative, and some still retain a degree of government control. These insitutions fall into two broad classes, those aimed at providing loans to farmers and those directed at mortgage lending. The former include the Federal Land Banks, which provide long-term loans to farmers; the Intermediate Credit Banks, which provide loans of up to five years to farmers to meet operating expenses and capital requirements; and the Bank for Cooperatives, which lends money to farmers' cooperatives. The latter group includes the Federal National Mortgage Association (now a private institution), which purchases mortgages, and the Federal Home Loan Banks, which provide credit to federal savings and loan associations.

All these agencies act as intermediaries. They obtain the funds they make available by issuing securities in the open market. Like the liabilities of other intermediaries, these funds compete for a place in asset holders' portfolios. At the same time, the assets the federally sponsored intermediaries hold must be obtained in competition with other financial institutions. Although not guaranteed by the government, the securities issued by these agencies are regarded as liquid and predictable by asset holders. The amount of assets held by each of the agencies named at the end of 1972 is listed in Table 13-4.

The important difference between these and other intermediaries is that the latter are organized for the benefit of their owners, but the former attempt to provide credit at reduced costs to sectors of the economy that are regarded by the government as especially deserving. These sectors (e.g., farmers) ob-

**Table 13-4   Assets of federally sponsored financial intermediaries
———————— December 31, 1972 (billions of dollars) ————————**

Institution	Assets
Federal Home Loan Banks	$10.6
Federal National Mortgage Association	17.8
Federal Land Banks	7.9
Intermediate Credit Banks	5.7
Banks for Cooperatives	2.1

Source: Federal Reserve Bulletin.

tain cheaper credit, since the securities of federally sponsored agencies can be issued at lower interest rates than those paid by private financial intermediaries.

SUMMARY

This chapter has described in some detail the activities of some major American financial institutions. In previous chapters we simply said that these institutions hold bonds in their portfolios and that their liabilities were either deposits or shares. In this chapter some of the differences in the types of liability offered by these institutions have been explored, and some of the differences in their portfolios behavior have been considered. In addition, an attempt has been made to describe the regulatory environment in which the institutions operate.

NOTES

[1] Maximum rates are established by the Board of Governors of the Federal Reserve system under provisions of Regulation Q. If the maximum established for banks in a state is less than the Federal Reserve ceiling, member banks are limited to the state maximum. Nonmember banks whose deposits are insured by the Federal Deposit Insurance Corporation are subject to the same ceiling applicable for member banks.

[2] Some banks, in attempting to raise the interest rate paid on time deposits above the legal ceiling, have offered free checking services to those holding savings deposits above a specified minimum amount.

[3] Recall our discussion of the transactions demand for money in Chapter 3.

[4] One should not conclude that loss of CDs from the banking system as asset holders shift to higher yielding assets necessarily leads to a decline in the reserves held by the banking system. To discover whether that is the case, we must trace the course of the funds withdrawn to purchase the other assets. If the sellers of the assets deposit the proceeds of the sales in commercial banks, or if they deposit the funds in institutions that hold reserves in commercial banks, the total reserves of the banking system need not change. To the extent that the new commercial bank deposits are of the demand type, which are subject to a higher legal reserve requirement than are CDs, however, the volume of assets that can be held by the banking system will decline, and this can occur even if currency plus demand deposits, increases. Chapter 12 provides a detailed analysis of this question.

[5] At the end of 1972 approximately 200 commercial banks holding less than 1 percent of all commercial bank deposits did not provide such insurance to their depositors.

[6] The maximum is currently $20,000 per depositor per bank. Thus a depositor holding two accounts of $20,000 each in a single bank will lose $20,000 if the bank fails.

[7] Probably a more important factor was that other banks were also forced to close because they could not quickly meet large deposit drains on demand owing to the illiquidity of many of their assets. (See the definition of liquidity in Chapter 2.) And this would even be true at present. But because of deposit insurance, the fear of

loss of deposits that prompted the runs on banks is less likely to occur than in the past.

[8] In New York, for example, branches were confined until recently to the county in which the bank's home office was located, except for New York City, where branching was permitted city-wide. Recent changes have permitted New York City banks to have branches in surrounding counties and banks in these counties to maintain branches in New York City.

[9] Bank holding companies are subject to federal regulation if they own 25 percent of the voting stock or otherwise control two or more banks. These holding companies are forbidden to engage in other than banking activities.

[10] Interestingly, some states (e.g., Texas) prohibit branching but place no limitation at all on group banking.

[11] Many of the most important bank mergers in recent years have been between very large banks.

[12] About 96 percent of all S&L deposits are insured by the Federal Savings and Loan Insurance Corporation.

[13] One of the most important reasons is that mutual savings banks tend to be located in the more slowly growing states and in the central cities, the areas of states having the slowest growth rates.

[14] Until fairly recently, savings banks and savings and loan associations have been forbidden by law to engage in checking activities. Thus commercial banks could compete with these institutions by offering time deposits and in lending activities of certain kinds, but savings banks and S&Ls could not participate in an important aspect of commercial banking, the provision of demand deposits. A new regulation, which has been little utilized to this point, permits savings and loan associations to transfer funds from their depositors' accounts to meet some regularly recurring payments. Thus a depositor might meet his rental or mortgage payment by instructing his S&L to transfer funds to his landlord or mortgage holder. This would permit the depositor to earn interest on funds that would otherwise be held in non-interest-earning demand deposits at commercial banks, thus encouraging shifts of funds from commercial banks to S&Ls.

[15] An interesting aspect of life insurance company activity concerns the tendency of policy loans to rise as interest rates rise. The interest rate on policy loans is fixed in advance; therefore, as interest rates at which households can borrow elsewhere rise, there is a tendency to look on policy loans as a low-cost source of funds. In 1961, for example, policy loans were only about $4\frac{1}{2}$ percent of all assets but this figure had grown to over 7 percent by 1970. During this period outstanding policy loans grew to $2\frac{1}{2}$ times their original value.

[16] In the early days of savings and loan associations, when they were called building and loan societies, this was also the case.

⚞14⚟
Monetary policy-making with incomplete information

Until now we have been concerned with the effects of changes in government policy on the economy in highly simplified situations. When policy makers know with precision the state of the economy at all times, when they have complete understanding of how the economy operates, and when the economy responds rapidly to changes in policy, the formulation of economic policy is relatively simple. Policy making consists simply of observing what must be done and arranging to do it.

The issues discussed in this chapter arise precisely because policy makers do not always know the state of the economy, nor can they be sure of rapid responses to changes in policy. Thus they may not learn for some time whether the actions they are taking have produced the desired results. It is, therefore, important to design procedures that produce good policies, given this handicap of ignorance.

There are a number of ways to deal with the problems of policy making just described. In the most ambitious of these, the policy maker employs an econometric model of the economy.[1] To use the model, goals for policy are established by determining desired values for certain of the variables with which the policy maker is concerned. The values of the policy instruments are then manipulated, and if the model is correct, the desired values of the goals can be expected to be achieved.[2]

This approach is seldom employed, at least in the formal manner discussed here. One reason is that policy makers, with some justification, have little faith in the econometric models that have heretofore been constructed. As a result, policy makers have turned to simpler methods. But even these methods require an understanding of the way in which the economy functions. They differ from the econometric model approach in that the objectives are far more modest and, as a result, far less knowledge about the structure of the economy is required. Rather than trying to achieve the policy maker's objectives at each point in time, they strive to avoid "large" policy errors. Given the gaps in our knowledge of how the economy works, these methods may be the best we can reasonably use at this time.

Here the policy maker seeks a variable, closely related to his ultimate objective, which (1) responds quickly to changes in policy and (2) is observable on a continuous basis. If the link between this variable and the ultimate objective is a close one, controlling the intermediate variable will involve controlling the ultimate objective, as well. This approach has the advantage that the policy maker can quickly learn whether his actions are having the desired effect on the intermediate variable. No such feedback is obtained if he attempts to operate directly on the ultimate objective, since the latter's performance can be observed only after some time has passed. Thus he requires a variable that satisfies the conditions 1 and 2, above. The search for such a variable is called the *target problem.*

The policy maker selects an intermediate target of policy, which ideally is linked closely to his ultimate objectives. He then decides what he believes the value of the target should be, to achieve his objective. If the intermediate target varies from its desired value, he takes whatever actions are necessary to restore that value. Sometimes keeping the value of the intermediate target at a constant value ends in the failure to achieve the ultimate objective, but a well-chosen intermediate target will have the effect of producing small failures.[3]

A number of variables have been suggested as appropriate intermediate monetary targets. All can be continuously observed, and all respond to changes in policy very quickly. They differ in that the use of each one as a target implies different beliefs about the underlying behavior of the economy and, consequently, leads to different policies in the face of disturbances in the economic system.

In the case of monetary policy, among the intermediate targets that have been suggested as meeting the foregoing requirements are the money stock, the rate of interest, and the level of net free reserves, which is excess reserves minus borrowed reserves of the banking system. In analyzing each of these proposed targets, we assume that the economy is initially in equilibrium at full employment and that one of the behavioral functions characterizing the economy shifts to reduce output.[4] We assume further that the government has chosen a value for the intermediate target that would, in the absence of the disturbance, produce full employment. We then ask whether the government's policy of maintaining a fixed value of the intermediate target is stabilizing. It is *stabilizing* if it serves to offset a portion of the deflationary stimulus. It is *destabilizing* if the deflationary stimulus is reinforced.

Each of the intermediate targets named—the money stock, the rate of interest, and net free reserves—is paired with deflationary shifts in the investment demand function, in the demand for money, and in the demand for excess reserves. There are thus nine cases to be considered.

DISTURBANCE FROM INVESTMENT DEMAND

A downward shift in the investment demand function shifts the *IS* curve to the left, causing it to intersect *LM* at a lower rate of interest and a lower income level if the government does not respond to the shift. In addition to the decline in the rate of interest, the quantity of excess reserves that banks wish to hold increases, and the volume of reserves that they wish to borrow decreases. As a result, the new situation is characterized by a larger volume of net free reserves and a smaller stock of money.

If government policy is to maintain the stock of money, open market security purchases can be made, to offset the effect of the lower rate of interest on the equilibrium stock.[5] As the interest rate declines, the quantity of unborrowed reserves must be increased to keep the stock of money from declining. The decline in the interest rate that follows a leftward shift in *IS* will therefore be larger if the stock of money is fixed than if it declines. The reason is, of course, that the public must be induced to hold the larger stock of money. Clearly a policy of maintaining the stock of money involves a smaller decline in income that would be called for if the quantity of unborrowed reserves was not changed and the stock of money was permitted to fall.

If the government policy target is to keep the interest rate from declining, then faced by the shift in the investment demand schedule, the government must engage in open market security *sales*. This policy is destabilizing, of course, since national income will decline by a larger amount than it would if the quantity of unborrowed reserves went unchanged. Thus when the intermediate target is the rate of interest and the disturbance arises from a shift in the *IS* curve, government policy will be destabilizing. It will serve to reinforce the deflationary effect of the decline in the investment demand schedule.

Finally, let us consider a policy of maintaining the net free reserves when investment demand declines. We have already seen that if the government does not respond to the shift in the investment demand function, net free reserves will increase. To induce them to return to their original level, the government must engage in open market security sales. If these security sales are sufficient to raise the interest rate to its original level, net free reserves will remain at their original level. That is because both excess reserves and borrowed reserves depend on the discount rate, which is being held constant, and the rate of interest. In this case, therefore, a policy of maintaining the level of net free reserves is equivalent to a policy of maintaining the rate of interest. A policy of stabilizing net free reserves has the effect of reinforcing the effect of the downward shift in the investment demand function. Although at the new equilibrium the volume of net free reserves is the same as at the original one, the stock of money is smaller than it would have been if the government had remained passive in the face of the shift in investment demand. And this is why the policy of stabilizing net free reserves is, in this case, destabilizing.

The three cases are depicted in Figure 14-1. The disturbance to the initial equilibrium at Y_0 is caused by the leftward shift in the IS curve to IS'. If the government maintains the volume of unborrowed reserves, the discount

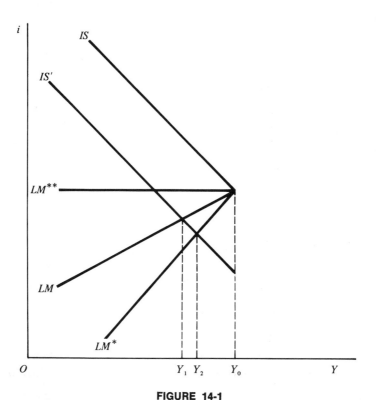

FIGURE 14-1

rate, and reserve requirements at their original levels, the appropriate *LM* curve to consider is *LM* along which the stock of money varies. If the government does nothing, income declines to Y_1. If government policy is to maintain the stock of money, however, the relevant *LM* curve becomes *LM** along which the quantity of unborrowed reserves varies. It is drawn more steeply than *LM* because with a larger money stock, the rate of interest must be smaller to induce the public to hold the stock. Since the money stock is maintained rather than being permitted to decline, national income falls only to Y_2. If on the other hand, the government wishes to maintain the rate of interest or, equivalently, to maintain net free reserves, the relevant curve becomes *LM***. The effect of this policy is clearly to make income decline by even more than it would if the government did nothing.

DISTURBANCE FROM THE DEMAND FOR MONEY

To see whether the conclusions we have reached about the usefulness of the various monetary policy intermediate targets still hold, we turn now to cases in which a situation of full employment equilibrium is disturbed by an upward shift in the demand for money. In the cases considered thus far, the use of the money stock as the policy variable was stabilizing and the use of the rate of interest or of net free reserves was destabilizing.

An increase in the demand for money shifts the *LM* curve to the left; and without any government action, national income will decline, the interest rate will rise, the stock of money will increase, and net free reserves will decrease.

Suppose that it is government policy to maintain the money stock. Since in the absence of government action, the rise in the rate of interest caused by the increase in the demand for money will cause the equilibrium stock of money to rise, open market sales of government securities are called for. Therefore, the government policy is destabilizing in that it reinforces the effect of the initial shift.

It is possible to compare the above-mentioned result with situations in which the government policy is to maintain either the interest rate or the quantity of net free reserves. For the government to keep the interest rate from changing in the face of an upward shift in the demand for money, it must engage in open market security purchases. And if it manages to keep the interest rate from changing, the equilibrium income level cannot change, since the *IS* curve has not shifted. Not only is the policy of maintaining the rate of interest in the face of a shift in the demand for money stabilizing, the size of the open market purchases called for actually succeeds in preventing any decline in income at all. The same result holds if the target is net free reserves.

DISTURBANCE FROM THE DEMAND FOR EXCESS RESERVES

Suppose that a full employment equilibrium is disturbed by an increased demand on the part of banks for excess reserves. At every interest rate–discount rate combination, banks now wish to hold a larger volume of excess reserves than previously. In the absence of any action by government, the income level will decline, the rate of interest will rise, the stock of money will decline, and net free reserves will increase. The stock of money is smaller than it was at the original equilibrium, even though the rate of interest is higher. The rise in the rate of interest offsets only partially the effect on the stock of money of the shift in the demand for excess reserves. A policy of maintaining the stock of money in the face of an increase in the demand for excess reserves results in a smaller decrease in national income than would occur if the government permitted a decline in the stock of money. And this should not be surprising: To keep the stock of money unchanged, government must engage in open market security purchases, an expansionary act that offsets partially the deflationary effect of the change in the demand for excess reserves.

If it is the policy of the government to maintain the interest rate at its original level, not only can the deflationary effect of the original disturbance be offset, but the offset is complete. National income does not fall because the *IS* curve has not shifted; therefore, if the rate of interest does not change, the level of national income cannot change.

Unlike the cases previously discussed, however, the demand for excess reserves has shifted; thus a policy of maintaining a constant rate of interest is not equivalent to a policy of maintaining a constant level of net free reserves. As a result, if the original interest rate is maintained, net free reserves will increase. Therefore, for net free reserves to be maintained at their original level, the rate of interest must rise. Yet the rise in the rate of interest induced by the increased demand for excess reserves is not large enough to prevent a rise in net free reserves. In the absence of any government policy action, net free reserves will be larger in the new equilibrium than in the original one. At a sufficiently high rate of interest, however, net free reserves will return to their original level. The decline in national income that occurs when the government stabilizes net free reserves is larger than would occur if government did nothing. This result should be expected, since to prevent net free reserves from rising, the government must engage in open market security sales. This action is deflationary and serves to reinforce the deflationary effect of the original shift in the demand for excess reserves.

OVERALL EVALUATION OF TARGETS

We are now in a position to compare the three targets, at least for the cases considered. In the following scoreboard (Table 14-1) a plus indicates that the use of the particular policy variable is stabilizing if the particular disturbance occurs. A minus indicates a destabilizing policy variable. None of the targets succeeds in being stabilizing for all three of the disturbances considered. When the use of the interest rate produces stabilizing results if the disturbance arises from the demand for money, it does not have this effect when the disturbance arises from investment demand. In the latter case the money supply is a better target variable. The interest rate seems to work at least as well as net free reserves, and better when a shift in the demand for excess reserves produces the disturbance. But it is probably possible to construct cases in which the use of net free reserves as the target variable provides better results than the use of the rate of interest.

The exercises in this chapter tell us that in choosing the appropriate policy target variable in an uncertain world, one must know a good deal about the factors that cause disturbances in the economy if destabilizing responses are to be avoided. The choice of the appropriate policy variable cannot be settled by theorizing alone. It should come as no surprise, therefore, that those who believe the demand function for money to be stable tend to focus on the supply of money as the appropriate policy variable, whereas those who believe it to be unstable regard the rate of interest as the appropriate object of Federal Reserve policy.

―――――――――――――――――**Table 14-1**―――――――――――――――――

	Policy Variable		
Disturbance	M	i	Net Free Reserves
Investment demand	+	−	−
Money demand	−	+	+
Excess reserves demand	+	+	−

MONETARY TARGETS AND THE MONETARIST CONTROVERSY

For the past decade or more one school of economic thought in the United States has held that the monetary authorities should aim for steady growth in the money stock.[6] This viewpoint stems from the beliefs that the stock of money is the appropriate monetary target and that steady growth in money provides the best hope of avoiding large errors in monetary policy. One of the major criticisms by the monetarist school of the use of the interest rate as a policy target is that interest rate is subject to many forces other than the actions of the monetary authorities. Although the same argument might be leveled against the use of the money stock, the monetarists argue that the demand for money is stable and the principal instability in the economy is in the goods markets.

The monetarist viewpoint has recently begun to have a direct effect on the conduct of monetary policy. In the past, money market conditions (primarily interest rates and the free reserve positions of banks) have tended to be the principal monetary targets. However, in 1971 the Federal Reserve adopted bank reserves as an additional monetary target. The Fed has aimed for stable growth of reserves, but it has continued to be concerned with interest rate movements. Thus when moderate growth of the money stock seemed to be leading to interest rates higher than those desired, the Fed apparently permitted faster growth in reserves than it would have preferred. The policy can be thought of as aiming for steady growth in the reserve base unless interest rates become too high. At that point, the reserve target is abandoned, or at least compromised, to keep interest rates from rising excessively.

SUMMARY

This chapter has focused on the difficulties confronting the policy maker when he does not have full knowledge of the behavior of the economy and when there is a lag associated with the effects of his own actions on the performance of the economy. We have described the "target approach" to making policy in such situations and have evaluated the usefulness of a number of alternative monetary targets.

NOTES

[1] An econometric model is a mathematical representation of the economy of the type analyzed in previous chapters, with the parameters estimated by statistical methods.

[2] In certain situations some of the stated objectives may be incompatible; in such cases success involves the achievement of a compromise established among the goals.

[3] A situation may arise in which the link between the target variable and the ultimate objective is broken. The policy maker must, therefore, have a signal that tells him that this has happened. The search for such a signal is called the *indicator problem*.

[4] To keep this chapter from being unduly long, the analysis is restricted to cases in which prices are rigid downward. With appropriate modifications, the analysis can be applied to cases in which prices are flexible but not flexible enough to prevent at least a short-term decline in output.

[5] It can also reduce the reserve requirement and/or the discount rate, but we restrict the analysis of this chapter to cases in which open market operations are the only means employed. In actual practice in the United States this is the case, and reserve requirements and the discount rate are changed infrequently.

[6] This viewpoint has had frequent and forceful expression. See, for example, Milton Friedman, *A Program for Monetary Stability,* New York, Fordham University Press, 1959, pp. 88–99.

Inflation

In Chapter 7 we developed a theory to explain the determination of national income and employment and the general level of prices. We showed how the equilibrium price level changes as the determinants of the behavior of the economy change. But we did not derive a complete theory of the inflationary process. In particular, we explained how the final price level differed from the initial one, but we did not fully describe the process by which the movement from one price level to another is accomplished. In this chapter we cover some theories of the inflationary process and analyze some of the effects of inflation.

CAUSES OF INFLATION

The search for the sources of inflation is almost as old as the study of economics itself. One of the earliest theories of inflation held that movements of prices can be traced to prior changes in the stock of money. This theory still has many adherents, and no economist would deny that large changes in the stock of money must lead to changes in the price level. An increase in the stock of money produces rightward shifts in the *LM* and *IS* curves. Even if there are underemployed resources and prices are rigid downward, a sufficiently large increase in the money stock eventually creates an excess demand for goods, and prices rise.

Some economists object to the foregoing description of the cause of inflation on the grounds that factors other than increases in the money stock can cause an excess demand for goods. As we have previously seen, shifts in the demand for money or the demand for goods can have a similar effect. In addition, increases in the volume of government spending, even if they are financed by the issuance of bonds, may also cause an excess demand for goods.[1] Taking a more eclectic view of the causes of inflation, we might say that inflation tends to be caused by an excess demand for goods. This excess can result from prior increases in the stock of money, but it can also have other sources.

The notion that inflation is produced by an excess demand for goods, whatever the source of the excess, is called *demand-pull inflation.* The rise in prices that occurs, by reducing the real value of the stock of money, is one way in which the excess demand is eliminated. If there is a once-and-for-all increase in the demand for goods, there is no further tendency for prices to rise when the new equilibrium price level is reached. This is the kind of situation we examined in Chapter 7. The price level can continue to rise only if there is a continuing increase in the demand for goods and services in excess of the growth of the capacity of the economy to satisfy that demand. If, for example, the stock of money continues to rise at a high rate, the price level will continue to rise over time.

A second kind of inflation that has been posited, *cost-push inflation,* arises either from an increase in wages or from an increase in prices produced by groups, large unions, or large firms, which are alleged to have substantial market power. Such groups are not price takers, as are participants in competitive markets, but they can influence the course of wages and prices.

Suppose that the economy is initially in equilibrium at full employment, with stable prices, whereupon the equilibrium is disturbed by an increase in prices brought about by powerful firms. We know from our analysis in Chapter 8 that if the price level is maintained above that required to bring about full employment, there will be deficient aggregate demand and unemployment will result. An upward movement in the price level at full employment thus has the same effect as a price level that is rigid downward in the face of a reduction in demand. In both cases, there is unemployment. The same result—higher prices and unemployment—occurs if the wage level is increased by powerful trade unions.

As in the discussion of demand-pull inflation, once the economy has adjusted to the new higher price level, the economy is in equilibrium (although the equilibrium is characterized by unemployed resources). Prices are higher than initially, but they have no tendency to rise further. For cost-push inflation to produce a continuing rise in prices, it is necessary to argue that firms (or unions) will continue to push up prices (or wages) in the face of growing excess capacity (unemployment of labor). This seems unlikely.

There is, however, a more plausible variant of the cost-push theory of inflation. Suppose that the government is committed to preventing unemployment of resources. Whenever unemployment develops, the government uses expansionary monetary and fiscal policies to increase aggregate demand. Thus whenever unemployment is produced by an upward movement in wages or prices, the government steps in to "ratify" the increases by expanding demand. In this view, the increase in demand follows the increase in prices.

The simple cost-push theory is thus deficient as an explanation of continuing inflation. Unless the government is pursuing a policy of preventing unemployment, all that firms or unions can do is to push prices or wages up, once and for all. They cannot promote continuing inflation because the result will be a continuing buildup of unemployed resources.

There is still another difficulty associated with the cost-push theory of inflation. In the late 1950s and early 1960s prices in the United States were highly stable. In the late 1960s and 1970s they rose rapidly. It seems implausible to suggest that these changes in the rate of inflation reflect changes in the market power of firms and unions. Changes in the rate of inflation occur too quickly to be explained by changes in the competitiveness of the economy. A better explanation would be either that periods of inflation were times of excess demand for goods and/or that the government was more willing to ratify previous wage and price increases then to let unemployment develop.

To summarize: Continuing inflation can occur only if the economy receives continuing increases in demand in excess of increases in the capacity of the economy to produce goods and services. These increases can be autonomous, or they can result from the need to prevent unemployment from developing after business and labor have pushed prices and wages to levels inconsistent with full employment.

INFLATION AND ASSET CHOICE

Suppose that an economy finds itself in the midst of a continuing inflationary process. The effect of the inflation is significantly dependent on the extent to which the event is anticipated. In a completely unanticipated inflation, the process itself causes gains and losses because a number of contractual relationships had previously been made on the assumption that prices would remain stable.

One of the major effects of an unanticipated inflation is the unexpected losses suffered by those holding assets whose returns are fixed in money terms. Holders of assets whose returns are not fixed do not lose when prices rise, and those who owe debts fixed in money terms gain. Among the assets whose return is fixed in money terms are money, private and government bonds, mortgage loans, and savings deposits. The assets whose return is not fixed in money terms include real capital and claims against the return on real capital, common stocks.

As the discussion in Chapter 2 indicated, the return from holding an asset is equal to its yield plus any change in its price. When the general price level is not constant, we must allow for changes in the price level in our calculation of the return from holding an asset.

Suppose that a bond sells for $100 at the beginning of the period and promises to repay its holder $104 at the end of one year. The holder of that bond will earn a 4 percent rate of return if there is no change in the price level. He will be able to purchase 4 percent more in goods and services as a result of waiting a year. But if the price level rises by 5 percent, at the end of the year the asset holder will be able to consume not 4 percent more goods and services but 1 percent less. The $104 he receives must be "deflated" by 1.05 to allow for the increase in the price level. Doing this, we discover that only $99.05 of goods and services can be purchased. The other side of the coin is, of course, that the issuer of the bond need pay back 1 percent less than he borrowed. Clearly, the effect of an unanticipated inflation is a redistribution of wealth between those holding assets whose return is fixed in money terms and those issuing these assets. If there is unanticipated inflation, borrowers gain and lenders lose.

Suppose, instead, that inflation is anticipated. In this case, we would expect that asset holders will wish to dispose of assets that are poor inflation hedges and to acquire assets that protect them against inflation. Thus, for example, people will attempt to dispose of money and bonds and to acquire real capital. In addition, they will try to find ways to hold smaller money balances. Equilibrium will be reached when the assets that provide effective hedges against inflation command a price reflecting this advantage.

What are poor inflation hedges? Any asset whose return is fixed in money terms is obviously a poor hedge. Consider holding money. When prices are rising, the holders of money suffer a decline in the real value of their money holdings. Similarly, the holder of a bond experiences a decline in the real value of his wealth under inflationary conditions, since the real value of each dollar he is repaid is smaller than the real value of each dollar loaned. Real assets are better hedges because the increase in the general price level is accompanied by a rise in the prices of the items the assets are used to produce.

The foregoing discussion suggests that when inflation is anticipated, people will wish to switch out of money and bonds and into real capital. The process drives down the price of bonds and raises the price of real capital. The decline in the price of bonds is, of course, equivalent to an increase in the rate of interest its holders earn in the future, although holders at the time of the decline in bond prices suffer a capital loss.[2] Equilibrium is reached when wealth holders are content to hold the amounts of money, bonds, and real capital, that exist. The price of real capital will be higher and the price of bonds lower than before the inflation became expected. The nominal rate of interest on bonds must be higher to offset the decline in the value of the dollars that will be repaid. The yield on real capital may be lower than before, but people are willing to hold it because it provides a good inflation hedge.[3]

INFLATION AND LABOR MARKETS

Still another effect of inflation results from the contractual relationship between workers and firms. Suppose that workers enter contracts to supply labor for a period of time. If they are free of "money illusion" (i.e., if the amount of labor they will offer depends on the real wage they are paid), they must estimate the prices that will prevail for the goods and services they will purchase after they have been paid for their labor. If the previous period has been one of stable prices, it is reasonable to expect workers to project that stability into the future, establishing their wage demands accordingly.

Suppose, however, that price increases occur. Then laborers as a group will have earned less, in real terms, than they expected; or, to put it slightly differently, they will have supplied more labor at the money wage that was paid than they would have, if they had known that the increase in prices was going to occur. In the next "period," the quantity of labor supplied at any money wage will have declined, since workers will anticipate continuing inflation. Workers who are free of money illusion can be bilked in the short run if an unanticipated inflation occurs. In the long run, however, their expectations will become adjusted to the actual rate of inflation.

THE PHILLIPS CURVE

In 1958 A. W. Phillips published a set of findings that profoundly influenced the subsequent study of inflation.[4] Phillips found that the rate of change of money wages in the United Kingdom varied inversely with the rate of unemployment. Years of rapid wage increases tended to be years of low unemployment. Stable wages tended to occur in years in which unemployment was high. A Phillips curve, as the relationship has come to be called, is shown in Figure 15-1. Phillips's results spawned the view that society faced a tradeoff between employment and inflation. Unemployment could be reduced only by accepting a faster rate of inflation.

This interpretation of Phillips's findings received a strong challenge in Milton Friedman's presidential address to the American Economic Association in 1967.[5] Friedman believed that Phillips had not observed long-run equilibrium positions. Assume that the economy is initially in equilibrium at

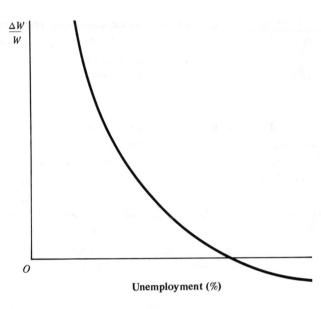

FIGURE 15-1

full employment with stable prices, say at point A in Figure 15-2.[6] Now suppose that an increase in aggregate demand occurs. Clearly there must be a
rise in prices. But will there be an increase in output? In Friedman's view
there will be, for a time.

Our analysis of the demand for labor in Chapter 6 indicated that the quantity of labor supplied depends on the real wage, if we assume that workers
do not have a money illusion. Similarly, business firms will hire labor until
the marginal physical product of labor is equal to the real wage. If prices
and wages rise by the same percentage as a result of the excess demand for
goods, the increase in aggregate demand will not cause an increase in output.
The only effect will be to raise prices.

But suppose that for a time labor anticipates stable prices, consistent with
the experience of the recent past. Thus if money wages rise, workers will
offer more labor, since they believe that this also represents an increase in
their real wages. If, at the same time, prices rise more rapidly than wages,
so that the real wage actually falls, firms will be willing to hire more labor.
While labor fails to allow for the increase in prices, then, output will increase.
Such a situation is represented by a movement to a point such as B in Figure
15-2. There is a higher rate of price increase at B than at A, and employment
is higher.

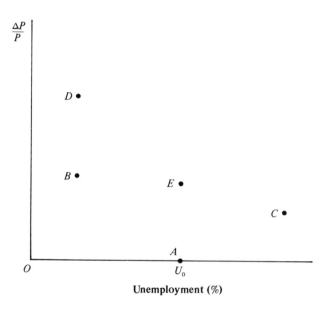

FIGURE 15-2

According to Friedman, however, a position such as *B* cannot be sustained for long. As soon as workers anticipate that inflation is occurring, they will reduce the quantity of labor they will offer at any money wage rate. This leaves the government three broad choices. It can do nothing, in which case economy will move to a less than full employment situation, such as *C* in Figure 15-2. Since the supply of labor is smaller at any money wage rate than initially, equilibrium will occur at an output level lower than the initial one. Second, the government can attempt to maintain the same level of employment as at *B*. But to choose this course in the face of a shift in the supply of labor, it must increase aggregate demand again. The increase in demand must produce an even larger increase in prices than in the first period, since labor supply already anticipates that amount of inflation. Such an equilibrium is at *D*. Finally, the government can attempt to move back to the original level of employment, but it must also increase demand to prevent a movement back to *C*. With the (temporarily) smaller supply of labor, demand must be increased beyond that prevailing initially to achieve the initial level of employment. Point *E* represents such an equilibrium.

But points such as *C*, *D*, and *E* are not sustainable for the same reason that point *B* was not. The rate of inflation anticipated by labor will turn out to be different from that which occurs. In the case of point *D*, the actual inflation turns out to be greater than anticipated, and the supply of labor falls further. For points C and E there is less inflation than anticipated, and the supply of labor increases.

The important lesson in all this is that rates of unemployment smaller than U_0 are not sustainable in the long run unless there is an ever-increasing rate of inflation. Furthermore, once inflation has begun and is built into the expectations of workers, equilibrium will be achieved only if the actual rate of inflation is brought below the expected rate.

This theory may help to explain the apparent paradox of a rising rate of inflation and rising unemployment during the late 1960s. According to the theory, the inflation that was experienced was an echo of the rapid inflation that began in the mid-1960s. As Table 15-1 indicates, as the rate of unemployment declined from 4.5 to 3.5 percent between 1965 and 1969, the annual rate of inflation rose from 1.9 to 4.8 percent. Since expectations of inflation had been incorporated into workers' behavior, even when unemployment rose to 4.9 percent in 1970, the rate of inflation climbed to 5.5 percent per year. As unemployment rose to 5.9 percent in 1971, however, the rate of increase of prices declined to 4.6 percent. Then, as unemployment dropped to 5.6 percent in 1972, the rate of increase of prices fell to 3 percent per year.

WAGE AND PRICE CONTROLS

Any discussion of inflation usually leads us to ask, Why not simply forbid wages and prices to rise? Under such an arrangement, the government would pass a law preventing the price of any commodity from changing. If we assume that such a law is enforceable in the face of an excess demand for goods, the problem becomes one of allocating the available supply of goods among competing demanders—for example, by requiring buyers to have government-

────────**Table 15-1   Unemployment versus inflation, 1965–1972**────────

Year	Unemployment, % of civilian labor force	Inflation, % change in GNP deflator
1965	4.5	1.9
1966	3.3	2.8
1967	3.8	3.2
1968	3.6	4.0
1969	3.5	4.8
1970	4.9	5.5
1971	5.9	4.6
1972	5.6	3.0

Source: Economic Report of the President, 1973.

issued coupons in addition to money to purchase a good, the government limiting the number of these coupons. This was essentially the rationing scheme used during World War II in the United States. An alternative is to have goods apportioned on a first-come-first-served basis. When inflation arises from an excess demand for goods, some form of nonprice rationing must be employed to allocate the available supply at existing prices. Under these circumstances it becomes difficult to prevent the development of black markets in which actual prices deviate from the government-established prices. The existence of black markets subverts the objective of stable prices, but such illegal institutions are often the inevitable outcome of attempting to limit price rises in the face of an excess demand for goods.

Although many would agree that stopping demand-pull inflation by means of price controls is difficult if not impossible, they still argue that there is a role for price controls. This opinion stems from the belief that much of the observed inflation in industrialized countries is of the cost-push variety. As discussed earlier, if wages or prices are pushed up by workers or firms with market power, the government can either allow unemployment to develop or it can increase the demand for goods, thus ratifying the initial wage or price increase. To avoid this dilemma, it is suggested that the initial price or wage increases be prevented by means of wage and price controls or guidelines.

If inflation is of the cost-push variety and if wage and price controls can be enforced, then in principle inflation can be controlled by means of controls or guidelines. Furthermore, since there is no excess demand for goods, the problem of rationing the available output by nonprice means does not arise. Unfortunately, this arrangement requires that either relative prices be frozen or that the government be in a position to determine which prices can rise and which must fall, while keeping the general level of prices unchanged.

As tastes and technologies change, the price system reacts by changing the relative prices of goods. The prices of goods that people come to favor rise, whereas goods that become less popular decline in price. Similar changes in relative prices occur as technological change takes place. If the government freezes all prices to prevent a cost-push inflation from developing, there may be an excess demand for some goods, even though no general excess demand for goods will develop. Once again, we are faced with the problem of rationing the available supply among competing users. Alternatively, the government may establish criteria for changing relative prices. Such criteria were included in the guidelines in force in the early 1960s when, for example, it was expected that prices would fall in areas of rapid technological progress, while where progress was slow prices would be permitted to rise. However, this approach requires that the government perform the function that markets are particularly well suited to handle—namely, responding to changes in tastes and technology by changing relative prices to direct the allocation of resources into the uses of highest value. And this places a burden on the government that is usually beyond its capacity.[7]

Wage and price controls in the 1970s

Wage and price controls are not, of course, of merely academic interest. In the late summer of 1971 the Nixon administration, acting under authority previously granted by Congress, imposed a program of controls. Phase I, as the first three months of the program came to be called, consisted of an across-the-board freeze on all prices and wages. No agency existed to administer the control program, and it was feared that unless a freeze was imposed, prices and wages would rise rapidly simply to "beat" the establishment of the agency. Subsequently, in Phase II, wage increases were limited and price increases were allowed in most instances only to permit firms to "pass through" cost increases, thus to maintain profit margins.

Since the administration had previously been on record as strongly opposed to wage and price controls, the change in policy in 1971 came as a surprise. The official rationale for the policy was that although price increases were slowing because of tighter monetary and fiscal policies being pursued, it was taking longer than anticipated to eliminate expectations of inflation, and unless such expectations were changed, undesirably high unemployment rates would be necessary to control price increases. The control program was intended to change expectations, thus to permit a more rapid transition to a period of lower unemployment and more stable prices.

The precise effect of wage and price controls is difficult to discern, since price increases were beginning to slow even before the controls took effect. As a result, some observers are inclined to give only limited credit to the program for the subsequent decline in inflation, and the question is likely to remain unresolved for some time, although it is clear that the slack in the economy did provide some assistance.

Those concerned with justifying wage and price controls argued that the program was needed only for a brief period and if monetary and fiscal policies were wisely managed, it would be possible to withdraw the controls without generating a new round of inflation. But when the controls were drastically eased in early 1973, a rapid burst of price increases occurred. The rate of price increase from late 1972 to late 1973 exceeded 7 percent per year, faster than before Phase I. Phase III, as the first half of 1973 was called, quickly gave way to Phase IV, which was basically Phase II reincarnated.

Why it proved so difficult to relax the control program once it was instituted is a subject that will doubtless concern economists for a long time. But one seemingly plausible explanation provides a further argument against imposing controls in the first place. According to this view, setting controls on wages and prices tempts the government to expand aggregate demand to increase employment. Rather than use the period of the controls to eliminate inflationary expectation, there is a tendency to attempt to exploit the controls by pushing hard to expand output while avoiding the cost of rapidly rising prices. But the situation cannot go on forever. If the control program is eliminated, the previously suppressed wage and price increases will occur, as they did in 1973. If the controls are maintained while there is a substantial excess demand for goods, there will be attempts to evade the effects of the control program. The most ardent proponents of the program saw it only as a device for "buying time" while price expectations were adjusted downward. But the program makes sense only if there is a return for the time "bought." If the period during which controls are in force is not also accompanied by stabilizing monetary and fiscal policy, the elimination of the program may well make the situation worse than it was when the program began. Perhaps the rapid rise in prices in 1973 supports that fear.

SUMMARY

Inflation can persist only if aggregate demand is continuously increased beyond the capacity of the economy to produce—for example, if government is committed to a full employment policy, hence must "ratify" wage or price increases produced by powerful unions or firms. The distribution of the effects of inflation and the effects themselves depend to an important extent on whether price increases are correctly anticipated. Once inflationary expectations are built into economic decisions, the ending of inflation and the return to equilibrium require that for a time the actual rate of price increase be less than that anticipated.

NOTES

[1] Recall, however, the discussion in Chapter 9 indicating that an increase in government spending financed by issuing bonds might be deflationary.

[2] Newly issued bonds will have to pay a higher rate of interest than in the past, when inflation was not expected.

[3] Another way to look at this is to say that because inflation lowers the real return from holding money, it must also lower the real return from holding assets that compete with money—in this case, real capital and bonds.

[4] "The Relation between Unemployment and the Rate of Change of Money Wage Rate in the United Kingdom, 1861–1957," *Economica*, 1958.

[5] "The Role of Monetary Policy," *American Economic Review*, 1968.

[6] The vertical axis in Figure 15-2 is the percentage change in prices rather than the percentage change in wages, as in Figure 15-1. Phillips curves of both types have been estimated.

[7] Some would accept the above characterization of the difficulties of using wage and price controls, arguing, however, that using controls for a short period may be useful to stop an ongoing inflation without introducing important distortions in relative prices.

16

Money and the international economy

Thus far we have been concerned with the behavior of a single economy viewed in isolation from all others. When only one kind of money is used for making transactions, a geographic entity has taken one step toward becoming a separate economy. The United States is an economy, as is France. If the nations of the European Common Market adopt a single currency, the member states will be, for many purposes, a separate economy. If all the countries in the world employed a unified currency, this chapter would not have to be written. Instead of discussing monetary policy for the United States, we could discuss it for the world and be done with it. But nations usually insist on monetary sovereignty in that each wants its own currency and its own independent monetary policy. This produces a set of problems in addition to those we have previously considered. These difficulties are the subject of this chapter.

MAKING INTERNATIONAL TRANSACTIONS

The purchase of goods in a foreign country requires a transaction in addition to those made when goods are bought domestically, namely, the conversion of domestic to foreign currency. Suppose that I wish to purchase a bottle of French wine, a Japanese automobile, or a bicycle made in England. The vintner or the auto manufacturer or the bicycle maker expects to receive payment in his local currency. I must therefore exchange dollars for francs, yen, or pounds sterling, at the prevailing price. Thus if the foreign exchange rate is £1 = $2.40, to purchase an English bicycle costing £50 I will have to convert $120 to British currency.

THE PRICE OF FOREIGN CURRENCY

What determines the price at which I can acquire pounds? In some foreign exchange markets the price of foreign currency in terms of dollars is determined by supply and demand. If many people decide to purchase the goods produced in a country, the price of a unit of its currency rises. If the nationals of that country decide to increase their purchases of imported goods, the price of a unit of its currency falls.

The vertical axis in Figure 16-1 represents the price of a British pound quoted in dollars. The curve *DD*, which represents the demand curve of Americans for pounds, slopes downward because we expect that the more dollars will have to be exchanged to obtain one pound, the fewer pounds will be demanded. Following up the example of the purchase of a £50 British bicycle, if a pound costs $4.80 instead of $2.40, I might decide to forego the purchase, preferring instead to buy an American bicycle. For similar reasons, the supply of pounds *SS* is upward sloping. British citizens will offer

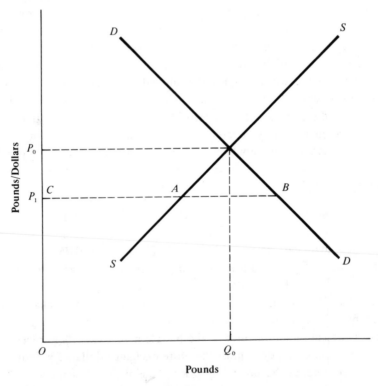

FIGURE 16-1

more pounds, the more dollars they can get for them. For the period in question, the price of a pound in terms of dollars is P_0, and Q_0 pounds are exchanged. If in the next period Americans develop a taste for Scotch whiskey, DD will shift to the right and the price of a pound in terms of dollars will rise.

It is rare for the price of one currency in terms of another to be determined entirely by market forces. For a considerable time countries have attempted to "peg" the relative values of currencies. The stated reason for this policy is the need to reduce uncertainty about what exchange rates might be, thus to encourage international trade.

How is the price of a currency pegged? In the case pictured in Figure 16-1, if the exchange rate is pegged at P_1, fewer pounds are supplied than are demanded. In the absence of intervention, the price of a pound would tend to rise to P_0. But suppose that the British government steps in and sells AB pounds. Some of the dollars supplied at P_1 are purchased by British nationals who wish to buy American goods. The rest are purchased by the British government.

If in the next period the supply and demand curves shift to create an excess supply of pounds at P_1, the British government would sell some of its dollar holdings, to prevent a drop in the price of the pound. This is how the fixed exchange rate system is supposed to work. In some periods a country accumulates the currency of others and in other periods it sells this currency. On balance, a country is expected neither to accumulate nor to decumulate foreign currencies. Governments take action to eliminate what would otherwise be short-run fluctuations in exchange rates about a long-run equilibrium value.[1]

There is another way to look at the quantity AB in Figure 16-1. The distances CB and CA represent pounds demanded by Americans and pounds supplied by the British, respectively. The pounds demanded by Americans reflect American demand for British goods, whereas the pounds supplied represent British demand for American goods. At P_1, in terms of pounds, the amount of American goods being demanded by the British is not as great as the amount of British goods being demanded by Americans. The difference AB is the excess of United States imports over exports.

INTERNATIONAL CAPITAL MOVEMENTS

The demand for foreign goods is not the only source of the demand for foreign currency. Americans may wish to purchase shares in foreign firms or the bonds of foreign governments, or they may want to construct branches in other countries. The acquisition of an asset in a foreign country requires the purchase of currency of that country, just as does the acquisition of a good for importation. Thus the demand and supply curves drawn in Figure 16-1 should include the demand and supply of currency for the purpose of engaging in foreign investment.

OTHER SOURCES OF THE DEMAND FOR FOREIGN CURRENCY

It should be clear by now that the demand for foreign currency can arise from a variety of sources. The demands for foreign goods and foreign investments are only two examples. If the United States wishes to maintain military forces in Europe, it will incur expenses that must be paid in foreign currency. If an American citizen wishes to send a gift of money to a relative living abroad, he must acquire foreign currency. Americans flying on a French airliner, purchasing insurance from a British company, or traveling in Japan, must acquire foreign currency.[2] All transactions such as these affect the demand for and supply of a nation's currency.

THE BALANCE OF PAYMENTS

It is clear from the foregoing discussion that if exchange rates were permitted to change whenever there existed excess demand or excess supply of a nation's currency, the problem of the balance of payments would not arise. If the demand by the British for American currency exceeded that of Americans for British currency, the price of the pound in terms of dollars would fall until the demands were equated.

Problems of the balance of payments arise when countries attempt to maintain exchange rates at disequilibrium levels for a long time. Suppose, for example, that the British attempted to maintain the pound per dollar price in the face of a persistent excess supply of pounds. To do this they would have to be prepared to absorb the excess supply by selling dollars. They could not do this forever, though, since their dollar holdings are limited.[3]

If the British persisted in trying to peg the exchange rate but realized that their resources were limited, they would have to resort to limitations on the international transactions in which their nationals engage. They could limit imports, restrict overseas investments, and reduce governmental spending overseas. As we shall see, there are yet other, more indirect, methods of dealing with the problem.

Calculating the balance of payments

In Table 16-1 we have summarized the international transactions for a hypothetical country during a year. The left-hand side of the table includes transactions involving a demand for the currency of the country, and the right-hand side contains transactions in which the currency of the country is supplied.

The *official settlements method* of calculating the balance of payments is performed by taking the difference between all private purchases of a nation's currency and all private sales or, alternatively, as the change in foreign currency holdings of its government plus the increase in the holdings of its currency by foreign governments. Since our hypothetical country was forced to sell gold and holdings of foreign exchange in the amount of $3 billion, and since foreign governments and central banks increased their holdings of its currency by $3 billion, the official settlements deficit is $6 billion.

The main difference between the *liquidity balance* and the official settlements balance is that the former treats changes in foreign private holders of a country's liquid liabilities as a method of financing a deficit, rather than as part of the calculation of the deficit to be financed. For the country being considered, if we regard the $2 billion increase in foreign private holdings of liquid liabilities in this way, the balance of payments deficit is $8 billion. The $2 billion is not regarded as an ordinary international transaction, such as long-term foreign investment, but instead simply one of the ways in which this country financed its deficit.

To summarize: There is no such thing as *the* balance of payments deficit. The identity of the transactions to be included in the balancing items is not always clear, and many economists prefer to use more than one measure, or to look at the transactions directly, to obtain a complete picture of a nation's balance of payments position. To indicate the differences that can be produced by the two methods, i.e., the liquidity balance and the official

—Table 16-1   International transactions of a hypothetical country—

Exports of goods and services	$63	Imports of goods and services	$59
Investments by foreigners	4	Foreign investment	12
Changes in holdings of gold and foreign exchange	3	Net governmental loans and transfers	4
Changes in holdings of liquid liabilities by foreigners			
Official	3		
Private	2		
	$75		$75

Table 16-2   Alternative measures of the United States balance of payments ($ billion)

Year	Liquidity balance	Official settlements balance	Net liquid private capital flows
1963	− 2.7	− 1.9	0.8
1964	− 2.7	− 1.5	1.2
1965	− 2.5	− 1.3	1.2
1966	− 2.1	0.2	2.4
1967	− 4.7	− 3.4	1.3
1968	− 1.6	1.6	3.3
1969	− 6.1	2.7	8.8
1970	− 3.9	− 9.8	−6.0
1971	−22.0	−29.8	−7.8
1972	−13.1	−11.6	1.5

Source: Economic Report of the President, 1973.

settlements balance, Table 16-2 shows both measures for the United States over the past decade.

During most of the 1960s, foreign individuals and firms accumulated liquid liabilities denominated in dollars; thus the official settlement deficit was smaller than the liquidity balance deficit. In three years the official settlements deficit was actually in surplus, although the liquidity balance deficit never was. But in 1970 and 1971 there was a net liquid private capital outflow of major proportions, which made the liquidity deficit smaller than the official settlements deficit.

THE ROLE OF GOLD

Under the international financial system prevailing between World War II and the late 1960s, the United States dollar was pegged in terms of gold. One ounce of gold was worth $35. This means that the United States government stood by ready to buy or sell gold at that price to anyone except its own nationals. The price of foreign currencies were also fixed in terms of gold, thus in terms of dollars.

The continuing United States balance of payments deficit during the 1960s resulted in a substantial reduction in the United States gold stock as possessors of dollars converted them to gold. United States gold holdings, which stood at $19.5 billion at the end of 1959, had fallen to $10.5 billion by the end of 1972. At the same time, foreigners were adding substantially to their holdings of dollars. It was soon clear that the pledge of the United States to convert its dollars to gold could not be honored. The country's response has been a small rise in the price of gold and, more importantly, the imposition of substantial restrictions on parties to whom gold could be sold. As of 1973 the United States had essentially dropped its commitment to sell gold to all potential buyers.

DEALING WITH DISEQUILIBRIUM IN THE BALANCE OF PAYMENTS

Suppose that a country experiences a continuing balance of payments deficit and does not wish to change its exchange rate. It cannot go on running deficits forever because foreigners are unwilling to keep acquiring its currency and its own resources are inadequate to sustain its price; therefore, it must bring about a change in some of its international transactions. We have already alluded to such direct methods as imposing tariffs or quotas on imports and placing restrictions on foreign investments. An alternative to direct controls is indirect influence on these transactions. A policy that reduces aggregate demand domestically can improve the balance of payments in two ways. First, by lowering domestic income the demand is reduced for all goods and services, including imports. Second, a fall in domestic prices reduces the demand for imports and increases the demand for country's own goods as exports. A decline in the United States domestic price level, or a slower rate of inflation in the United States relative to that in other countries, will increase the demand for dollars and reduce the supply of dollars in foreign exchange markets.

Promoting unemployment to improve the balance of payments is clearly not a viable long-run solution to a deficit in the balance of payments. And, as we have seen in the previous chapter, it may be difficult to reduce the rate of inflation without producing unemployment. Robert Mundell has proposed an interesting scheme for attaining equilibrium in the balance of payments without sacrificing the goal of full employment.[4] Mundell argues that international capital movements depend on the rate of return from holding assets domestically as compared with the rate of return on holding assets abroad. Other things equal, increase in the domestic interest rate should result in a net inflow of capital. He assumes further that imports depend on the level of national income. If a country is at full employment and is experiencing a balance of payments deficit, a policy of higher interest rates will reduce capital outflows (or increase inflows). Thus a monetary policy that produces a rise in interest rates will result in improvement in the balance of payments. But unless offset, such a policy will produce unemployment. According to

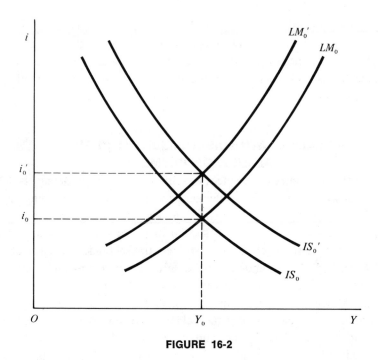

FIGURE 16-2

Mundell, the offset should come from an expansionary fiscal policy, tax cuts, or government spending increases.

The initial situation is depicted as the intersection of LM_0 and IS_0 in Figure 16-2. If the IS curve is shifted to the right through fiscal policy to IS_0' and the LM curve is shifted to the left to LM_0' so that the curves continue to intersect at Y_0, the interest rate will be raised to i_0'. Imports will be the same as at the initial equilibrium, since national income has not changed. But the increase in domestic interest rates, assuming that it is not accompanied by higher rates abroad, will increase capital imports. Thus the balance of payments will improve.

SUMMARY

So long as all nations do not have a single currency, the monetary effects of international transactions must be accounted for. Under a system of flexible exchange rates, variations in the demand for and supply of a nation's currency are reflected in the terms at which its currency exchanges for that of other countries. When exchange rates are pegged, the monetary authorities step in to prevent changes in exchange rates. If imbalances in payments persist, however, international transactions must be restricted or exchange rates must be changed.

NOTES

[1] Whether the system in fact works in this fashion is a subject to which we return shortly.

[2] Even if the price is quoted in dollars, the foreign firm is likely to convert the dollars acquired into its own currency.

[3] Alternatively, the United States might be willing to absorb pounds continuously. This is unlikely to happen, however, since in taking such action Americans would be sending goods abroad in return for pieces of paper.

[4] "The Appropriate Use of Monetary and Fiscal Policy for Internal and External Stability," *International Monetary Fund Staff Papers,* 1962.

Index